The Gnostic

A Journal of Gnosticism, Western Esotericism and Spirituality

Issue 3

Copyright Page and acknowledgments

The Gnostic 3, Summer 2010.

Opinions expressed are those of the contributors and not necessarily those of the publisher.

Editor: Andrew Phillip Smith

Published by Bardic Press
71 Kenilworth Park
Dublin 6W
Ireland.

ISBN: 978-1-906834-05-0

Thanks to the contributors and all others who have made this possible, including but not limited to: Tessa Finn, Lance Owens, David Tibet, Miguel Conner, Bill Darlison, Elan Trinidad, Daniel Matt, Jacob Needleman, Anthony Blake, William Kennedy, John Freeman, Reggie Freeman, Jeremy Puma, Mike Grenfell, Karl Le Marks, Andrew Criddle, W.W. Norton & Co., Xochi Adame and Quest Books, Watkins Books, Apocryphile Press, Watkins Books, Arcturus Books.

The Gnostic

A Journal of Gnosticism, Western Esotericism and Spirituality

Issue 3

Lance Owens, David Tibet, Miguel Conner, Bill Darlison, Elan Trinidad, Daniel Matt, Jacob Needleman, Anthony Blake, William Kennedy, John Freeman, Reginald Freeman, Jeremy Puma, Mike Grenfell, Karl Le Marks, et al

Edited by Andrew Phillip Smith

Bardic Press

Dublin 2010

Contents

Editorial

From the Mouth of the Demiurge

When I began *The Gnostic* I promised myself that I would keep it going for at least three issues and then see what happens. This is, of course, the third issue, and something has to change, perhaps the frequency (which has already been adjusted to two issues a year rather than the proposed three) perhaps the format.

This issue is again larger than the previous issue. The circle of contributors widens, bringing with them new possibilities. It is due to the determination of Lance Owens, author of the important article on the Red Book of C.G. Jung, that we have Jung's painting of Philemon on the cover. Our interviews are with musician, Coptologist and apocalyptic Christian David Tibet, philosopher and Gurdjieffan Jacob Needleman and *Zohar* expert Daniel Matt. Elan Trinidad gives us our first comic.

The Gnostic has a lot more potential, and I really enjoy the work of commissioning and articles and working with the authors. But the production of the journal takes me far too long and my enthusiasm wanes in that crucial final phase. Yet The Gnostic is a zero-budget publication and we have no money for a designer.

Should *The Gnostic* continue as it is? Or switch to a more standard paperback book format? Can we really continue to produce two issues a year? Or should we keep the format and frequency but change the subject matter to, for example, heating engineering, the artificial language Esperanto, or the sex lives of Disney cartoon characters? Should it even continue at all?

Personally I'm inclined to keep going but to simplify the format and reduce the content to articles, interviews and reviews and market it as a paperback anthology.

Let's hope we get another issue out before the end of 2010.

From the feedback that I've received, it seems that readers of the second isssue were, very imprssed by the comparative lack of of typos.. My thanks again to the contributors, each of whom will receive the grand sum of a free copy of this issue.

As ever, letters, gifts, monetary donations, rare codices and Egyptian cat mummies may be sent to:

The Gnostic Magazine
71 Kenilworth Park
Dublin 6W
Ireland.

Channelled apocryphal gospels are also accepted via PayPal. Emails are welcome to

andrew@bardic-press.com

We have a working website, http://www.the-gnostic.com, which includes some extra material including audio clips. The most convenient way to order *The Gnostic* is via Amazon.com and its international sites. It may also be ordered from most booksellers and is stocked in selected bookstores. If you have trouble ordering, please contact us directly via email.

Andrew Phillip Smith,
Dublin, Summer 2010

Andrew Phillip Smith

An Interview with David Tibet

APS: Hello David. You're a musician and you've been recording since the early 1980s. You're a scholar of Coptic, and you have unorthodox Christian beliefs.

DT: Well, I wouldn't say that I'm a musician for a start.

APS: No?

DT: No, I can't play any instruments, and I wouldn't think that I was a scholar of Coptic. I read a lot of Coptic and I recently got my M.A., and I did very well in that, I won the relevant prizes. But I'm not an academic really. I love Coptic, and I'm fascinated by Gnosticism, of course, and the noncanonical texts, and also monasticism, Shenoute's writings, through Stephen Emmel and Heike Belmer, who are the main two people I studied under when I was doing the M.A. That has led me, not away from Gnostic texts, because I still love those, but they suggested that I should look into Egyptian monastic texts, because there is so much there that hasn't been translated all right. The Gnostic texts are fascinating of course—I love them deeply—but there's a lot of work done on them already, and I think also that it was important for me to try and be able to read all sorts of Coptic. Emmel said to me that if you concentrate just on the Gnostic texts, which are the Nag Hammadi texts and so on, let's say that they are usually translated from a Greek original, as a general observation, you could learn to read Gnostic texts in Coptic, but it doesn't mean that you can then read other texts in Coptic. If you read Shenoute, for example, someone who was a writer in Coptic—and these aren't translations—is to enter a very different world

of literature or writing as well as imagination. There are references to heretics and pagans, so he's not unaware of the competing ideologies, he does refer to them. His sentences can be incredibly long and quite difficult to follow. He often changes subject within the area of his sermon or discussion. So I try to really read as much as I can of everything. I read Gnostic texts, and noncanonical, Shenoute, I read letters, these amazing mostly Manichaean letters that come from Kellis. You probably know about those, do you?

APS: Only vaguely.

DT: They're really fascinating. There's literary texts and documentary texts from Kellis which are edited by Iain Gardner. And there's just remarkable stuff there. They tend to be short and their letters or parts of psalm books and so on, very often Manichaean. So I'd call myself as an enthusiast. I'd be happier with that and scholar, because I'm not an academic. I'd like to start a Ph.D. later this year, maybe next year, but I'd have to try and fit it in with all the other things I'm interested in and do.

APS: And with someone like Shenoute, there is the linguistic interest and everything, and it's unexplored territory, but do you find any edifying spiritual content in his works as well?

DT: I think I'd have to be pretty weird to be edified by it. He's not a gentle person. I wouldn't say it's stuff I would read for my edification. It's quite ferocious and very moralistic, and obviously that was an important strand of Christian thought and Christian monasticism. But—Emmel pointed me towards it—there's a really beautiful apocalypse that I translated, by Shenoute, a vision, that I'm still hoping to publish. I haven't done it properly yet. But I wouldn't sit down and think and feel and get guidance from the Lord from Shenoute. I'm just trying to follow his sentences and see if he can cap one ferocity with another ferocity, which he normally does.

APS: You mentioned that he refers to heretics and the like, is there anything that might interest the reader of the Gnostic that you've discovered, that might not be well known, in his works?

DT: That's something for me to think about actually, and I'm not an expert on Shenoute. Emmel has written very well about his destruction of pagan Temples, which is of course not Gnosticism, although some Gnostics may well claim some link with the Egyptian "paganism", pharaonic pre-Christian religion. Offhand I can't think of anything which I could quote and say, well, he says this about this and this about this. Of course the problem with a lot of these people like Shenoute or other "orthodox" Christians of the times is that anyone who disagreed with their pretty narrow opinions would be called a heretic or a Gnostic or a pagan. It's not the main thrust of his argument. The main thrust of his text is, again on a general level, about trying to rule the monks and the nuns under his charge, and he himself is living in the desert and in the monastery, so there's a lot of stuff, a lot of material where he's trying to stop people fighting, squabbling with each other. There's a great book by Rebecca Krawiec, called *Shenoute and the Women of the White Monastery*, which is an academic work on how he tries to deal with the nuns, who are often squabbling, and there's problems with lesbianism, problems with vanity, and are they getting too friendly with the monks? And they made a cloak, and the cloak wasn't nice enough, and it wasn't well made and so... So he's not a heresiologist in the sense that we look at the great Christian heresiologists, who are often going for the Gnostics, as we call them now. That goes into a whole other problem of what is Gnosticism, was there a Gnostic religion, were there Gnostic sects, was there anything that

really linked these people together?

APS: And what are your own thoughts on that currently?

DT: I'm saying this as an enthusiast and as someone who is equally excited and enthused by rigid monastic texts in Coptic and Gnostic hallucinatory vision texts... I think we just don't know enough. What is orthodox Christianity? When did orthodox Christianity finally conquer Egypt? It's difficult because so many texts have disappeared. I'm sure you've looked into the Nag Hammadi problem as to what were these, were these in fact texts from the nearby monastery that they had to get out quickly, but they loved them too much and they were still referring to them? One of the things you asked me in a question was: am I a Gnostic? What are my thoughts on contemporary Christianity? On orthodoxy, you know, not Russian Orthodox, but accepted Christianity... I think that's linked to this question of what do we know? We know of course what the victorious side said, we know what Shenoute said, we know quite a lot of what Shenoute said. The Gnostic texts, how many were lost? We know what the canon contained fairly quickly, but we also know what Tatian wrote in the Diatessaron, and there were also different ideas on what the gospels were, some of the noncanonical gospels were kept in the canon of the Syrian or Armenian churches—the official bible canons. It just seems to me to be very fluid and I don't think we're ever going to know enough. So much has gone. Manichaeism, which today so many more people are looking into, so much of it is gone. Then you've got the Manichaeism that we had in India, you've got the one we had in China... Things are constantly shifting and all it would take is some other... I'm not saying the *Gospel of Judas*, because it was fascinating, but it didn't really overturn anyone's ideas on what Gnosticism was... But who knows what will turn up? That's another thing that makes this fascinating. I mean, we can't even say what was the early church? If people want to return to a form of primitive Christianity, and I don't mean that in a disparaging way, if they want to return to the purity of the early church, what was that?

APS: Yes, I quite agree there.

DT: It's difficult to say. Is it Pauline? Paul is always saying in his letters about other churches competing with mine, and they're getting a bit free in their doctrine, but we don't know much about them.

APS: So would you subscribe to the multiple early Christianities, at least by the second century? That the Gnostics are basically a form of early Christianity just as the proto-orthodox were another form of Christianity.

DT: Again, I would be hesitant to say that I would say that. We've got lots of orthodox early Christian material that was kept by the church. I think too much of the rest has been lost. Of course, there were competing early Christianities, but whether they were competing in the sense that is often meant now, where you had Valentinianism and, let's just say, orthodox Christianity, and then you've got Manichaeism, and you've got Sethianism, or something like that, they all had as good a chance to become Christianity. My feeling is that isn't the case. There's wealth and, again just as an enthusiasm, as an enthusiast and not as a scholar, I think that the complexity of the ideology or the doctrine that we see in the Gnostic texts, certainly in the Manichaean

texts, these are very, very complex cosmologists. It doesn't mean that they are wrong of course. The orthodox Christian cosmology is fairly simple. It might be a absurd to many people, but it wouldn't take long to describe it. If we tried to describe various layers of pleroma and we went all through the different levels in the Manichaean model of the universe, the spiritual universe, it would take a long time. I think, generally, the simpler a faith is, the quicker it spreads. I think if there is conviction in the prophets, in the evangelists and the missionaries, if they have conviction in their faith, I think it spreads quicker. The Manichaeans are equally convinced of the truth of what they're saying. It slightly eludes me just how popular Manichaeans was, how massive it was, because it was very complex indeed. And I think that's important because it does make us realise that would not talking about missionaries going in with a bunch of stupid peasants with donkeys trying to survive. They're interested in pretty complex spiritual concepts. Of course there were peasants who were Manichaeans, I'm sure, and I'm not saying they understood the complexity of Manichaeans doctrines any more than a Catholic Farmer in Ireland or Spain knows what Aquinas is going on about. There's different matters of faith, but Manichaeism is so complex. So then the Manichaeism that we see in the material from the Dakkleh Oasis, the Kennet stuff, is fairly simple credos, just letters from one family member to another with a blessing in the name of Mani, and so on, very simple forms. I don't know how anyone, without having all the evidence one could have—and we can't have that—how can we say? There's been so many ideas about Gnosticism, this or that, and then something else has turned up which changes at all. I was reading a book recently about Mithras, where the old idea was it was just a straight import, or at least a fairly direct import from Persia, and what the nature of the mythos of slaying the bull was... In this fascinating book by David Ulansey, *The Origins of the Mithraic Mysteries.* He says that the classical view that you and I had or have, or the view that people generally think of, seems to be absolutely incorrect, and the famous tableau of Mithras slaying the bull is totally astrological, and representations taken from Zoroastrianism, dualist representations, simple symbolic dualism. So who knows? When we die we'll find out. We'll have to ascend through about 4000 pleromas and see Sophia falling the other way when we're ascending. Then I think you'll probably have to chuck away the rosary that you've got and use a Gnostic rosary which probably has about 9072 beads on it.

APS: Talking about the Manichaeans, I went along to the Manichaean exhibition at the Chester Beatty Library.

DT: When was that?

APS: It finished late last year I think.

DT: Because there was a conference there, wasn't there? The Manichaean conference. I was going to go to it but I didn't have the time.

APS: I don't go to the conference. I did get the tour of the exhibition from the curator, who was a manuscript expert rather than a Manichaean expert. He couldn't read Coptic himself actually. There was a codex there which they called the "sod of turf" because it's in such bad condition —I think it was salt crystals that did it, it was

damp and then dried and everything—and it was basically this organic lump. It's a 200 page codex.

DT: And have they been able to get into it?

APS: No, it might be impossible to restore, even to separate the pages out from each other. So there's a couple of hundred pages of Manichaeans texts there, and nobody knows what's in it at all.

DT: It sounds like it's pretty much fused.

APS: It would take a massive amount of effort to restore it, an awful lot of fund raising and everything.

DT: Where was that found?

APS: It might have been from the Medinet Madi find. So we have talked a bit about the difficulty of historical reconstruction, based on how little survives. But that's not your only relationship to the apocrypha and the Gnostic texts, or to the New Testament. You are also inspired as an artist and as an individual by these things.

DT: I was talking to somebody about this in an interview recently. I really wouldn't consider myself an artist. It's always sounded very precious, and again I would say I'm an enthusiast with a deep belief in what I do. I never considered it as some sort of artistic expression. All the stuff I have done, all the records and the books and the translations and the painting, have just been things that I was driven to do for my own sake. It was purely for me, and the fact that some people have found it of interest is sweet, and it's flattering, and I'm delighted, but one thing I can say is that there are more people in the world who don't know it or don't like it than do like it, so I claim modesty there. But just as a child growing up in Malaysia I was fascinated by religions generally. And of course around me there was a lot of Hinduism, Chinese Buddhism, and Islam, Daoism and so on. And there was also the New Testament, and I read the New Testament quite young, and as time went along I was reading the Bhagavad Gita, the Upanishads and various Vedic things and things like that. I was always fascinated by the New Testament especially, rather than the Old, and Revelations. The Book of Revelation really struck me with great force when I was young. I wanted to find out more about it, and when I was at school I read a ghost story by M.R. James, then I read all of his ghost stories, then I wanted to find out more, then I came across the *Apocryphal New Testament*, and for me that was already interesting because I was already interested in the New Testament. When I was at school I was given the Old testament apocrypha for a prize of some sort and that fired up my interest in books that were not part of the proper canon. And I like the Old testament apocrypha a lot. Bel and the Dragon I thought was a wonderful story. So I came across the New Testament apocrypha, bought that, really read it all and just became fascinated by this whole world. We're talking of 1972 or something like that, and it was a very hidden world then, to a kid from Malaysia in a prep school in England. As with a lot of things when you're young, I read it, drifted away for a bit, but it was always something that was in the back of my mind. About seven years ago, because I was interested in a lot of other areas like Tibetan Buddhism, and as a young boy I was always interested in Crowley, his doctrines and the western hermetic tradition, I investigated those things more, and then about seven years ago I was reading a more and more Christian texts again and books on the early Christianity, and I wanted to learn New Testament Greek to read the gospels, or to read the New Testament. I know New Testament Greek, which I didn't much enjoy. I'm okay with it still, but it wasn't really beautiful for me. It's beautiful to read the New Testament in Greek, but the language just didn't come alive for me, which is my loss of course. And then I decided, well, I'm interested in the Nag Hammadi texts as well, so I'll learn Coptic. So I bought Lambdin's *Introduction to Sahidic Coptic* and started teaching myself. As soon as I opened it I felt an immediate familiarity. I don't mean this at all as a mark of how intelligent I am or anything. I have a facility. It made sense. I felt a recognition, I suppose it's one of those things where the pop psychology is maybe I was a Copt, or something

like that. I don't mean that's the case at all, I'm not sure I believe in reincarnation, but it just felt natural. I don't mean that I found it all easy, or that there were no problems in learning it, but it had heart and I loved it and I didn't begrudge learning it, whereas with Greek, I kept on thinking, "oh no, not another middle, what's the point? A middle subjective? Why?" So once I got into Coptic, that was it. I think sometimes it would be nice to learn Syriac or Ge'ez, but I think it's better to be focused. I'm not great at languages. I'm not one of these people who I so much envy who can pick up lots of different languages. So I just have to stay with Coptic and enjoy that and get as deep into it as I can. I started quite late, I guess I was 46, something like that. I probably went off the subject a bit, didn't I?

APS: No, there's no rod to keep us in line or anything.

DT: You were just asking what I liked when I was younger. In a sense, the things that most touch me and moved me as a child, in a profound way as you might say, are the things that still touch me and move me on a profound level now. I don't read Jennings books any more, or Just William, but apart from that… There are certain areas that I've gone into more than others. I was interested in Tibetan Buddhism for a long time and studied with a lama, a Tibetan lama called 'Chi.med Rigs.'dzin Lama Rinpoche, and that was really fascinating for me. He was a really fascinating, wise and sometimes very difficult man. But my interest in Buddhism of all types always engaged my head rather than my heart. I didn't necessarily feel that it was true. For me. And that is finally I think why I returned to what I felt did engage my heart and I think is true— again, whatever that means, true. But it was, I wouldn't say Christianity, because Christianity so often now means Christendom, and it's a political imperium, or moral imperium, that doesn't have much to do with what Christ says in the gospels, I believe myself. It may be he has a lot to do with what Shenoute is talking about, and I think that that story is a true story. C.S. Lewis said once that the story—the basis of

Christianity, that which Christ came to do, and did—he said was a fairy tale, but it was different to all the other fairy tales in that this was a true fairy tale, and it did happen. And that's my belief still. At that particular time Christ was born and Christ was crucified something so enormous happened that we still haven't understood it. I don't mean that in the sense of the cliché that he affected western civilisation or eastern civilisation, that area, I just mean that I believe that something so extraordinary happened that the divine in a very beautiful, and also in a very terrifying way, snapped into the world for 33 years, or however long, and it really cut time in half. There is before that and there's after that. That's also why it's important for me that there are still so much we don't know. I believe that the gospels are essentially accurate. There's a lot in the Gnostic gospels, or Gnostic texts let's say that I also believe to be accurate, although I think that often they're working on a more dreamlike, more mystical level, not because they're more spiritually profound, but because they're talking about things which in a sense the gospels and talking about. The gospels are fundamentally a narrative, aren't they? They're about a story that happened, and there's Christ speaking about his beliefs, and in John we find that in a much more mystical form. But the Gnostic gospels and things like that, I think they're dealing with what happened with Christ on a more poetic level. Putting aside the fact that a lot of them are written considerably after, one would think, the four gospels, nonetheless I still think they're a continuing reaction—and I am not alone in saying this, I'm not claiming it is a great insight—to something so awesome and life changing that happened, they're constantly trying to reinterpret what it was that happened. How could God send his son? It must be docetic. So they're just trying to think what happened, how could this have happened?

APS: On your Facebook page you had a quote, "docetic or just mimetic?" Can you expand on that?

DT: On the last album, *Alef on Hallucinatory Mountain*, there's a line where my text goes,

"docetic or just mimetic? Dying or running or hiding from the stauros [cross]?" It's just a reference to that, really. I'm interested in the idea of docetism, but I'm not a doceticist. I don't think it was a docetic appearance of Christ. It could have been a docetic crucifixion, why could have been a docetic body on the cross for some people, I don't know. I think it says in some of the Gnostic texts, that sometimes Christ appeared as a young child and sometimes he appeared as a man. And I think he appeared in many different forms, and perhaps some people did see it as docetic, and that was their intuition, and that was their truth, and from that they receive more illumination. Perhaps. Nobody has been able to, as you know, classify what happened. Nobody has come near to the truth of it, so they're all handy, and sometimes not so handy, ways of trying to describe the indescribable. Did the son of God suffer on the cross and die as a human being, and if so what was the nature of the godhead within him? Maybe he did, but how are we going to define it? It's not possible for us to grasp what happened, so we come up with docetic, patripassionist, all these different very beautiful ways, but not necessarily very clarifying ways, of trying to understand what the mystery of Christ was. I don't know, I don't think anybody can know, unless it's through direct experience of Christ, and if they have that direct experience of Christ, then Christ may well appear to them as a docetic child or as a he's-as-real-as-fish-and-chips physical body.

That's what I think, that there is something about Christ which was incredibly earthy, so we read in the gospels, and also in the *Gospel of Thomas*, not really so much in the Gnostic gospels—and I'm using the word advisedly of course, I'm not saying that they are gospels—he is appearing in all these different forms. I think, I hope and believe that he appears to people who are really searching for him and searching for the kingdom. I think he appears in a different way for all of them. I'm suspicious of mass movements which have the same Christ. It's the problem in institutionalised churches, not

From the series "I Arose as Aleph, the Speller, the Killer"

that they're don't recognise that themselves, I'm not saying that all the Catholics and Lutherans are blind to the problems of having a mass movement that must finally be built on having a personal experience of God or the godhead or whatever you want to call it, but I don't like to see armies marching behind crosses.

APS: In terms of these different christologies, which ones have you found more illuminating for yourself? I know you mentioned patripassionism.

DT: Well patripassionism... What really brought me to read into patripassionism and to try to understand it was Pascal's comment in the *Pensées* that Christ must be in agony until the end of the world, must not rest in the meantime, and the idea that Christ is still on the cross now, and we're living in the Roman Empire, or a type of Roman Empire, a type of imperium, really affected me strongly. Of course, Philip K. Dick wrote about this a lot, well he did in his later works, but it was Pascal who arrived first and I was living in Japan for a while, and I was never really a science fiction fan. When I was a kid I really loved Narnia and *Lord of the Rings*. I liked fantasy, though generally then there wasn't an awful lot of fantasy, but people like E.R. Edison didn't really move me, or Dunfany or…

APS: H.P. Lovecraft?

DT: Lovecraft came a bit later. I was going to say George MacDonald. Lovecraft is one of those people I still love the idea of, and I read all of his books in the Panther editions when I was a kid voraciously, and then I found I could never read them again. I tried, and I really admire him, I admire his imagination. I know a lot of people say a great imagination but a clunky writer. It's not to do with that, I mean I don't mind clunky writers. I just got tired of it all. There wasn't a continual thread through it I suppose. I like the works of authors or musicians to have some conceptual thread. When I was young I liked a lot of prog rock, and I still do, Emerson Lake and Palmer and Yes and Judas priest—they weren't really conceptual, but they are now because their last album *Nostradamus* was a concept album which I loved, a tremendous album, one of my favourites. I was in Japan, I didn't really have anything new to read and a guy I knew there said why not read Philip K. Dick. He was a huge fan and he had everything in paperback. So I tried one and I really enjoyed it. It was one of the earlier novels, so then I had an idea where to go next, you know, *Do Androids Dream of Electric Sheep* and so on, but the ones that most moved me were the last ones, *The Transmigration of Timothy Archer*, *Radio Free Albemuth*, and then his writings on… Are they Gnostic?

APS: His *Exegesis*, do you mean?

DT: Yeah. They are Gnosticish, whatever that means.

APS: We've had some articles on Dick in the first two issues, including an interview with his widow.

DT: I knew Paul Williams, who wrote *It's Only Apparently Real*. He was a friend of Dick and he interviewed him a lot and he knew him well. Previous to reading Dick in Japan I'd been very taken by *Pensées* by Pascal. We got on to this because you were asking me about the christologies. So patripassionism, I found it academically interesting, not academically, intellectually interesting, and I also found it moving because I have believed for a long time that we are living in the end times, but I think those end times started when Christ was crucified. This is still the end time. It was the end time then, as it was spoken of in the Bible, and this is still now the end time. In terms of time, 2000 years or so as not very much and have been living in a continual expectation of parousia, but generally I'm not really a fan of christologies in a sense, beyond finding parts of them that moved me and parts of them that don't. The christologies that most move me aren't really christologies. There is the work of Kierkegaard, the book the *Way of the Pilgrim*, and the *Sayings of the Desert Fathers*. And also Pascal's *Pensées*. There is other people who touch me a lot like Soloviev, but really it's Kierkegaard, Pascal, the Desert Fathers and the *Way of the Pilgrim*. It's those books and then all the other stuff I was referring to, the New Testament, Gnostic texts, noncanonical texts. And finally they are all poems, they are all people trying to make sense of their personal relationship with something that cannot be described and cannot be classified in any way whatsoever except as a poem. So another book is the *Cloud of Unknowing* and Julian of Norwich's *Revelations of Divine Love*. They really meant a lot to me as well. There are christologies in there, but they all personal christologies and there are always shifting, because they are humans trying to come to terms with something, and as humans always do, they move. They take one position, then they're not so sure about it, and that seems to be the reality, the most honest way of reacting to something that cannot be definable. It cannot be defined unclassified. We cannot say he, okay, this is absolutely what Christ was, the exact balance of his godhead and humanity, 60% of this, 40% of that, it's just not doable.

APS: Sometimes I think those heretical christologies and different versions of the Trinity are just the working out of the logical permutations of having three things, the Father and Son and the Holy Spirit, plus the nature of Christ. If you work through the logical permutations you actually come up with all the different versions that have occurred in history.

DT: Yeah, but the other thing is, as you yourself, if you work out the logical permutations… So we're working out the logic, in a human language of logic, what is not definable, not describable. So it's just impossible. It's not feasible. What is Aquinas's masterwork about? He's trying to formularise the definitive statement of Christ. What Christ was, what the churches, the mystical church, the church on the earth. And he's done an amazing job, of course, but he's done it himself. It can't be for anyone else. I'm not slighting him. I love Aquinas and his many profound insights, and of course we remember that at the end of his life he said that everything I wrote was like a bundle of straw, didn't he?

APS: Yes, yes.

DT: That bundle of straw is the desert fathers speaking, that's the pilgrim of the *Way of the Pilgrim*, that's Kierkegaard talking about the need for poverty and the leap of faith while he's drinking an expensive brandy and smoking cigars. In a top hat. I think that's what Christ is like. Christ is the person who comes sometimes and says, "I do not bring peace but a sword." Sometimes he says, "Love your neighbour as yourself." I find that strange: I bring not peace but a sword; unless you hate your mother and father; leave all and come and follow me; let the dead bury their dead. There is a ferocity there, or something that we describe as ferocity, and when we try to saying what Christ really meant was this, I feel we're missing it. We're missing this absolutely unpredictable being. The person who taught me New Testament Greek, he always

said—he read Greek and Hebrew and he was a Christian a questioning Christian, a sort of interested Christian—he said, "What's your favourite Christ, in the book?" And I said, "Well I like the Gospel of John a lot. We were just talking about the canon, the Old testament, the New Testament, and I said, "I like the Christ of John a lot, its mystical and the idea of the Logos and so on," and I said, "What you like?" And he said, "I like the God of the Old testament." And I said, "Anywhere in particular?", and he said, "No, all of it." And I said, "Why?", because Christians tend to be a bit embarrassed about that, and he said, "Because that to me is the real God. He's not the God of 'its okay, he's a gentle Jesus, he's going to hold your hand,' he's the God who says, 'I'm going to do this really good thing, but only if you slaughter all the tribes next door.'" And that was really fascinating to me because, in a sense, it's one of the main Gnostic conundrums isn't it? Why is he slaughtering and raping all the people and then if you do all that he's going to give you a city for 10 years before he brings the Babylonians on to you? God is unpredictable, Christ is unpredictable, we live in an unpredictable world. Its beauty and terror. It's often hell, it's often heaven, but generally people think more of hell because they're surrounded by so much pain and horror which leaks in. Why does it leak in? Well, it leaks in from the media, but it also leaks in I believe because we're in the middle of the war, and we've always been in the middle of the war, we are surrounded all the time by demons and angels and they both are struggling for us. And that's the history of mankind, being told by one extreme of beauty to another extreme of cruelty. How are we going to build ourselves a satisfactory Christ under a satisfactory God that will be suitable for the entire world? I remember there's something that really struck me as being a sad non sequitur, whether it's true or whether it's just apocryphal, but it could be true, and I'm sure you know the story. There are Jews and Christians in a concentration camp and they're being tortured and murdered and gassed, and somebody is being hung, and a non-believer turns to Christian and said, "where's your God now?" And the Christian points to the man hanging and said, "that's our God now." It's meant to show that Christ suffers with this at all times, but I don't think that's a very good proof of God. That's the non sequitur. Well, it can't have been very comforting to the non-believer who heard that. But perhaps to the person who said it, it was a true story, it was absolutely comforting that that was his personal experience and in that person he saw the Christ that suffers for us all. But again it was absolutely personal. How can that be encouraging to other people who don't have that same insight?—and I don't mean the same level of insight, I just mean the same angle of insight. So what I like is people who struggle with belief and are never satisfied with what they have, because I believe that when they're satisfied with what they have, when they have reached enlightenment or are absolutely in the presence of Christ they stop writing, and when they stop writing there's nothing there to lead us, or to spark in us the same imagination and poetry and beauty that took them to their epiphany.

APS: Going back to what you were saying about the Old Testament God, do you see a role for a demiurge in whatever form?

DT: Well, it's a good question. I think not for me personally. It's just more layers of complex theology, so there is a good God, but the God who has created this world is about God, but then Christ came, in whatever form, in terms of the different Gnostic senses of whom Christ was, and then he saved us from it, or he's showing us the way to get it back to the light. It's a beautiful idea but none of these are helpful for me because it's the same problem: if the good God is all powerful, why then has he allowed the demiurge to impregnate one of his emanations and now we have to eat watermelons and cucumbers, as the Manichaeans said, to get the light to ascend again? And again, it may be true, but it's not true for every one I believe. But it doesn't explain or solve the problem of there's evil in the world and there is a good God, and that good God is all powerful, then somewhere along the line he has been fooled, he has had something stolen from him, someone has one

over on him. Well, what do you think? Do you think the demiurge explain anything?

APS: I wouldn't say I have it as a personal belief. But I think the good God doesn't necessarily have to be all powerful. In the classic Gnostic myth he emanates, and the emanation furthest away from him becomes interested in something outside of the pleroma, and then you get the whole problem. Of course, there's also the benign platonic demiurge. I think Origen had Christ is the demiurge, didn't he?

DT: Yeah. I suppose it makes me think of an intellectual fascination and a beauty of profoundly moving, imaginative and often pretty cunning explanations of the world. It doesn't make me feel any clearer. I said to a friend once, Christ gave the Sermon on the Mount. It was pretty basic. There weren't many points, it was pretty simple, very clear, very difficult for us to do of course. If you want to follow them, they're there. He did the Sermon on the Mount, and then what we have in theology is someone will write a five volume treatise on the Sermon on the Mount telling us what he really meant and giving us loopholes so we can sort of be doing it and not be doing it. So with the platonic demiurge or the Gnostic demiurge, they are kind of fascinating ideas, but still it's a conceptual framework which is trying to explain something, as I've said before, which is absolutely, absolutely, absolutely not explicable. Really, the benign demiurge or hostile demiurge, the docetic or patripassionist, all these concepts don't really get us out of the question or solve the problem of who are we and what is Christ. They are ways of avoiding the target, it seems to me. As you said, the platonic myth is really beautiful, it's a useful model to see the world I think, at times. I do have to say, does that make me clearer about my world knowing there is a benign or hostile demiurge, has that made it made more sense? It hasn't really. Not at all. I think in many ways I'm quite dualist, very dualist. I think there are powers for good and there are powers for evil. Why they should both exist if there's an all powerful "good" God is beyond me. All I can do is saying it's incomprehensible, the only way to reach it is through personal experience, and we have to be ready when we do meet God to realise that it is certainly not what we think it is and it will be beyond the moral constraints that we have put on this God. A lot of the things that he, say, did were bad. These are classic Christian apologetics, but in the context of time, of what God sees, they weren't bad. They're actually good in the long run, but they were bad at the moment. But nobody can be satisfied with that on a deeply personal level, I think, as an explanation in words of something that can't be explained.

APS: I see that in your own work you have all the strange, vivid images throughout your songs. For example, "Judas as Black Moth," "Black Ships Ate the Sky." You presumably find that a more satisfying way to relate to these things.

DT: A lot of my texts and ideas come in dreams. I'm not trying to sound mystical. I just do get a lot of ideas from dreams. I wake up and I start writing it down. *Black Ships Ate the Sky* was a concept album about the coming of the anti-Christ and the second coming of Christ. They are my ways of explaining the world, the material and spiritual world around me to myself. That's how I see the world and how I interact with it and how I make it emotional sense of it to me. People say to me, when you talk about the second coming of Christ, David, you're not being literal, it's a mystical, poetical thing. And I say, no, it's completely literal. I think that the sky will open and return on a white horse, and that's what black ship set the sky is about, or one of the things it's about. That's what I expect to see at the moment, and it's how I interpret the mystery of Christ and the parousia. I'm not saying this is the truth and everyone else has to believe it or else wrong, I want to make it really clear that I'm singing and I'm writing and I'm doing all of this work just purely for myself. Just to explain myself to myself. I'm looking in the mirror I suppose. "Judas as Black Moth," again that was a dream. I heard a beating at the window in the dream. When you have a dream things from the real world go into the dream world. I heard a beating from the window and I looked out of the

window and I thought in the dream I saw it was Judas, it was identified as Judas with a human face beating at the window. Judas as black moth. And when I looked at the window there wasn't a moth. I think there may have been a bat or a bird, something like that, because there was a garden with a lot of trees near the window. It could have been a moth that had flown away, but moths tend to not make very much noise outside the window. It made me think that, possibly, Judas is now a moth, a black moth, that's what it meant to me, and that's how he was at that moment. Again, I'm not saying that's an important part of my personal christology, that Judas is in fact a black moth. It's just the way I see and feel, and I'll write it down for myself and I'll perform it or release it or whatever and I'm not attempting to make a consistent christology or way that my belief can be presented. I was interested in Crowley for a long time of course as I said, and I found most of his writings absolutely incomprehensible. I don't mean that I didn't intellectually understand them. I did, but there was just too much there. There was just too much. I think he should have written less and the books should have been shorter. I love his paintings and I collect his artwork. I've got about nine paintings or so. But even that I can see… That's where I see him. I see his quest and his belief and his dreams and nightmares sometimes. That's clear to me in reading *Magick in Theory and Practice*. It's too long, as I said. Everything I've done, especially since my work started becoming a lot more autobiographical, in, say, 1992 with the album *Thunder Perfect Mind*, it's just for me, and if are other people find it interesting or moving, I'm really delighted. If they find it absolutely unbearable and hate it, that's really fine too, but it's not for them. If people find something in it it's really fine. I haven't made the effort to push it. I'm not constantly doing interviews. I'm on this way and this is what I do, and I can't really do anything else. I can't do everything and it gets frustrating at times. When I was much younger I listen to music I really liked, the *Court of the Crimson King* by King Crimson, T. Rex, stuff that really moved me, and I'd think this is absolutely

From the series "I Arose as Aleph, the Speller, the Killer"

fantastic, I love it so much, but it's still not mine. But there's something I can do which will move me more because it will be more truly my story. So really that's how I started doing what I do, just for myself, not thinking that people would say, "Oh the *Court of the Crimson King* is okay, but wait till you hear *Baalstorm Sing Omega*, it's much better than the *Court of the Crimson King*," or David's songs are much more worthy of Top of the Pops than T. Rex, it's not really that. I believe everyone has their own song and their own story. We're put here for a reason, or many reasons, and one thing we must do is to be open to ourselves and open to others, to singing that song or telling that story, and just to take off our masks, to be as honest ourselves as we can and to other people, because when we day will be stripped naked by God and the more masks we have on the more painful and terrifying it will be when we're naked in his, her or its presence. Using multi-gender language. Really that's what I feel. We all have to answer for ourselves, not for anyone else, just to our souls. And we just have to do the best that we can, to be as true as we can to ourselves, and we nearly all fail. I'm sure I'm failing, but we have to try to do our best. If I feel that the work's honest to myself then that something. It was Samuel Johnson, wasn't it, who said—I really love Samuel Johnson—about a writer or maybe a dramatist, if the public is pleased it is well and good, if the public isn't pleased by the work it doesn't behoove the creator to tell them why they should have been pleased. When people say that some so and so, it's the best record ever made, or that U2 are the best group in the world, it's just absolutely meaningless. What does it mean? That there is an objective best in the world and U2 have the slot? So from U2 to Gnosticism I feel the same way about all these christologies. U2 is definitely the best for somebody, and patripassionism is definitely the best for somebody else, but I really wonder how many people who have achieved personal enlightenment and personal liberation and personal knowledge of the mystery of Christ through reading lots of books about patripassionism. I think in the *Way of the Pilgrim* you've got a man whose humility is so extraordinary. I'd rather spend time with somebody like that. There'd be more to learn from him than from… I was going to say Augustine, but I Augustine would have a lot to tell us about early Christianity, wouldn't he? Who would be more interesting, Aquinas at the end when he had seen everything as a straw, or Aquinas part of the way through the *Summa Theologica*? I'm fascinated by people really, and their own experience, even if it's not for me. I'd rather come across somebody who has some true beliefs… not just a platitude. You know what I'm saying.

APS: Yes, yes.

DT: I was thinking that often the groups that I most like, is the album where they've really tried and come out with an album which doesn't work for me all. Often it doesn't work for the fans generally, they're not so keen on it, but I often find those the most fascinating. Then you can see all the flaws, and the decision to do something different, and I think it's gorgeous.

APS: So, *Thunder Perfect Mind* is obviously of interest to readers of the Gnostic. You produced that album a long time before you learnt Coptic, and you just mentioned that this was perhaps a change in your approach to something more autobiographical. Could you talk about that a bit?

DT: I'd done some shows in Tokyo and I decided to stay there for a while. A lot of my music had been instrumental, just with soundscapes or lots of loops or maybe howling, and there were texts, I used metaphysical poetry, English metaphysical poetry, sometimes I'd turned traditional folk songs, sometimes I had done lots of things, and it felt very personal but… There was a woman I went out with at university. I was there from 1978 to 81 and there was a woman called Suzanne and treated her badly. Not violently, but just in the way that when you are at university. People often at that age are selfish and promiscuous and I remember feeling that she really meant a huge amount to me and I started reflecting generally on the way that I had been selfish when I was at university. I decided I'd tried to get in touch with all the girlfriends or women I'd been having relationships with. I wasn't always A…

APS:… A cad?

DT: A cad or a bounder, but there was something that came to me very strongly. I'd abused people's trust and love, and I just felt really I'd needed to clean things up. So I got in touch with the ones that I could and said that I'm really sorry for letting you down and betraying your confidences and cheating on you, and I know I caused you a lot of pain, and it certainly caused me a lot of pain, and I just wanted to say sorry. Some of these women, as was the case at university, it's not as if they were all… I'm sure there was something on the other side as well, but it was something I had to do. There was one woman, she's married now, her maiden name was Suzanne Riddoch, and I couldn't get in touch with her, and she meant a lot to me. If I think if her now I really get quite emotional. I just wanted to say sorry to her and I couldn't find her. I did have an address for her. But I started thinking about the nature of why was I so driven to apologise to these people and try and get some—I'm searching for a phrase because I hate healing and I hate closure—just to feel that they know that I knew that had been discourteous really. And I couldn't get in touch with her, so I wrote a song about her called *Lament For Suzanne*. And that was when I was scuttling back from Japan to England, I went back and forth a few times, and I wrote that about her and at the same time I started writing another album which was going to be a concept album called *Long Satan and Babylon*, which was also going to be a novel, which was about two demonic forces sent by Satan—meant generally, I'm not making a specific theological type of Satan—to the world in preparation for the second coming. There was a set of keys in the centre of the world, and that was obviously referring to Christ, I give you the keys of heaven and hell, to Peter, and they had to get the keys in order to stop the successful return of Christ. It wasn't meant to be a thriller, I know I have made it sound a bit Dan brown there, but it was a long sort of dream novel. I started writing that as well, and only two songs remain from that, a track called "The Descent of Long Satan and Babylon," which is on *Thunder Perfect Mind*, and another track called "All the Stars are Dead Now," and that was on *Thunder Perfect Mind* as well. It's a mad mixture of Gnostic, apocryphal, noncanonical, apocalyptic Christianity, which was one thing that was very strong for me at the time, and the other thing was this set of personal reminiscences and emotional exploration connected to Suzanne and who I was as a person and what I'd done as a person. And that's when I started reading, not in Coptic, but I started looking at the Nag Hammadi texts again, and I decided to call the album *Thunder*

Perfect Mind, because that was the text I found the most beautiful. And I mention that to Stephen Stapleton of Nurse With Wound, one of my closest friends and longest musical partners, and he said, "Oh yeah, what does that mean?" And I said, "I'll tell you tomorrow," because we had been out or something, and he said that that night he had a dream where I came to him and gave him an album, and I said, here's your new album Steve, and on the album it had Nurse With Wound, *Thunder Perfect Mind*. So when he woke up in the morning, he had been working on an album which he had nearly finished, and he said, can I call it *Thunder Perfect Mind*, and he told me the dream. And I said, "I think that's a wonderful idea." And then I had been thinking about what do it had said about the nature of Sophia, and also Soloviev, the 19th century Russian mystic, really beautiful, and friend of Dostoevsky. You know Dick talks in his diaries and so on about Sophia moving from one person to another in dream, and that was also an idea that I got from Soloviev, because Soloviev wrote a lot about Sophia as well, and in the British Museum reading room in the late 19th century Soloviev had a vision of Sophia, and obviously Soloviev was Russian orthodox, in which the female principle and Sophia is so powerful. And that's how Steve took the title of *Thunder Perfect Mind*, and when I in fact realized that everything I had done before was only partially about myself, and I know that could sound quite solipsistic, now everything is just about me, but in a sense it is. Because the work that we do is finally just about us. So everything just became far more personal, and following my rediscovery of the Gnostic texts and the noncanonical texts, and my rediscovery of how I'd treated people. I'm sure I was over emphasizing what I'd done. What I'd done was in the scheme of things not great. I had a girlfriend and I also had another girlfriend on the side. It's not a war crime, its common, especially when you're younger, but it just struck me as being essentially dishonest. I'd betrayed other people, and in betraying other people I'd betrayed myself. So I just continued on that same path of going into myself and my work and my manifestation, in the way that we all manifest as Crowley would say in the outer: the inner manifests in the outer, that's just what I do now. The Coptic and Gnosticism of course still absolutely fascinates me, but it's just generally Coptic and the insights one can have through this remarkable body of literature. It's very odd. It's not very wide in topic, there are no plays or novels and so on. It's very determined and single minded and it is brought me a lot of joy. And it keeps on informing my work. So the new album, which is out in a couple of weeks, *Baalstorm Sing Omega*, even the title of that came from when I was reading a Coptic text. I do a little translation of it in the album. It's just a quick translation, and I'm not pretending that its academically correct—well it is correct. Shenoute is talking about an observation by Pachomius. I don't know if you remember from your own Coptic but there is the verb *jo, janja omega,* which means to say or to sing. Then the text was translated by Jerome, and Pachomius from the Greek, he translated it not as speak in Latin, but as *cantare,* "to sing." But I read it as "Sing Omega." So the title of the album came directly from this text by Shenoute's in which he quotes Pachomius, the "Sing Omega."

A good and wise Father, truly pious, said in his writings (which are) in his letters, "Speak Omega, and do not allow Omega to speak you." For my part, I think it was this that he said—Speak to the world, from which you will go into the presence of God, saying "The love of money and the impiety which are in the world are unable to force me to be impious in all things". Do not let the world say to you—"I have caught you and I have bound you with the love of possessions and fornication and adultery and violent actions and thefts and foulnesses and impurities and other things contrary to our nature which are numberless."

APS: Lastly, I see that you had an exhibition of visual art, *Invocation of Hallucinatory Mountain:*

Some Gnostic Cartoons.

DT: *Invocation of Hallucinatory Mountain,* there was one in London, one in Rome, one in Denmark, Copenhagen. I do a lot of paintings, and often do the covers for my albums. I do a lot of paintings for the covers. The paintings in *Invocation of Hallucinatory Mountain* are Gnostic. There's one called "Yaldabaoth," so there are often references to Gnostic ideas as well as standard Christian apocryphal stuff.

APS: What Gnostic themes were you addressing in the cartoons?

DT: They weren't really themes, just the ideas I've been talking about, there's a war on, blah blah. They're just really things that move me and interest me. So that's the Gnostic influence. Again it's just the texts that touch me and I'm influenced by, but they're certainly not portrayals in pastel or ink of Gnostic theology or anything similar to that.

Lance S. Owens

The Hermeneutics of Vision
C.G. Jung and Liber Novus

On the evening of 12 November 1913, Carl Gustav Jung arrived at the mythic crossroads of his life. A power emerging from the depths was compelling him toward a journey he did not comprehend. Unexpected words were demanding his voice. He reached into a desk drawer, retrieved the journal he had abandoned eleven years earlier, and opened it to a blank leaf.

Jung was thirty-eight years old, a famous doctor, clinical investigator, and leader of Freud's revolutionary psychoanalytic movement. He sat in the study of the new mansion he had built for his family on the shores of Lake Zurich. But this night he faced the darkness of a starker interior fact: during a decade of meteoric success, he had lost something precious. Jung had lost his soul.

Now She awaited. He turned to the empty page, scribed the date at top, and began:

My soul, my soul, where are you? Do you hear me? I speak, I call you–are you there? I have returned, I am here again. I have shaken the dust of all the lands from my feet, and I have come to you, I am with you. After long years of long wandering, I have come to you again....

Do you still know me? How long the separation lasted! Everything has become so different. And how did I find you? How strange my journey was! What words should I use to tell you on what twisted paths a good star has guided me to you? Give me your hand, my almost forgotten soul. How warm the joy at seeing you again, you long disavowed soul. Life has led me back to you. ... My soul, my journey should continue with you. I will wander with you and ascend to my solitude.[1]

I.

The odyssey that commenced that evening and proceeded intensely for the next five years would transform Jung. In old age he testified:

The years ... when I pursued the inner images were the most important time of my life. Everything else is to be derived from this. It began at that time, and the later details hardly matter anymore. My entire life consisted in elaborating what had burst forth from the unconscious and flooded me like an enigmatic stream and threatened to break me. That was the stuff and material for more than only one life.... Everything later was merely the outer classification, the scientific elaboration, and the integration into life. But the numinous beginning, which contained everything, was then.

But exactly what it was that happened—what he experienced, what he saw and heard and recorded in his ledger of the journey—remained Jung's hidden mystery.

Historians, biographers and critics struggled to explain this seminal period in his life.

They called it a creative illness, a period of introspection, a psychotic break, or simply madness.[2] Lacking any factual foundation, all these words were vessels of pure speculation. Jung's own record remained hidden.

And Jung had kept an extensive and detailed record. First, there were six sequentially dated journals, known as the "black books", which he began this night in November of 1913 and continued through the early 1920s. These journals might be best described as his primary and contemporaneous ledger of a voyage of discovery into imaginative and visionary reality, what he termed "my most difficult experiment".[3] By 1915, as the magnitude of his experience penetrated him, he felt the need for a more formal and elaborate recording of the visions. With great artistic craft—employing antique illuminated calligraphic text and stunning artwork—Jung labored for sixteen years translating the primary record of his experience from the black books into an elegant folio-sized leather-bound volume: this is the famous but long-sequestered *Red Book*. Jung titled it *Liber Novus*, "The New Book".

Throughout his life the Red Book, *Liber Novus* remained veiled. Only a handful of his closest students and colleagues were allowed to examine it; after his death in 1961, his family refused all requests (and they were frequent) for access to the volume or to the secret Black Books.[4] For the last several decades, the Red Book was closed away in a Swiss bank vault, unseen by anyone.

Now nearly a century after the record began, both the book and the experience that produced the book have been opened. With the full cooperation of Jung's heirs and after thirteen years of exhaustively detailed editorial work by Dr. Sonu Shamdasani, in October of 2009 W.W. Norton published The Red Book in a full-sized folio facsimile edition, complete with an English translation, a comprehensive introduction, and over 1500 extensive editorial notes including excerpts from the black book journals and other previously unknown contemporaneous documents.

In sum, this publication signals a watershed in the understanding of the life and work of C. G. Jung. It is a revelation. In its light, our understanding of the story and history of Jung begins anew.

THE WAY OF WHAT IS TO COME

Liber Novus is the long occulted key to comprehending everything Jung said and wrote after 1916.[5] But it is also a singularly modern document, a book unlike any other, defying categorization or comparison. It fractures expectations; it speaks with voices beyond common ken.

Whether one approaches *Liber Novus* as an historian, a psychologist, a literary critic or simply as an interested reader, the puzzle is the same: What was the man doing, what was happening to him? Is this record to be read as an imaginative literary creation, a psychological work veiled in prophetic language, an epoch-defining revelation, or as pure madness? How do we interpret Jung?

Jung well understood the problem. In private comments recorded by a close associate during the 1920s, he expressed his own doubts about whether the work could ever be revealed or understood.[6] Modern language lacked words with meanings vital enough to convey the nature of what he had experienced. He himself struggled to understand it, find words to contain it or explain it. After more than a decade besieged with the burden of his revelation, and nearly as many years transcribing that revelation into *Liber Novus*, Jung concluded it could not be disclosed. No one would understand.

First must come another crucial work. He had to establish again in history a method to his madness, a hermeneutics to his vision. In 1928, Jung set aside work on *Liber Novus* and turned to that task.[7] It would occupy the remaining decades of his life. Throughout this extended enterprise, the seminal experience he faithfully served would remain hinted but hidden.

We now have the record of his experience, a transformative journey of discovery that lasted in intensity for about five years.[8] And we have the corpus of Jung's public enterprise, the hermeneutics to his vision, extracted from that crucible over the forty following years. Finally, together, we see how in Jung they wed.

But like much of Jung's work, this too is a circular course. *Liber Novus* and the hermeneutic enterprise it fomented form a paradoxical *complexio*. Neither can be what it was until it has the other with it, as it is. The experience, and the knowledge granted by the experience, is one. Vision revealed a hermeneutics. The hermeneutics demands confrontation with the vision.

Once we enter the realm of *Liber Novus,* it is impossible to read Jung's collected writing without hearing its echoing voices. Encountered anew, with *Liber Novus* in hand, the greater sum of Jung's subsequent writings is revealed as a vast hermeneutical project intent on opening to modern comprehension his experience, its record, and its centering fact: the forgotten reality of the Soul.

MY SOUL, MY JOURNEY SHOULD CONTINUE WITH YOU…

But what was the man doing, what was happening to him?

In early 1913 Jung's six year long association with Freud acrimoniously dissolved. These years had brought both frenetic activity and what Jung later identified as escalating self-alienation. It was a short passage in Jung's long life and it is best understood in the negative context of its failure.

When the two men first met in 1907, Jung was thirty-two years old and just finding professional footing. The elder Freud proffered exactly what the younger doctor then dearly sought: a comprehensive theory, seemingly built on years of clinical insight, that added order to Jung's own puzzle of observations and nascent intuitions about the psyche.

Jung initially embraced Freud with an almost religious zeal. Freud responded to this "Father complex" by precipitously proclaiming Jung a

Joshua to his Moses, his successor and crown prince in the psychoanalytic movement. Of course, along with immense intellect and enthusiasm, Jung brought Freud something else dearly needed: an exponent with international stature from outside the marginalized Jewish circle surrounding him in Vienna. The association with Jung and his respected Swiss colleagues put Freud on a much larger stage.

Jung was not an obedient son. His own distinct intellectual background, powers of observation and natural predilections inexorably drew him toward views that Freud's dogma did not abide. Freud had firmly delimited the unconscious psyche as a midden of life's infantile traumas and sexual repressions, a dank cellar of personal pathology. Jung differed. He sensed in the soul not just the refuse of repression, but beneath that undeniable personal layer, deeper healing strata running to yet indeterminate sources.

In the visions of his psychotic patients and in the dreams and fantasies of more balanced individuals Jung had discerned primitive mythic motifs and symbolic images—evidences augmented by his own self-observation. What these espoused, how deeply they were rooted, he did not know. But this question became his central focus. When Jung published his massive—if somewhat chaotic—mythologic and symbolic study of the psyche, *Wandlungen und Symbole der Libido*[9] in 1912, Freud saw final evidence of heresy. Jung saw in Freud a quasi-religious fixation on a theoretical creed. By hypostatizing his own sexual dogma, Freud had cut short the psyche.

The severing of his relationship with Freud was not "the cause of Jung's impending mental breakdown", as past critics have facilely suggested. With new facts at hand, the end of that association appears more a byproduct of Jung's own relentless quest. And to this, Freud remained peripheral.[10]

The psyche—the soul—was an experienced force. But Jung could now say nothing more. He explained in the draft manuscript of *Liber Novus*, "I had to accept that what I had previously called my soul was not at all my soul, but a dead system that I had contrived."[11]

During the early months of 1913, his dreams presented puzzles he could not order. Inchoate forces stirred in the unconscious, petitioning a voice he did not own. This activation climaxed in October of 1913 with two repeated spontaneous visions:

> In October, while I was alone on a journey, I was suddenly seized by an overpowering vision: I saw a monstrous flood covering all the northern and low-lying lands between the North Sea and the Alps. When it came up to Switzerland I saw that the mountains grew higher and higher to protect our country. I realized that a frightful catastrophe was in progress. I saw the mighty yellow waves, the floating rubble of civilization, and the drowned bodies of uncounted thousands. Then the whole sea turned to blood. This vision lasted about one hour. I was perplexed and nauseated, and ashamed of my weakness.
>
> Two weeks passed; then the vision recurred, under the same conditions, even more vividly than before, and the blood was more emphasized. An inner voice spoke. "Look at it well; it is wholly real and it will be so. You cannot doubt it."[12]

The eruption of over-powering visual hallucinations caused Jung to fear that he was "menaced with a psychosis."[13] He had witnessed the disastrous sequels of such phenomena in many patients. Commenting in a private seminar twelve years later, he explained, "I thought to myself. 'If this means anything, it means that I am hopelessly off.'"[14]

Over the next weeks, he surveyed his situation, delving for any brand of insight that might staunch seeming insanity. He found none. There was no way back, no way around.

From this crossroads, one solitary path awaited him: It went in.

And so, on the evening of 12 November 1913, Jung sat at his desk, opened his journal and addressed the mystery:

Meine Seele, Meine Seele, wo bist Du? (My Soul, My Soul, where are You?) …[15]

A year later, in reflection on these initial words, he added commentary:

> The spirit of the depths forced me to say this and at the same time to undergo it against myself, since I had not expected it then. I still labored misguidedly under the spirit of this time, and thought differently about the human soul. I thought and spoke much of the soul. I knew many learned words for her, I had judged her and turned her into a scientific object.
> I did not consider that my soul cannot be the object of my judgment and knowledge: much more are my judgment and knowledge the objects of my Soul. Therefore the spirit of the depths forced me to speak to my soul, to call upon her as a living and self-existing being. I had to become aware that I had lost my soul.
>
> From this we learn how the spirit of the depths considers the soul: he sees her as a living and self-existing being, and with this he contradicts the spirit of this time for whom the soul is a thing dependent on man, which lets herself be judged and arranged, and whose circumference we can grasp. I had to accept that what I had previously called my soul was not at all my soul, but a dead system. Hence I had to speak to my soul as to something far off and unknown, which did not exist through me, but through whom I existed.[16]

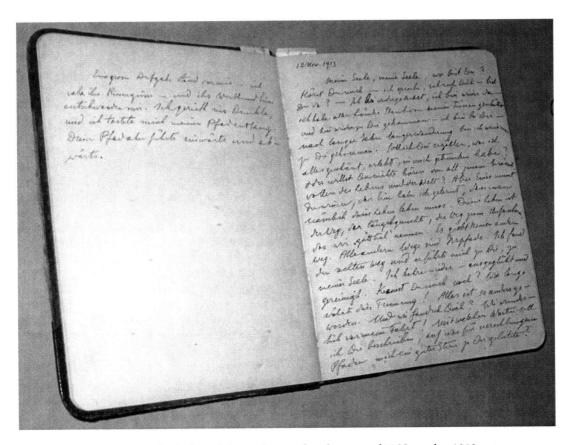

Figure 2: Jung's Black Book journal, opened to the entry of 12 November 1913,
the night his journey began.

WHO ARE YOU? ARE YOU GOD?

A journey had begun, but the course before him was obscure. He had no theory or concept to explain what he was doing, whom he was addressing, or how he should proceed. He simply had to let things happen, let the unconscious find its voice. How else could he hear its intent, see its point of view, probe its depths? Two nights later, on 14 November 1913, he called out to his soul:

I am weary, my soul, my wandering has lasted too long, my search for myself outside of myself. Now I have gone through events and find you behind all of them. For I made discoveries on my erring through events, humanity, and the world. I found men. And you, my soul, I found again, first in images within men and then you yourself. I found you where I least expected you. You climbed out of a dark shaft....

I wandered for many years, so long that I forgot that I possessed a soul. I belonged to men and things. I did not belong to myself. Where were you all this time? Which Beyond sheltered you and gave you sanctuary? ... How should I decipher you?

Who are you, child? My dreams have represented you as a child and as a maiden. I am ignorant of your mystery. Look I bear a wound that is as yet not healed: my ambition to make an impression. Forgive me if I speak as in a dream, like a drunkard—are you God? Is God a child, a maiden? ... How strange it sounds to me to call you a child, you who still hold the all-without-end in your hand.[17]

And the next night:

What strange things are happening to me? ... Where are you leading me? Forgive my apprehension, brimful of knowledge. My foot hesitates to follow you. Into what mist and darkness does your path lead? ... I limp after you on crutches of understanding. I am a man and you stride like a God.... I should give myself completely into your hands—but who are you?[18]

Then came a portentous quiet. "I wanted to throw everything away and return to the light of day. But the spirit stopped me and forced me back into myself."[19]

Jung had addressed his Soul, felt the penetrating reality of the Soul. He had heard a call from the Depths. But the dialogue he was attempting was, so far, very one-sided. For twenty-five nights he persisted, petitioning communication. He sensed himself in a desert: an anchorite wandering in his own internal and barren wasteland under a burning sun. He had to wait, stay present in that interior fact, turn off conscious and exterior critical thought: observe the empty, listen to silence. Wait.

Slowly a response began to come, finding voice through him. The words began as short phrases and cryptic comments. He explained, "Sometimes it was as if I were hearing it with my ears, sometimes feeling it with my mouth, as if my tongue were formulating words; now and

then I heard myself whispering aloud."[20]

Jung had arrived at the threshold of vision.

II.

In 1925, about twelve years after these events, Jung gave a seminar to a small group of individuals then working with him in Zurich. The group wanted to know more about the formation of his psychological views, and specifically, details of what happened during this decisive confrontation with his unconscious a decade earlier. Jung complied, giving his most explicit—yet still highly abbreviated—public account of the experiences recorded in *Liber Novus*.[21] Selecting from the critical landmarks of his passage, Jung discussed at length two opening events. They might be described as the "threshold" and "doorway" of his journey, and occurred in December 1913. To this pair, in late life Jung added to the public record two more landmarks, recorded in *Memories Dreams Reflections*.[22]

These four beacons help orient us in a brief survey of the journey recounted in *Liber Novus*. Long established in Jung's literature, they also allow us to compare Jung's abbreviated renditions of the story with his direct record. I would descriptively title these passages (and this is entirely my own apparatus): "The Cave"; "Elijah's Door"; "Meeting Philemon"; and "The Summary Sermons". I will touch upon each in my ensuing comments.

During his "twenty-five nights in the desert", the period between mid-November and December 1913, Jung was struggling to go deeper into what he now conceived as "the depths". To aid the progress, he began to work intentionally with visualizations:

Not knowing what would come next, I thought perhaps more introspection was needed. When we introspect we look within and see if there is anything to be observed, and if there is nothing we may either give up the introspective process or find a way of "boring through" to the material that escapes the first survey. I devised such a boring method by fantasizing that I was digging a hole, and by accepting this fantasy as perfectly real. This is naturally somewhat difficult to do—to believe so thoroughly in a fantasy that it leads you into further fantasy, just as if you were digging a real hole and passing from one discovery to another. But when I began on that hole I worked and worked so hard that I knew something had to come of it—that fantasy had to produce, and lure out, other fantasies.[23]

He labored, imaginatively: Digging, digging, digging. Watching, hearing. Digging.

Finally, I felt I had come to a place where I could go not further down. I said to myself that, that being the case, I would then go horizontally, and then it seemed as if I were in a corridor, and as though I were wading into black slime. I went in, thinking to myself that this was the remnant of an old mine....

ENTRY OF THE CAVE

A full account of what followed is recorded in his journal, dated 12 December 1913, and thence in *Liber Novus:* "The spirit of the depths opened my eyes and I caught a glimpse of the inner things, the world of my soul, the many-formed and changing....

I stand in black dirt up to my ankles in a dark cave. Shadows sweep over me. I am seized by fear, but I know I must go in. I crawl through a narrow crack in the rock and reach an inner cave whose bottom is covered with black water. But beyond this I catch a glimpse of a luminous red stone which I must reach. I wade through the muddy water. The cave is full of the frightful noise of shrieking voices. I take the stone, it covers a dark opening in the rock. I hold the stone in my hand, peering around inquiringly. I do not want to listen to the voices, they keep me away. But I want to know. Here something wants to be uttered. I place my ear to the opening. I hear the flow of underground waters. I see the bloody head of a man on the dark stream. Someone wounded, someone slain floats there. I take in this image for a long time, shuddering. I see a large black scarab floating past on the dark stream.

In the deepest reach of the stream shines a red sun, radiating through the dark water. There I see—and a terror seizes me—small serpents on the dark rock walls, striving toward the depths, where the sun shines. A thousand serpents crowd around, veiling the sun. Deep night falls. A red stream of blood, thick red blood springs up, surging for a long time, then ebbing. I am seized by fear. What did I see?"[24]

He concluded his summary of this first invoked vision, saying to the 1925 seminar group:

When I came out of the fantasy, I realized that my mechanism had worked wonderfully well, but I was in great confusion as to the meaning of all those things I had seen....[25]

"I was in great confusion..." He had no conceptual framework, no map, for what he would encounter on his exploration. Jung was entering an unknown or forgotten dimension of reality, a place as close as the beating heart in his breast, and yet as distant as the faintest stars of heaven. Everything he had held as a theoretical concept would be discarded before the reality of the experience.

Dr. Shamdasani explains, "His procedure was clearly intentional—while its aim was to allow psychic contents to appear spontaneously."[26] And now, "The spirit of the depth opened my eyes and I caught a glimpse of inner things, the world of my soul."

Jung had crossed the threshold, and his sight had opened to an inner vision. A year later he added commentary to his initial account:

> Because I was caught up in the spirit of this time, precisely what happened to me on this night had to happen to me, namely that the spirit of the depths erupted with force, and swept away the spirit of this time with a powerful wave. But the spirit of the depths had gained this power, because I had spoken to my soul during 25 nights in the desert and I had given her all my love and submission. But during the 25 days, I gave all my love and submission to things, to men, and to the thoughts of this time. I went into the desert only at night.
>
> Thus can you differentiate sick and divine delusion. Whoever does the one and does without the other you may call sick since he is out of balance. [27]

At this point in the story and history, a question inevitable arises: "Was Jung insane? Is this a psychotic episode, marked by auditory and visual hallucinations?" The answer, based on extensive historical documentation, is: "No."

During this period, and over the next several years while pursuing his "nocturnal work" Jung continued to function in his daytime activities without any evident impairment. He maintained a busy professional practice, seeing on average five patients a day. While undeniably complex, his family life was full. He lectured, wrote, and remained active in professional associations. In addition, he gave obligatory service as an officer

in the Swiss army and served on active duty over several extended periods during each of the following years.[28] In the balance between his night and day he found sanity: "Whoever does the one and does without the other you may call sick since he is out of balance".

This is our conundrum: in modern conception an individual who claims to have "visions" is either insane, or using the wrong word. Finding the right word—faced against the spirit of the times—was a chore for Jung. In the remarks above, Jung employs the word "fantasy" to describe his night work. But elsewhere he declares his dislike for "fantasy" and the limited meaning it conveyed in modern usage.[29] Alternative terms he used to circle the experience are "imagination" and "vision". Unfortunately, they all suffer the same limitation: common parlance either pathologizes or trivializes the words.

Jung fractures this conundrum with his own paradox. In subsequent years, we follow him in his writings struggling to revalorize the barren conceptual vessel of the Word with a living and experienced fact.[30] This endeavor was crucial to his extended hermeneutic project.

ELIJAH'S DOOR

Jung had found a "glimpse of inner things". He wanted to follow this inner path further. About ten nights later he attempted to do just that. And this time the doors of perception swung wide open. He explained to the 1925 seminar,

"The next thing that happened to me was another fantastic vision. I used the same technique of descent, but this time I went much deeper. The first time I should say I reached a depth of about one thousand feet, but this time it was a cosmic depth. It was like going to the moon, or like the feeling of descent into empty space."[31]

In *Liber Novus* he recounts the vision:

> On the night when I considered the essence of the God, I became aware of an

image: I lay in a dark depth. An old man stood before me. He looked like one of the old prophets. A black serpent lay at his feet. Some distance away I saw a house with columns. A beautiful maiden steps out of the door. She walks uncertainly and I see that she is blind. The old man waves to me and I follow him to the house at the foot of the sheer wall of rock. The serpent creeps behind us. Darkness reigns inside the house. We are in a high hall with glittering walls. A bright stone the color of water lies in the background. As I look into its reflection, the images of Eve, the tree, and the serpent appear to me. After this I catch sight of Odysseus and his journey on the high seas. Suddenly a door opens on the right, onto a garden full of bright sunshine. We step outside and the old man says to me, "Do you know where you are?"

I: "I am a stranger here and everything seems strange to me, anxious as in a dream. Who are you?"

E: "I am Elijah and this is my daughter Salome."…

The visions that followed and continued intensifying over three nights form one of the longer encounters in *Liber Novus* (and here "vision" is the precise word Jung used to describe the experience). They are also highly complex and meaningful, and impossible to summarize adequately. Jung called the visions the "mystery play", the *Mysterium*. He describes it as his "transformation".[32] One finds the personages of Salome and Elijah repeatedly referenced in Jung's later writings, though never explicitly linked to this experience.

Sometime later Jung penned a psychological reflection on the figures encountered: "They are certainly not intended allegories; they have not been consciously contrived to depict experience in either veiled or even fantastic terms. Rather, they appeared as visions."[33]

At the conclusion of the first night's vision, Jung exclaims to Salome and Elijah, "You are the symbol of the most extreme contradiction." Elijah corrects him: "We are real and not symbols."

Elijah explains that he and his daughter, his Wisdom, have been one from the beginning. Salome declares her love for Jung, and explains that she is his sister; their mother is Mary. At the denouement of the vision, which occurred on Christmas 1913, Jung is Christed—he suffers the last hour on Golgotha. Here, *Liber Novus*:

Salome says, "Mary was the mother of Christ, do you understand?"

Jung: "I see that a terrible and incomprehensible power forces me to imitate the Lord in his final torment. But how can I presume to call Mary my mother?"

Salome: "You are Christ."

I stand with outstretched arms like someone crucified, my body taut and horribly entwined by the serpent: "You, Salome, say that I am Christ?"

It is as if I stood alone on a high mountain with stiff outstretched arms. The serpent squeezes my body in its terrible coils and the blood streams from my body, spilling down the mountainside. Salome bends down to my feet and wraps her black hair round them. She lies thus for a long time. Then she cries, "I see light!" Truly, she sees, her eyes are open. The serpent falls from my body and lies languidly on the ground. I stride over it and kneel at the feet of the prophet, whose form shines like a flame.

Elijah: "Your work is fulfilled here. Other things will come. Seek untiringly, and above all write exactly what you see."

Salome looks in rapture at the light that streams from the prophet. Elijah transforms into a huge flame of white light. The serpent wraps itself around her foot, as if paralyzed. Salome kneels before the light in wonderstruck devotion. Tears fall from my eyes, and I hurry out into the night, like one who has no part in the glory of the mystery. My feet do not touch the ground of this earth, and it is as if I were melting into air .[34]

In his later reflections,[35] Jung explains that no other event in *Liber Novus* shared the same quality as these visions. This experience marked a doorway of mystery. Jung passed through.

III.

At the end of the *Mysterium*, Elijah gave an explicit mandate: "Other things will come. Seek untiringly, and above all write exactly what you see." Jung complied.

His journey had commenced forty-five days earlier. Now the imaginal realm lay opened before him, and he engaged it untiringly, almost nightly, throughout the winter and early spring months of 1914. The kaleidoscopic series of adventures, the imaginative figures and the dialogues that ensued cannot be briefly summarized with justice.

Jung's experiences varied in both intensity and mode of expression. Many of the experiences he recorded are highly visual, others are more auditory and conversational. The literary flow of several passages suggests an imaginative encounter written in progression. Jung's comments in later years on "active imagination" accepted a broad range of experience in the imaginative mode: it involved the whole being. But ultimately every sensory metaphor for the experience of the imaginal fails to the degree that it remains single-sighted, bound by the exterior light of day.

In the opening passages of *Liber Novus*—written about a year after the initial experiences and interpretively reflecting upon them—he attempts explanation:

> If you remain within arbitrary and artificially created boundaries, you will walk as between two high walls: you do not see the immensity of the world. But if you break down the walls that confine your view... then the ancient sleeper awakens in you.... There in the whirl of chaos dwells eternal wonder. Your world begins to become wonderful. Man belongs not only to an ordered world, he also belongs in the wonder-world of his soul....
>
> If you look outside yourselves, you see the far-off forest and mountains, and above them your vision climbs to the realms of the stars. And if you look into yourselves, you will see on the other hand the nearby as far-off and infinite, since the world of the inner is as infinite as the world of the outer. Just as you become a part of the manifold essence of the world through your bodies, so you become a part of the manifold essence of the inner world through your soul. This inner world is truly infinite, in no way poorer than the outer one. Man lives in two worlds. [36]

The key is immersion and involvement in the mythopoetic imagination: grasping the independent reality of imaginal voice and vision, and participating with it. I do not say "granting reality" to the experience—that would imply the sovereignty of the granting observer. The shattering fact that Jung knew is that the ego sacrificed all sovereignty in the experience.[37] The demiurge was deposed: daylight consciousness was not the sole creator of the real.

ΠΡΟΦΗΤωΝ ΠΑΤΗΡ ΠΟΛΥΦΙΛΟC ΦΙΛΗΜωΝ

Figure 2: Philemon, painted by Jung around 1924 in Liber Novus

MEETING PHILEMON

By January 1914, Jung had received a gift of magic. But he knew not how to explain it, interpret it, or use it. What was magic? He needed the help of a magician. The event that follows is the third landmark Jung gave to his journey[38] and it forms a major section of *Liber Novus.*

In a dream (apparently about this time) Jung had met an impressive figure,

> It was an old man with the horns of a bull. He held a bunch of four keys, one

of which he clutched as if he were about to open a lock. He had the wings of the kingfisher with its characteristic colors. Since I did not understand this dream-image, I painted it in order to impress it upon my memory.[39]

Jung sought out the figure in vision and "after a long search I found the small house in the country fronted by a large bed of tulips. This is where ΦΙΛΗΜΩΝ [Philemon], the magician, lives...."

But in this first imaginative encounter, Philemon appeared feeble, senescent, and of improbable aid:

Why is ΦΙΛΗΜΩΝ a magician? Does he conjure up immortality for himself, a life beyond? He was probably only a magician by profession, and he now appears to be a pensioned magician who has retired from service. His desirousness and creative drive have expired and he now enjoys his well-earned rest out of sheer incapacity, like every old man who can do nothing else than plant tulips and water his little garden.[40]

Over the coming years, Philemon's mask of senescence transmuted as he disclosed himself to Jung in progressive emanations of timeless grandeur. In his 1916 commentary for *Liber Novus* on the initial encounter, Jung would pen a long ode to Philemon and express understandings recast by further experience:

You know, Oh ΦΙΛΗΜΩΝ, the wisdom of things to come; therefore you are old, oh so very ancient, and just as you tower above me in years, so you tower above the present in futurity, and the length of your past is immeasurable. You are legendary and unreachable. You were and will be, returning periodically. Your wisdom is invisible, your truth is unknowable, entirely untrue in any given age, and yet true in all eternity, but you pour out living water, from which the flowers of your garden bloom, a starry water, a dew of the night.[41]

In *Memories, Dreams, Reflections*, Jung hints at the nature of his relationship with Philemon, "At times he seemed to me quite real, as if he were a living personality. I went walking up and down the garden with him...." Jung names Philemon as his teacher and "guru". But in private comments to Cary de Angulo in 1923, Jung describes Philemon as something ineffably greater. He was, in multiform manifestations, an avatar of "the Master",

...the same who inspired Buddha, Mani, Christ, Mahomet - all those who may be said to have communed with God.[42]

Above Philemon's image painted on page 154 of *Liber Novus*—and this is one of the few images from the book released for publication in prior decades—Jung penned an appellation in Greek: "Father of the Prophet, Beloved Philemon". [43]

But the deepening understanding of Philemon came only in the next two years and as a result of the revelatory power of other visions. In the initial encounter during the winter of 1914, Philemon was simply a mysterious old magician, a strange dream figure with the blue wings of a kingfisher, holding a key.

THE CONCEPTION OF *LIBER NOVUS*

By the summer of 1914, the initial imaginative flood ebbed and then ceased entirely. Jung had accepted Elijah's vocation, he had recorded in his ledger all he had seen and heard. But what was its meaning? How should he interpret it?

Beginning with the spontaneous visions of destruction flowing over northern Europe in October of 1913, and then in other images throughout his months of descent into the imaginal, Jung had repeatedly confronted dark portents of war. Initially, he worried they reflected his own internal state, the danger of being rent apart by psychic dissolution. The Great War loomed unsuspected over Europe.

When war did erupt in August of 1914, Jung's understanding of his private journey reformed. The visions had actually been precognitive and prophetic, and not entirely personal. His experience had been entwined with forces acting upon the exterior world. As he explained in a letter to Mircea Eliade many years later:

> Now I was sure that no schizophrenia was threatening me. I understood that my dreams and my visions came to me from the subsoil of the collective unconscious. What remained for me to do now was to deepen and validate this discovery. And this is what I have been trying to do for forty years.[44]

Working from his ledger of the experience, the black books, he began a new draft manuscript. It appears he was considering compiling a record for publication. And here he engaged a first interpretive endeavor. The visions from his journals were faithfully transcribed, but to each sequence now was added a secondary commentary or meditation. Upon completion of this draft, the next phase of work commenced: a medieval artistic calligraphic labor of elaborating the text onto folio-sized parchment with historiated initials and interspaced images.

After transcribing material up through the *Mysterium* onto seven parchment leaves,[45] he envisioned yet something more. He commissioned a beautiful folio-sized volume containing about 600 blank pages, and exquisitely bound in fine red leather. On the spine, in golden lettering, Jung put the title: *Liber Novus*.

Now he began transcribing the contents of the draft manuscript directly into the Red Book. The effort would continue slowly and with great artistic craft over the next 15 years. The book was never completed. Of the draft material he had compiled, only about two-thirds of the text was eventually transcribed into the red leather volume of *Liber Novus*.[46]

SEVEN SUMMARY SERMONS

In the late summer and autumn of 1915, after having completed his first draft manuscript, a new stream of imagination erupted. These deepening experiences continued over the next year, through the summer of 1916, and formed the last sections of *Liber Novus*. From this time on Philemon is an increasingly central figure in Jung's imagination.

Philemon first reappeared on 14 September and greeted Jung with a long enigmatic statement on the mystery of gold, "A blazing hoard is piled up, it awaits the taker." He informed Jung that "Hermes is your daimon." Both these cryptic comments would only reveal their means to Jung two decades later.[47]

The tone of the encounters in this second phase of experience seems subtly changed from the earlier material. Jung has spent a year compiling and reflecting on his initial experiences. He is differentiating and integrating the voices that have emerged from the depths, and gaining perspective on his own voice relative to them. The visions are working towards a coalescence.

A critical juncture in this distillation came on 16 January 1916 when Jung's Soul delivers an astounding mythologic statement about the nature of God, man, and creation. In tone and content, it reflects an ancient Gnostic myth—the story of Sophia (who speaks here as his Soul) and of Abraxas, the creative Demiurge who had separated from Sophia:

> *You should worship only one God.* The other Gods are unimportant. *Abraxas is to be feared.* Therefore it was a deliverance when he separated himself from me. You do not need to seek him. He will find you, just like Eros. He is the God of the cosmos, extremely powerful and fearful. He is the creative drive, he is form and

formation, just as much as matter and force, therefore he is above all the light and dark Gods. He tears away souls and casts them into procreation. He is the creative and created....

But you have in you the *one* God, the wonderfully beautiful and kind, the solitary, starlike, unmoving, he who is older and wiser than the father, he who has a safe hand, who leads you among all the darknesses and death scares of dreadful Abraxas. He gives joy and peace, since he is beyond death and beyond what is subject to change....
This one God is the kind, the loving, the leading, the healing. To him all your love and worship is due. To him you should pray, you are one with him, he is near you, nearer than your soul.[48]

Two weeks later, Jung was visited by a ghostly horde. They demanded a statement from him. In the form of seven sermons, he gave the ghosts the summary revelation of his experience, reflecting all he had so far integrated from the visions, and including insights granted by the revelation from his Soul, above. This event is the final major landmark Jung publically disclosed about the experiences forming *Liber Novus*.

In *Memories, Dreams, Reflections* Jung offers an account of what happened:

It began with a restlessness, but I did not know what it meant or what "they" wanted of me. There was an ominous atmosphere all around me. I had the strange feeling that the air was filled with ghostly entities. Then it was as if my house began to be haunted....

Around five o'clock in the afternoon on Sunday the front doorbell began ringing frantically ... but there was no one in sight. I was sitting near the doorbell,

and not only heard it but saw it moving. We all simply stared at one another. The atmosphere was thick, believe me! Then I knew that something had to happen. The whole house was filled as if there were a crowd present, crammed full of spirits. They were packed deep right up to the door, and the air was so thick it was scarcely possible to breathe. As for myself, I was all a-quiver with the question: "For God's sake, what in the world is this?" Then they cried out in chorus, "We have come back from Jerusalem where we found not what we sought." That is the beginning of the *Septem Sermones*.[49]

Over the next nine nights, Jung composed and presented to the dead his *Septem Sermones ad Mortuos*.[50]

The *Seven Sermons to the Dead* present a vast cosmogonic myth, a discourse on the progressive emanation and evolution of human consciousness from the first unconscious source, an ineffable, undifferentiated fullness Jung calls the *Pleroma*.[51] Though using terms common to ancient Gnostic mythology such as *Pleroma* and *Abraxas*, this is not a recapitulation of any single extant mythologic progenitor. An incautious reader, unaware of the true authorship, could however easily locate it within the framework of ancient Gnosticism.

From his diaries, it appears that Jung wrote the sermons with his own voice. As he later reflected on the experience, however, he saw that it was Philemon who had spoken them through him. When he transcribed the *Septem Sermones* into his final manuscript of material for *Liber Novus*, Jung made Philemon voice:

Behold, ΦΙΛΗΜΩΝ came up to me, dressed in the white robe of a priest, and lay his hand on my shoulder. Then I said to the dark ones, "So speak, you dead." And immediately they cried in many voices, "We have come back from

Jerusalem, where we did not find what we sought. We implore you to let us in. You have what we desire. Not your blood, but your light. That is it."

Then ΦΙΛΗΜΩΝ lifted his voice and taught them….

Jung adds something more to the text of the sermons in *Liber Novus*. After each of the seven sermons, Philemon offers exegetical comments, in dialogue with Jung. Philemon declares his statements are not declarations of "belief", but are avowals of his sure knowledge (*gnosis*).

Jung stated, as recorded in *Memories, Dreams, Reflections,*

> These conversations with the dead formed a kind of prelude to what I had to communicate to the world about the unconscious: a kind of pattern of order and interpretation of its general contents.[52]

They are also the only part of *Liber Novus* which Jung disclosed during his lifetime. Around 1917 he had a small number of copies of the *Septem Sermones ad Mortuos* printed. In the printed version, Jung pseudepigraphically attributed them as: "Seven exhortations to the dead, written by Basilides of Alexandria, the city where East and West meet."[53] Basilides of Alexandria was an early Gnostic Christian about whom very little documentation now survives.

Throughout his life Jung occasionally gave copies of this small book to trusted friends and students, but it was available only as a gift from Jung himself. Those who received copies usually held them in strict confidence.

Septem Sermones ad Mortuos, a summary statement coalesced from Jung's experience of the Depths, brings *Liber Novus* toward a close. There is, however, one last detail about Philemon disclosed on the final of page of the text that must be mentioned.

In the ultimate vision recorded in *Liber Novus*, Jung meets both Philemon and Christ in his garden. Philemon addresses Christ as "my master, my beloved, my brother!" Christ sees Philemon, but recognizes him as Simon Magus—one of the first historical figures of ancient Gnosticism. Philemon explains to Christ that once he was Simon Magus, but he is Philemon now.

This needs consideration: Jung is the voice of the sermons in his first journal rendition. In the version of the *Septem Sermones* transcribed into the Red Book manuscript, Jung gives Philemon as the voice. When Jung transcribes the *Septem Sermones ad Mortuos* to be printed as an independent text, they are attributed pseudepigraphically to yet another historical second century Gnostic teacher, Basilides of Alexandria. Then it is revealed that Philemon is Simon Magus! Thus Jung, Philemon, Simon Magus, and Basilides are all finally conflated together in the voice of the Gnostic prophet who speaks the *Septem Sermones ad Mortuos*.

At this point in his journey, the sum of evidences suggests Jung associated something very central in his experience with an ancient nexus of Gnosis. This was, of course, not the end of Jung's journey. His encounters with the imagination continued into the early 1920s. Final disclosure of that material, contained mainly in Black Books 6 and 7, will hopefully be forthcoming in future years.

IV.

CRYSTALLIZING A STONE

From the very beginning of his journey in November 1913, Jung struggled with an interpretive task: translating his imaginative encounters—his visions—into words. The translators of *Liber Novus* comment,

> At the outset of *Liber Novus*, Jung experiences a crisis of language. The spirit of the depths, who immediately challenges Jung's use of language along with the spirit of the time, informs Jung that on the terrain of his soul his achieved language will no longer serve.[54]

The theoretical, didactic and discursive forms of his previously well-honed scientific jargon would not carry the fact of this experience. Jung confronts the challenge before him in his introduction to *Liber Novus,* and he makes this petition to the reader for understanding:

My speech is imperfect. Not because I want to shine with words, but out of the impossibility of finding those words, I speak in images. With nothing else can I express the words from the depths.

Near the end of life, Jung spoke of the visions as "the fiery magma out of which the stone that had to be worked was crystallized."[55]

The first task—the primary hermeneutic task—was a crystallization of the stone.

That stone, the fact he would work for the rest of his life, originated in a protean visionary experience playing over several years, a descent into mythopoetic imagination. Now he needed to give this experience firm form. This was an intensely focused and deeply considered interpretive process. The voice of the depths spoke in images, and so, in translating his experience, must Jung. Even the graphic expression of words on the page needed to speak with image.

Jung further intuited that his experience was not *sui generis*, but rather somehow linked with something else, something that existed earlier in history.[56] With parchment and pen, and archaic calligraphic script, he had to bridge an invisible chasm in time, linking past and present. And future.

The process unfolded in a dynamic progression. As the transcription proceeded, parchment pages changed to paper ones, artistic images imaginatively brought to the text became more abstractly expressive, the calligraphic hand appeared less archaic. The sum reveals these temporal strata. But it is all stone crystallized from one same source.

Jung recognized that what he had experienced was not personal. It was epochal. Commenting on signal imaginative creations across the ages, in 1930 he states that great imaginative art

... draws its strength from the life of mankind and we completely miss its meaning if we try to derive it from personal factors.

Whenever the collective unconscious becomes a living experience and is brought to bear upon the conscious outlook of an age, this event is a creative act which is of importance for a whole epoch. A work of art is produced that may truthfully be called a message to generations of men.... This is effected by the collective unconscious when a poet or seer lends expression to the unspoken desire of the times and shows the way, by word or deed, to its fulfillment....[57]

He was occultly speaking in kind of his own hidden book, *Liber Novus*: the primary translation to word of vision, a multifaceted layering of word in image and image in word, reaching back and forward in time, "a creative act which is of importance for a whole epoch ... a message to generations of men."

WORKING THE STONE

By the end of the 1920s, C. G. Jung had emerged from the crucible of his experience. He held a stone, a crystallization of vision. How he worked it over the remaining four decades of his life constitutes one of the most multifaceted and complex hermeneutic projects in human history.

I cannot here give full voice to deciphering the layered meanings in that declaration. Jung turned two million words and more to the story of his stone. Here I will open just three aspects of the way his interpretive project developed.

PHYSICIAN AND WOUND

A decade earlier Jung had been thrust into a difficult and dangerous self-experiment. As a physician he had already spent years studying the power of psychic functions to gravely wound as well as to mysteriously heal. But he had no idea what these powers were or from where they originated. His therapeutic model had proved inadequate. Finally it seemed his own sanity hinged upon finding answers.

What happened in the course of his journey of discovery was unexpected, extraordinary, creative, imaginative, artistic. And more. Jung had rediscovered the depth and vitality of the mythopoetic imagination. A doorway had opened upon the forgotten "other pole" of human nature, the fact behind human consciousness.

Jung had experienced his "empirical man" entering a greater dimension, a "divine" realm, the realm of the greater "self".[58] In the union of inner and outer, above and below, he had discovered the image of God. To this witnessed experience he poignantly gives early testimony in September of 1915:

Through uniting with the self we reach the God. ... I have experienced it. It has happened thus in me. And it certainly happened in a way that I neither expected nor wished for. The experience of the God in this form was unexpected and unwanted. I wish I could say it was a deception and only too willingly would I disown this experience. But I cannot deny that it has seized me beyond all measure and steadily goes on working in me. ... No insight or objection is so strong that it could surpass the strength of this experience.[59]

But Jung did not seek the mantle of prophet to the God. Nor was he called to be an artist. And he was certainly not a madman. At the end of his journey, he remained a physician confronting the festering wound of his age: Modern man had lost his Soul. The stone now crystallized in his hand held healing powers. But it needed to be worked to that purpose.

First he had to awaken his age to the fact of the existence of the psyche. This awakening uniquely required an experiential encounter with the Soul. Dream was one ubiquitous evidence of psychic activity, but there were others, including the royal road of imagination and vision. With interest aroused in the phenomena, Jung would encourage inner exploration, show doorways and paths. He would become a guide to many. Those whom he judged had successfully journeyed themselves and encountered the terrain would join him as guides, as analysts—understanding always that a guide or "therapist" can help others only through lands they themselves know. And Jung would aid the task with maps of the terrain, signaling the prominent landmarks, translating what he had learned from his own travels into tools of discovery.

To speak of the psychic terrain meaningfully, a new vocabulary was needed. Words that had been cut from their roots by modern culture needed to be revitalized, valorized, and grafted to the perennial radix of experience. This was a task of vast hermeneutic complexity.

The core of Jung's psychological terminology is figuratively a map of his own journey. Archetype, active imagination, collective unconscious, anima, animus, persona, and individuation: All these words were first spoken descriptively by Jung between the years 1916 and 1918 in the early development of this second layer of the hermeneutic project. And the words imagination, vision, God, symbol: these were sound vessels to be refilled with the elixir of experience.

Jung the physician had been called to treat a terrible wound. He offered his unguent, artfully compounded from a rare and healing stone.

VISION AND HISTORY

By the late 1920s Jung had fleshed out his map of the psyche along with a descriptive vocabulary. These were not theoretical constructs, but rather tools for deciphering human experience. Any understanding of their practical utility required contact with the phenomena of the psyche. As a physician, he dedicated himself to personally guiding patients into that phenomenal realm, pointing out landmarks in their personal chaos and paths with healing potential.

In his duty as a scientist, however, he faced a different and broader task. He needed now to collect his evidences and elucidate the phenomenology of the psyche at a generic level. The facts needed to be summed. And though he worked a lifetime collecting specific case histories and clinical fragments of psychic phenomena, no sum of study could substitute for the touchstone resting in his study, opened on his desk: *Liber Novus*. The empirical foundation, the bedrock to his science, was already crystallized there. But he could not reveal it.

Jung knew his book would not—not yet—be understood. The primary ledger of his most difficult experience, and the material formed in *Liber Novus*, had to remain concealed. Then in 1928, another road opened.

In that year, Richard Wilhelm sent Jung a Chinese meditation text he had recently translated, *The Secret of the Golden Flower*, and asked for Jung's comment. Jung was stunned. In the treatise he saw a clear description of what he had been doing. Not only was the visionary technique described in the text similar to his own, but also the result of the process described there mirrored his own result, imaged by his mandala paintings in *Liber Novus*. Suddenly he saw a path by which the contents of his book could find "their way into actuality." [60]

The Secret of the Golden Flower figuratively maps passage through a little-evidenced experience. By fact of his own journey in that terrain, Jung immediately recognized what was being described. He had been there, done

that. Jung turned his interpretive skills to commentary, using this independent document to illustrate and amplify his discoveries. From this point onward, *Liber Novus* remained the occult Rosetta Stone, the unseen intertext, to his hermeneutics.

Jung searched through esoteric literature seeking other material that fit into this hermeneutic method. He had long recognized in ancient Gnosticism the analog of his experience, but the fragmentary literature available at the time, in the early twentieth century, remained too limited and corrupted to sustain his full development. Then Jung discovered remnants of the Western alchemical literature. Here awaiting him was a magnificent locked library of experience—and he had been given the key.

The medieval alchemists had been brother physicians, seemingly seared and marked by a molten *prima materia* Jung too had known. He would apply the hermeneutics of his vision to that historical record, the quest for the Philosopher's Stone. Using this documentary source, he could establish extensive evidence, drawn from many centuries of recorded experience, for the generic outlines of his science, elucidating the phenomenology of the psyche.

Over the next twenty-five years Jung worked, resurrecting deciphering, refining, and illuminating the alchemists' forgotten old books. And preparing way for his new one: *Liber Novus*.

HERMENEUTICS AND TRADITION

The revelation of *Liber Novus* and other related primary documents opens new perspectives on the life and work of C. G. Jung. One of the most important of these focuses attention on his multifaceted vocation as hermeneut.

I have mentioned very briefly two aspects of Jung's approach to the interpretation of his experience — how he worked the stone in his roles as physician and as scientist. But there is another vital and complex issue that must be considered: Jung had received a revelation.

How did he interpret this fact in the context of Western religious tradition, and what was his reading of *himself*, the one chosen to receive the revelation?

To say he rejected the archaic role of prophet is both accurate and completely insufficient. This is a critical issue in understanding Jung and his hermeneutics, and simply saying, "No, he didn't do *that*" is no answer at all. Over many years, Jung reflected deeply upon the answers to these final questions; in the last two decades of his life, he directly confronted the soteriological implications of his experience within the contexts of Christian history. In conclusion, I will focus attention here.

Among the astounding source materials Dr. Shamdasani provides in the editorial apparatus of *Liber Novus* is a section from Jung's journal dated 5 January 1922. [61] Jung entered a conversation with his soul about his vocation. The dialogue he recorded adds perspective on the immensity of the burden Jung felt resting upon him:

Jung has not been able to sleep, and addresses his Soul, asking why. She says there is no time to sleep, he has great work to begin, he must go to "a higher level of consciousness". Jung asks, "What is it? Speak!"

Soul: You should listen: to no longer be a Christian is easy. But what next? For more is yet to come. Everything is waiting for you. And you? You remain silent and have nothing to say. But you should speak. Why have you received the revelation? You should not hide it. You concern yourself with the form? Is the form important, when it is a matter of revelation?
Jung: But you are not thinking that I should publish what I have written [*Liber Novus*]? That would be a misfortune. And who would understand it?
Soul: No, listen! … your calling comes first.

Jung: But what is my calling?
Soul: The new religion and its proclamation.
Jung: Oh God, how should I do this?
Soul: Do not be of such little faith. No one knows it as you do. There is no one who could say it as well as you could.
Jung: But who knows, if you are not lying?
Soul: Ask yourself if I am lying. I speak the truth.

Three days later, his soul explains further:

"You know everything that is to be known about the manifested revelation, but you do not yet live everything that is to be lived at this time…. The way is symbolic."

He knows everything to be known about the revelation. Now he has to live it. The way is symbolic.

It appears Jung is confronting not just the "revelation" but also the fact of himself, a modern man, being the "revelator". How could he live *that* peculiar fact "at this time"? He faces not only the hermeneutics of a vision, but of himself as hermeneut.

Behind the word "hermeneut" resided a mythic and symbolic history of meaning. Jung knew it. Hermes was the interpreter of the words of the Gods to Men, the mercurial messenger imaged in his planetary aspect: a tiny celestial luminosity visible only occasionally in twilight hours between light and dark, on swift journey between the gates of the sun and the land of human dreams.

Old theological discussions of the hermeneutical art worked principally within a horizontal axis: the methods of interpreting meanings from an object (classically, a sacred text, the "word of God") in comparative historical, ethical, allegorical and metaphorical modes.

However, another mysterious mode of interpretation was mentioned in medieval commentaries. It was called *anagoge*.[62] Its methods remained perpetually vague in many centuries of commentary. The Greek word itself means to lift up, or elevate. Hermeneutics in the anagogical mode cleaves all other approaches with a vertical axis: it reads mystical meanings. Here the hermeneut directly bridged above and below, thus witnessing the visionary fact veiled by words.

Jung traveled that high way—the vertical axis—the ancient road of Hermes. Understood symbolically, in image of the hermeneut, he stood as nexus between inner and outer, hidden and seen, above and below, Gods and Men.

In this symbolic task, Jung had duties to his own time. He described his situation:

> There were things in the images which concerned not only myself but many others also. It was then that I ceased to belong to myself alone, ceased to have the right to do so. From then on, my life belonged to the generality.[63]

Many evidences suggest Jung understood himself as a link in a golden chain, the hermetic "…*Aurea Catena* which has existed from the beginnings of philosophical alchemy and Gnosticism".[64] The chain was forged from individual human lives, each link binding an epoch with ageless reality.

Jung stood himself within a tradition that was not defined by creed or dogma, but instead by an experience: a baptism in the mythopoetic stream of imagination, an entry into the ardent furnace of the primal fact. In myth and symbol and text, wayfaring men who returned from the ancient highway worked the interpretive art. In the records they left, Jung recognized signal images of his own experience.

In his scientific writings, Jung repeatedly pointed to these specific historical manifestations of the tradition, drawing upon that record to help amplify his own. Most specifically, he pointed at early Christian history where the tradition had been called Gnosis, and at the textual traditions of Hermeticism and the hermetic "yoga" of alchemy. Both of the latter, Jung stated, were entwined in origins with Gnosticism, and complexly mingled in Western Christian tradition over more than a millennium.

Through the seer's stone of his own experience, Jung read the marks in history of a visionary hermeneutics. What he saw and attempted to explain often remains entirely obscure to his readers. And he understood their problem. Only those who had traveled the inner world, and been wayfaring men, could clearly recognize these ancient maps for what they were. To explain what he saw, he had to help others take the journey into psychic reality. Then they too would see. This was a difficult and circular course. He gave his life to it.

In the end, Jung did not proclaim a new religion. Instead, and with increasing focus during his last years, he turned his vision to revealing the living stream from which the myths, rituals and symbols of Christianity took source. He said we stood beside a great river. If a bridge over it was to be built, it must start from the ground where we stand. And we stood upon a great wealth and we did not see. The discarded and forgotten but still precious stone from the past would be the cornerstone of that bridge to the future. But first, humankind must return to the source, find the imaginative fire from which experience wrought the myths and images of old. In that molten basalt emerging in imaginative channels from ageless depths, our destiny would crystallize.

In an interview coinciding with the publication of *Liber Novus*, Dr. Sonu Shamdasani was asked to prophesy on ways the Red Book would affect Jung's image in coming years. By way of answer, Shamdasani referenced the immensely important collection of Gnostic texts rediscovered in 1945 and first published in 1977 as the *Nag Hammadi Library*—texts widely recognized to be long lost primary documents of the ancient Gnosis.

Looking to the future, he replied:

The publication will be seen to mark a caesura comparable to the effect of the publication of the Nag Hammadi library on the study of Gnosticism—finally, one is in the position to study the genesis of Jung's work and what took place in him during this critical period, on the basis of primary documents....[65]

I vision Dr. Jung smiling broadly over the mysterious conjunction within that comment.

V.

Jung wrote the conclusion of *Liber Novus* not with pen upon its many remaining blank pages, but in stone at his Bollingen Tower on the shores of Lake Zurich. This was his shrine to Philemon, his repentance of the Faustian sin—the hubris of modern consciousness that refused a place of welcome to the Gods.[66]

In 1950, in remembrance of his seventy-fifth year, Jung worked the last "page" of *Liber Novus* from a large square stone resting beside his tower. As he began work on the front surface, the stone showed him a circle: it looked out at him like an eye.

With chisel, he cut deep the round circle, and then the central pupil. In the pupil of the eye—at the doorway between inner and outer worlds—he saw and carved a small figure, the cabiri Telesphoros. His vestment is marked with the symbol of Hermes. In hand, he bares a lantern. Around him in ancient Greek, the stone speaks this proclamation:

> *Aion* is a child playing—Wagering on
>   draughts—Kingship of a Child
> Telesphoros traverses the dark
>   regions of this Cosmos
> A flashing Star from the Depths
> Guiding way to the Gates of the Sun
>   and to the Land of Dreams [67]

There, at the threshold of vision, we meet the final mystery of Carl Gustav Jung and his *Liber Novus*.

Figure 3: Jung's Lapis at Bollingen, completed in 1950

NOTES

I wish to express my gratitude to Dr. Stephan A. Hoeller, who several decades ago introduced me to the wisdom of C. G. Jung and guided me through the great gateway of the Septem Sermones ad Mortuos. *This commentary reflects many years of our conversations. Along with a generation of Jung's students, I respectfully thank Dr. Sonu Shamdasani, whose editorial work and scholarship provide the historical foundations for this commentary.*

1 C.G. Jung, *The Red Book: Liber Novus*, ed. Sonu Shamdasani, tr. John Peck, Mark Kyburz, and Sonu Shamdasani (WW Norton & Co, 2009), p. 232 i. (hereafter, LN) Given the large size of the folio pages of LN, citations are to page and page column, column given as i or ii.

2 For extensive review of biographical treatments of Jung and this period in his life, see, Sonu Shamdasani, *Jung Stripped Bare Jung by His Biographers, Even* (Karnac, 2005).

3 LN p. 200 ii.

4 There are seven journals, the first dating from before 1902. The events beginning 12 Nov 1913 are recorded in Black Book 2 through 7. The last five of these journals had black covers, the cover of Black Book 2 is a dark brown. Somewhat confusingly, Black Book 2 is often referred to as the "first journal", since it is the beginning the record pertinent to LN.

5 Sonu Shamdasani, Oct 9 2009 address delivered at New York Academy of Medicine, author's transcript; and LN p 221 ii.

6 LN p. 212ff.

7 By 1928 Jung had transcribed only about two-thirds of the draft material he had prepared, and apparently intended, for inclusion in *Liber Novus*. In the published edition, this draft material is include within the translation of the manuscript text. See Shamdasani's editorial notes in LN.

8 Events continued intensely through 1918, and then less intensely into the early 1920s. LN includes events up through summer 1916, with commentary add up until about 1918 (based on my reading of Shamdasani's notes). Diary material from 1916 onward will almost certainly reach publication at a future date.

9 First published in a flawed English translation by Beatrice M. Hinkle in 1916, under the title *Psychology of the Unconscious*; thereafter heavily revised by Jung and published in the Collected Works as *Symbols of Transformation*, CW 5.

10 See, Sonu Shamdasani, *Jung and the Making of Modern Psychology: The Dream of a Science* (Cambridge University Press, 2003) for a comprehensive evaluation of the many intellectual currents to which Jung was exposed, and the relative influence of Freud.

11 LN p. 232 n39.

12 C. G. Jung, *Memories, Dreams, Reflections*, ed. Aniela Jaffe (revised edition, Pantheon, 1993) p. 175 (hereafter MDR).

13 MDR p. 200; LN p.198 ii.

14 C. G. Jung, *Analytical Psychology: Notes of the Seminar Given in 1925*, ed. William McGuire (Princeton University Press, 1989), p. 40; LN p. 198 ii. Ten months later, he recognized this as a pre-cognitive vision of the Great War that erupted in August of 1914. During this period, there were several others vision that he late understood in this context; see LN p. 202 i, and below.

15 LN p. 232 i. The text following this invocation is given at the beginning of this paper. I have reproduced the repeated words, "Meine Seele, Meine Seele", as written in the original diary entry.

16 LN p. 232 i.

17 LN p. 233 i.

18 LN p. 234 ii.

19 LN p. 235 ii.

20 MDR p. 178.

21 *Analytical Psychology*. At least one of those present, Cary de Angulo (later, Cary F. Baynes) had read manuscript material prepared for *Liber Novus*. It is likely that a few others present, including Jung's wife Emma, had read material in *Liber Novus*.

22 The rendition of events given in 1925 was subsequently adapted, with many deletions and additions—including these two mentioned signal events—for inclusion in *MDR* chapter 6, "Confrontation with the Unconscious".

23 *Analytical Psychology* p. 47.

24 LN p. 237 ii.

25 *Analytical Psychology* p. 47-8.

26 LN p. 200 ii. Apparently paraphrasing comments made by Jung to Aniela Jaffe, Shamdasani adds: "In retrospect, he recalled that his scientific question was to see what took place when he switched off consciousness. The example of dreams indicated the existence of background activity, and he wanted to give this a possibility of emerging, just as one does when taking mescalin."

27 LN p. 238 ii.

28 LN p. 201 i.

29 Jung objected: "I really prefer the term "imagination" to "fantasy"... fantasy is merely nonsense, a phantasm, a fleeting impression; but imagination is active, purposeful creation.... A fantasy is more or less your own invention, and remains on the surface of personal things and conscious expectations. But active imagination, as the term denotes, means that the images have a life of their own and that the symbolic events develop according to their own logic—that is, of course, if your conscious reason does not interfere." *Tavistock Lectures*, CW 18 p. 171.

30 Jung begins *Liber Novus* quoting Isaiah and the Gospel of John.

31 *Analytical Psychology* p. 63.

32 LN p. 250 n197.

33 LN p. 356 i This commentary was probably written in the early 1920s, and is given as Appendix B in *Liber Novus*.

34 LN p. 252 ii.

35 LN p. 356 i.

36 LN p. 264.

37 *The Collected Works of C. G. Jung*, (Princeton University Press), Vol 11, p. 157 (hereafter, CW; references are to volume and page, not paragraph number).

38 MDR p. 182ff.

39 MDR p. 183.

40 LN p. 312 i.

41 LN p. 316 i.

42 Cary F. Baynes papers, Jan 26, 1924, LN p213 ii.

43 This appellation and painted image of Philemon in *Liber Novus* was probably completed in late 1924 or early 1925, base on surrounding dates in the text.

44 Shamdasani reviews this matter in detail, LN p. 201ff.

45 He would subsequently title this section of the account *Liber Primus* ("Book One").

46 The published edition of *Liber Novus* contains the complete text of the drafts in English translation, including material apparently intended for, but never entered into, the Red Book volume. The seven original parchment leaves, *Liber Primus*, would subsequently be place by Jung interleaf into the beginning of the big book. Material transcribed directly into the Red Book constitutes *Liber Secundus*, relating to events from late December

1913 through about April 1914. The last draft pages of *Liber Secundus* were never transcribed, and none of the material from the third section of the draft material, *Scrutinies,* appears in the Red Book volume. By my examination of the original volume, I surmise approximately 400 pages at the back of the volume remain blank.

47 Reflecting on these statements in the 1930's, Jung undoubtedly saw alchemical gold. LN p. 337 n25.

48 This journal entry is in Black Book 5 and does not appear in *Liber Novus*. LN Appendix C, p. 370. During coming weeks, Jung sketched in his journal the outlines of his first "mandala", the *Systema Munditotius*, which forms a schema of this statement and the vision conveyed in the *Sermones,* LN Appendix A, p. 363-4.

49 MDR , p190-1. Based other dated events in his journals, the Sunday referred to in this account is probably Sunday, 30 January 1916. Shamdasani also gives Cary Baynes' remembrance of Jung's account of the event, LN p. 205 ii.

50 From Dr. Shamdasani's notes in LN, it appears that the Seven Sermons are recorded in journal entries in Black Book 6, dated 31 January to 8 February 1916.

51 The best available analysis of the *Septem Sermones ad Mortuos* remains the seminal 1982 exegesis by Stephan A. Hoeller, *The Gnostic Jung and the Seven Sermons to the Dead* (Wheaton, IL: Quest , 1982).

52 MDR p. 192.

53 Hoeller translation, *The Gnostic Jung*, p. 44.

54 John Peck, Mark Kyburz, and Sonu Shamdasani, LN p. 222.

55 MDR p. 4 Shamdasani translates the passage less poetically and more precisely, "The first imaginings and dreams were like fiery, molten basalt, from which the stone crystallized, upon which I could work." LN p. 219 ii.

56 At the end of *Liber Secundus*, Jung wrote: "I must

catch up with a piece of the Middle Ages—within myself. We have only finished the Middle Ages of—others. I must begin early, in that period when the hermits died out." LN p. 330, 216 ii.

57 CW 15 p. 98.

58 CW 11 p. 157.

59 LN p. 338 ii.

60 Jung's 1957 "Epilogue" to *Liber Novus*, LN p. 360.

61 LN p. 211-2.

62 See for example, Hugh of St. Victor (c. 1078 –1141), *De scripturis et scriptoribus sacris.*

63 MDR p. 192.

64 MDR p. 189.

65 "Inside Jung's Red Book: Six Questions for Sonu Shamdasani", *Harper's Magazine*, Oct. 2009.

66 Over the gate at the Bollingen Tower, Jung engraved this dedication: *Philemonis Sacrum— Fausti Poenitentia* (Shrine of Philemon— Repentance of Faust). MDR p. 235n.

67 This is my translation. The first phrase references a fragment from Heraclitus of Ephesus (c. 535 BC), and can be read on the stone as a coherent statement. MDR translates Jung's amplified German rendition of the inscription: "Time is a child— playing like a child—playing a board game—the kingdom of the child. This is Telesphoros, who roams through the dark regions of this cosmos and glows like a star out of the depths. He points the way to the gates of the sun and to the land of dreams." MDR p. 227.

Karl Le Marks

Déjà vu, Consciousness, Time & English Pubs

If I had ever been here before I would
     probably know just what to do
Don't you?
If I had ever been here before on
     another time around the wheel
I would probably know just how to deal
With all of you.
And I feel
Like I've been here before…
We have all been here before.
Crosby, Still, Nash & Young, "Déjà vu"

Sometimes I feel like there has been a skip in reality and I get this overwhelming sensation that I've been here, and lived this moment, before. I feel locked in a film, one I know I've seen before, and know just what is going to happen next or what those around me are about to say but I feel if I were to say anything at that time then the whole of reality would collapse upon me, and then I'm out of the moment and the sensation has gone….

Melanie, 29, New Hampshire, USA

Paramnesia (from the Greek *para* (parallel) and *mnēmē* (memory)), in psychiatry, is a disorder of the memory or the faculty of recognition in which sensory experience or dreams may be confused with reality, often accompanied by the feeling that one has experienced the present moment before, but a

more familiar term is déjà vu (literally translated as "already seen") which was first used by Emile Boirac in 1903 in his book "*L'Avenir des sciences psychiques*" ("The Future Of Psychic Sciences"). However, déjà vu is just one of a whole myriad of names given to a variety of such memory and sensory experiences and is often used incorrectly to describe what the individual is experiencing and what the cause of such experience may be. I have been interested in déjà vu and all the scientific, philosophical and spiritual explanations for the phenomena for many years so I recently sent a questionnaire to a controlled group of scientists, philosophers, spiritual practitioners and people who live with déjà experiences in order to collate some thoughts and opinion regarding the subject from a professional and personal perspective. What made my research all the more interesting is that I personally, have never had a déjà vu, whilst around 70% of the population respond to having done so. However, something very strange did occur to me last year, which this year has proven to be true and I will outline that experience and my new term for it, within this paper.

It happens when I am generally not thinking. I mean when I'm just doing normal things like making the bed or driving the car or shopping. Suddenly it's like everything feels familiar, like I'm watching a replay but I'm there, living in it and then it just goes again. 10 seconds at most and I look at the people around me hoping that someone else just saw that as well.

Lucy, Manchester, UK

Dr. Arthur Funkhouser is one of the world's leading authorities in déjà experiences. He is a Jungian Psychotherapist in Bern, Switzerland and he defines three types of déjà vu experience in an attempt to more clearly delineate between associated, but different, neurological experiences. These are *deja vecu* (already lived), *deja senti* (already felt) and *deja visite* (already visited). Déjà vecu is the most common déjà vu experience and involves the extended temporal sensation of having done something or having been in an identical situation before, combined often with a sense of knowing what will happen next. Whereas a déjà vu can be a fleeting moment of sensation, a flash of memory or an immediate sense of familiarity, a déjà vecu has a longer time-span often utilising all the senses combined with an occasional cognition of what is about to occur.

I've been honoured to know Art for a couple of years now and had access to some of the voluminous data he has collected on the whole spectrum of déjà experiences and it is interesting to hear his thoughts on possible explanations, coming from a scientific and professional perspective but also from a personal one as he himself has had déjà vu.

I do not have an explanation for how it is possible for my psyche to take a peek into the future, I just know that it can do so. I am aware of many hypotheses that have been put forward, but I have found no reason to choose one over another. "

"For me, the events involved in such experiences are always very banal and ordinary. I would think that if my unconscious would want to show me a preview of some future happening, it would choose something memorable like the birth of my first child. That is why I question the extent of the control that my unconscious is able to exercise in giving me such previews.
Dr Art Funkhouser, Bern, Switzerland.

This seems to be a striking commonality in the responses I've received to my questionnaire and the research conducted for this paper – the unremarkable nature of the moment in which the déjà experience is experienced. Taking a psychological look at the neurology it is almost as though such experiences require an *unconscious-competent* modality to connect with our consciousness.

The last déjà vu I had was just yesterday. I was cleaning the inside of my kitchen window and suddenly my eyes went to a nearby tree as I knew exactly what was going to happen. As I stared at the tree while continuing to clean the window, a large ball from next door's garden hit the tree and knocked several leaves into my garden, right where I had just cleaned half an hour ago.

William, Cambridge, UK

Do these déjà experiences require a kind of lowered state of consciousness to connect with us? One where we are functioning almost on auto-pilot; an unconscious-competent state of activity which is largely unconscious in function thereby leaving our consciousness open to such communication, or is it all easily explained with science and that most elusive of ephemera, Time?

In 1963, Robert Efron published a paper entitled "Temporal perception, aphasia and déjà vu", in which he proposed déjà vu was explained as delayed intra-hemisphere transmission over the corpus callosum (the central white matter within the brain that links the left and right hemispheres). The Efron Thesis is still amongst one of the most suggested explanations for the whole of the déjà experience spectrum, but does it truly provide the answer?

THE FOUR PSYCHOLOGICAL STAGES OF LEARNING

Unconscious - Incompetent: *You are not aware that you can't do something!* (the person is not aware of the existence or relevance of the skill area)

Conscious - Incompetent: *You become aware that you can't do something!* (the person becomes aware of the existence and relevance of the skill)

Conscious - Competent: *You start doing the thing but have to think about it!* (the person learns it reliably but will need to concentrate and think in order to perform the skill)

Unconscious - Competent: *You do the thing without conscious thought!* (the skill becomes so practised that it enters the unconscious parts of the brain - it becomes 'second nature')

The human brain consists of two identical hemispheres connected by the corpus callosum and Efron suggest that what is presented to our consciousness is not what is actually perceived by our senses at that exact moment, in fact that our conscious awareness is functioning in a time frame that is running behind the time of our observations, so what we see at any one moment is not happening right now, but had already occurred just seconds before. This temporal time delay between what is observed and what is then presented to our consciousness via our senses has been experimentally documented many times since Efron's suggestion that this was the cause of déjà experiences.

Noetic Scientist Dean Radin in his books *The Entangled Mind* and *The Conscious Universe* provides a number of experiments in which such time delay to cognition has been proven to exist, so could what Efron proposes be the explanation?

He suggests that we initially observe the situation through one or both eyes and then this is processed in our brain crossing the corpus callosum to integrate the functioning of both hemispheres before being presented to our consciousness as reality. What déjà vu is,

therefore according to Efron, is just a temporal skip within the neurology of our brain so we are presented with the situation a fraction of a second after we have consciously become aware, and thus it appears familiar.

However, recent investigations into the suggested explanations of the Efron Thesis have produced very interesting results, especially at Leeds University in the UK where Dr Chris Moulin has been looking into more of the déjà vecu elements of continual déjà vu.

In a paper published in the journal *Brain and Cognition*, Leeds University researcher Akira O'Connor worked with Dr Moulin to relate how mundane experiences—undoing a jacket zip while hearing a particular piece of music; hearing a snatch of conversation while holding a plate in the school dining hall, etc. were examples of how déjà vu experiences were triggered in a subject who was blind, and therefore receiving no visual input, on which the whole Efron Thesis argument is founded.

It is the first time this has been reported in scientific literature. It's useful because it provides a concrete case study which contradicts the theory of optical pathway delay. Eventually we would like to talk to more blind people, though there's no reason to believe this man's experiences are abnormal or different to those of others.

Optical pathway delay is a quite antiquated theory, but still widely believed -- and was the basis for the déjà vu sequences in Joseph Heller's novel *Catch-22*. But this provides strong evidence that optical pathway delay is not the explanation for déjà vu. The findings are so obvious, so intuitive, that it's remarkable this research has never been done before.

Akira O'Connor – Leeds University, UK

O'Connor admits that to the person experiencing déjà vu, it feels almost inexplicable.

"And because it feels so subjective, psychology, in striving for objectivity, has tended to shy away from it. But psychologists have gone some way to illuminating things like the 'tip of my tongue' sensation when you can't think of a particular word. We just wanted to get to the same sort of understanding for déjà vu. We now believe that déjà experiences are caused when an area of the brain that deals with familiarity gets disrupted."

In one experiment, students are asked to remember words, then hypnotised to make them forget - and then shown the same word again to induce a feeling that they have seen it before. Around half said this brought on a sensation similar to déjà vu – and half of whom said it was definitely déjà vu.

The suggestion here is that through the examination and experimentation into the induction of déjà vu through hypnosis that memory is proven to function with a far wider vista that our consciousness presents.

The sense of time in a trance is diminished. This is particularly evident in post-hypnotic amnesia. We, in our normal states, use the spatialised succession of conscious time as a substrate for successions of memories. Asked what we have done since breakfast, we commonly narratize a row of happenings that are what we can call "time-tagged".

Julian Jaynes – *The Origin Of Consciousness in the Breakdown Of The Bicameral Mind*

So, what about those instances where the déjà experience seems to envelop the person in an almost literal playback of memory?

I was sitting on the train with my partner opposite me coming back from a trip to London and was gazing out the window really not concentrating on anything when I heard what, to me, sounded like a crack of a whip from the end of the carriage but when I looked away from the window all I saw was everybody motionless, but on closer look saw they were very, very slowly moving and my partner was turning the page of his book in slow-motion. This seemed to go on for minutes, probably 5 or so before the train seemed to jerk and like pressing play on a DVD from pause, the carriage came to life. While in the fugue I felt my partner would say to me something about Russell Brand and when everything returned to normal he closed his book, looked at me and said "Shall we go and see Russell Brand live, I think he's touring…

Stephanie, Nottingham, UK

Diana E. Zimmerman lives within a seemingly functioning permanent state of déjà vecu and I asked her how the experience feels to her.

When I'm happy, I enjoy it, appreciating each moment. But sometimes I'm lonely, because I don't know others who are like me, and sometimes I wish I could experience something NEW, like others seem to do. I occasionally wonder, what's it like to watch a movie you haven't seen before? To take a trip you haven't taken before? To get together with family and friends and have conversations you've never heard before? To go to work and do a task you haven't already completed before? Conversely, it's come in handy on many occasions, for me to be déjà familiar with the road I'm on, and then I'm thankful, and am awed again by the déjà mystery.

Diana's questionnaire that she kindly completed for me was one of the most fascinating I received and I could quote many more instances from her experiences, but to me the whole concept of perpetually being in such state would either suggest that the Efron Thesis was wrong, in its temporal anomaly state, or raise the question whether such temporal time delay could have a neurological permanence, given certain conditions.

> I began to déjà vecu continually in August of 1972. It was the culmination of 18+ years of sporadic, relatively odd temporal perceptions (including occasional, fleeting déjà vus), for a toddler/child/adolescent growing up. Having continually déjà vecue'd for more than 37 years now, I usually tend to ignore it, somewhat like you might ignore the intricacy of your hands, even when you're using them to accomplish something. I pay more conscious attention to it when I'm in the midst of obviously novel experiences, either pleasant or unpleasant. At those times, I seem to have no choice but to pay attention. During mundane or repetitious circumstances, the sense of déjà vecu is somewhat diminished, yet remains at the fringe of my conscious awareness, much as do your hands (or face, arms, legs, feet, torso, head…). On those occasions, it becomes apparent to me if and when I choose to notice it.

This was particularly interesting to me because in the vast majority of cases I've researched, the déjà vu experience often occurs whilst the mind and body are operating in a kind of symbiosis of repetition and mundane activity, whereas here, Diana states that during those circumstances her déjà vecu is in fact diminished. As Diana herself suggested to me:

> For example, I'm aware of the "déjà vu" of filling out this questionnaire; it takes no pointed concentration on my part for that awareness to rise to my conscious mind, whereas conscious awareness of my breathing process is seldom so close

to the surface.

I began to wonder if there may be a correlation between levels of awareness and consciousness in relation to déjà experiences as a mediator to how cognisant the whole experience becomes. Perhaps our psyche requires a certain state of equilibrium between the conscious, subconscious and unconscious functioning to communicate such states. Similar in concept to "the zone" of sportsmen or "the muse" of actors and cultural inspiration: Perhaps equitable to the Buddhist concept of Jhana, a state of serene contemplation or unconscious absorption.

> My girlfriend and I went on holiday a few years ago to Madeira in Portugal, somewhere that we both had often said we wanted to visit. Neither of us had been before nor knew why we both had an interest in the place but when we arrived there we both looked at each other and knew we had been before. In my dream the night before we travelled I pictured us walking down this cobbled street near some bushes down to a road with a view over some water and then there I was in the very spot the following day, my dream had shown to me my memory of the view and I knew it was then that I had to ask my girlfriend to marry me. I looked at her and she said "before you ask, you already know it is yes.

Graham (& Michelle), Edinburgh, UK

I was intrigued to consider how not one, but two people could seemingly have a déjà experience if such were explained as mere time anomalies within the neurology of the brain's processing of our independent empirical inputs. Our brain indeed does house two symmetrical hemispheres with different functioning areas depending on the sensory input and intended output, so could there be a system by which we are not just experiencing something for the first time, but where we are actually remembering the first time when we did?

> Two subjects, living side by side, but possessing different psychic apparatus, will inhabit different worlds - the properties of the extension of the world will be different for them.

P.D. Ouspensky, *Tertium Organum*

Anthony Peake is author of a fascinating hypothesis in relation to the whole spectra of déjà experiences and the subjectivity of consciousness. His *Cheating The Ferryman* thesis was introduced in his first book *Is There Life After Death: The Extraordinary Science Of What Happens When We Die* and suggests that we have indeed lived our lives before and are now experiencing them again much in the style of the movie *Groundhog Day* so such déjà experiences are, to Tony, evidence of our reliving the experience and becoming more aware of such.

If, like Neo at the start of the film *The Matrix*, we are all living inside a pre-recorded simulation then there must be an occasional glitch in the playback, a tell-tale sign that proves that this is all an internally generated holographic image. Again the writers of *The Matrix* show how this may be implied. In the film Neo experiences the phenomenon commonly known as a déjà vu. He sees a cat cross his path twice. This, it transpires, is evidence that the matrix programme was being altered. Could this be what is really happening in a déjà vu experience? If the holographic theory of experience is right then all a déjà vu is, is a judder in the playback process, a situation where the same information is presented to consciousness twice.

In essence, a reflection again on the suggestion that our perception of Time is at the heart of such phenomena. Einstein's special theory of relativity suggests that Time is relative to the observer and does not flow at a fixed rate. Time also flows at differently perceived rates to our own consciousness as evidenced when sleeping or when watching something particularly boring.

So, if Time is malleable as a concept and equates to consciousness in its immediacy then surely our perception of reality within such a transient frame of reference will have these anomalous moments that we term déjà vu?

> Because it is not proved by other than itself to itself, we say that consciousness of consciousness is immediate. "Immediate" means "not mediated", not using anything other than itself to know itself.

Eugene Halliday – *Reflexive Self-Consciousness*

Perhaps the immediacy of Time, within the immediacy of a subjective consciousness, presenting to our consciousness the data of our empiric experiences or the development of a super-aware higher self with a memory of our future? Are we living our experiential lives in a continuum of "Now" moments, being fractions of a second in length. What Roger Penrose termed "Objective Reductions" within the neurology of our brain could explain our consciousness but our perception of Time, given the human eye can function at rates of frame per second between 24 and 120 could equally reflect such phenomena as déjà experiences.

> There is no difference between the past and the future in the four-dimensional space-time-world. The present is only an illusion.

Albert Einstein

> When I consider the small span of my life absorbed in the eternity of all time, I am

frightened and astonished to see myself here instead of there now instead of then.

Blaise Pascal

But as I showed in relation to the Moulin/ O'Connor work, déjà has been shown to be inducible using non-visual means, so is déjà a purely visual phenomena? Does the brain compensate for lack of visual input by increasing the functionality of the remaining senses to induce a déjà?

One day, I decided (more or less out of the blue) to go visit my childhood home. (We had moved away about six years earlier, when I was thirteen.) It was probably a two-hour drive from where I was living. I didn't have a car, so I hitch-hiked. When I arrived at the house, I knocked on the door and an older woman opened it. I explained who I was. She kindly invited me in, introduced me to her husband, and they took me through the house and back to see my old bedroom. She and her husband had it fixed up for their granddaughter. It was arranged and decorated much the same as it was when I'd lived there, with the exception that where my bulletin board had hung on the wall by the door, hung a large poster, instead. The poster said,

I AM NOT AFRAID

OF THE FUTURE

BECAUSE

I'VE BEEN THERE

BEFORE.

Anonymous, in response to my questionnaire.

I shall now relate the only experience of my own life which seems to have any linkage to déjà experiences as I have never had a déjà vu, nor sense of having been somewhere before,

although I have had several, what are called, *Jamais Vu* in which one feels sure they have been somewhere but when they get there it is completely new to them.

As the bus wound its way into the town I felt an overwhelming sense of familiarity, unlike anything I have experienced before or since. I did not recognize landmarks and I couldn't have found my way around without the help of a map and obliging English-speaking tourists, but this does not mean that the sensation was not incredibly strong. I felt intense joy at being there that is so hard to explain.

Sophie, UK, discussing her first visit to Shimla in India.

FUTURE ANTICIPATED RECALL – (FAR)

It was around September 2008 and I had not long since met my now partner and was visiting her in the Midlands of the UK one weekend. She was working as a Nurse at the hospital in Solihull and I had taken the train to meet her there.

This was my first visit to Solihull and we walked from the train station into town towards the shopping centre. After a short while my partner took me out of another door of the shopping centre onto this unremarkable, but quaint looking, short, straight street of shops and business. Immediately I felt a sense of remembrance and with each stride up the street, as I looked at the front of the shops and the people milling around, I felt a strange sense of me remembering this very walk. Not a sense of already having done it, in the traditional déjà sense, but a strong sense of my fond recall and I had a very fleeting vision of myself remembering in the future the first time I had walked this street that I somehow knew I was going to walk many times in that future.

It was then that my partner showed me that at the top of this short street was a particular chain of public house that I often frequent in order to write and research while enjoying one of the UK's spectacular varieties of real ale and she told me that if we were to continue up the street and cross the road at the top we would come to the hospital where she worked.

Immediately I understood my strange sensation, because I would indeed be walking that very stretch of small street many times in the future as I would be meeting my partner from work by walking from the shopping centre, to the pub and then onwards to the hospital.

Over the last year this has proven to be very true indeed as I must have walked that same street a hundred times if not more, and then, a few weeks ago as I sat in that bar waiting for my partner, I sat back and remembered the first time I walked it and the cycle was complete.

I have termed this experience, Future Anticipated Recall (FAR), because that is exactly how it felt. I never felt like I had been there before or that I was remembering doing it. It felt like my future self was remembering the first time: in essence I was anticipating the future recall of the experience as I experienced it for what I perceived to be the first time.

In a 2001 paper, "Intense and recurrent déjà vu experiences related to amantadine and phenylpropanolamine in a healthy male", Satu Jääskeläinen and T. Taiminen reported their findings that certain drugs increased the occurrences of déjà experiences in neurologically healthy males.

A particular instance saw a man within their study group take the drugs *amantadine* and *phenylpropanolamine* to relieve flu symptoms which resulted in his vastly increased déjà experiences which he found so intriguing that he continued to take the medication long after his flu had cleared up in order to fully report his experiences. As a result, Jääskeläinen and Taiminen consider déjà experience to be hyperdopaminergic action in the mesial temporal areas of the brain.

Despite the vast quantity of qualitative and quantitative data, some deride déjà experiences as trifling incidents of no real importance; others live with the experiences daily and offer the exact opposite opinion. Some suggest a neurological condition and associations with *temporal lobe epilepsy* or a serious psychopathology such as *schizophrenia* and *dissociative identity disorder*, but surely such would logically conclude that everyone who experiences a déjà has some neurological anomaly. Which is clearly not the case.

To me, a deeper understanding of these phenomena is absolutely necessary towards a fundamental understanding of our consciousness and the nature of reality. We are often deceived by our senses and our pre-conceptions so that we can never truly know what is outside of our own perceptions and thus our entire universe is often constructed within our own conditions.

Sigmund Freud regarded déjà vu as evidence of sub-conscious activity, he thought that it happens when one is reminded of a sub-conscious fantasy. Carl Jung wrote an account of déjà visité" (*a form of déjà vu involving a sense of knowing a place that you've never been to before*) in a famous 1966 paper called "On Synchronicity".

We have all some experience of a feeling, that comes over us occasionally, of what we are saying and doing having been said and done before, in a remote time - of our having been surrounded, dim ages ago, by the same faces, objects, and circumstances —of our knowing perfectly what will be said next, as if we suddenly remember it!

Charles Dickens, *David Copperfield*

Many who do experience déjà say that the frequency of the sensation declines with age, in effect that we get fewer déjà experiences as we get older. Again, there are contrasting theories as to why this may be from a levelling out over time of the neurological temporal timings to the suggestion that we have already created a new life for ourselves by changing some aspect of our past as we live our lives again.

When I have a déjà vu or déjà vecu or any sense of a precognition or familiarity with my life I smile and register it as simply my consciousness reminding me that what I think is the sum total of reality is just a speck in the sand of the oneness of consciousness and the universe.

Ally, Hamburg, Germany

In my mind we are all of one consciousness that is experiencing itself subjectively and the separation of our individual consciousnesses is purely an illusion. Time has no definition outside of an observing consciousness and as the earlier Eugene Halliday quote shows, "consciousness mediates itself, and so does Time, hence we mediate our own subjectivity of consciousness and perception of Time."

Whether you view déjà scientifically, philosophically, spiritually or neurologically it appears to be a widespread phenomenon across all ages, creeds, cultures and beliefs. Are we in fact remembering an unconsciously stored dream imagery or simply stuck in a momentary matrix like glitch of time perception? Are we to believe the entirety of what our sensory input suggests?

Until we truly have a more fundamental understanding of what it means to have a subjective conscious experience and how such independence of mind is produced from the material realm of our brain functionality it is unlikely we will ever reach a universally agreed conclusion to the causes of déjà experiences.

When you see familiar faces
But you don't remember where they're from
Could you be wrong?
When you've been particular places
That you know you've never been before
Can you be sure?

'cause you know that this has
   happened before
And you know that this moment
   in time is for real
And you know when you feel deja-vu
Feel like I've been here before
Ever had a conversation
That you realise you've had before
Isn't it strange
Have you ever talked to someone
And you feel you know what's coming next
It feels pre-arranged.

Iron Maiden, *Déjà vu*

"Have you not done tormenting me with your accursed time! It's abominable! When! When! One day, is that not enough for you, one day he went dumb, one day I went blind, one day we'll go deaf, one day we were born, one day we shall die, the same day, the same second, is that not enough for you? They give birth astride of a grave, the light gleams an instant, then it's night once more."

Samuel Beckett, *Waiting For Godot*

Andrew Phillip Smith

The Hard Choice:
The Authoritative Discourse on the Soul

The soul does not exist for herself. This is the central message of the *Authoritative Discourse*, the third tractate in Codex VI of the Nag Hammadi library. The soul rightfully belongs to the hidden heavens; from these she came, with these she is one, to these she will return. But while she is in the visible material world, she is joined to a material body, and through this body she experiences the travails and the sinfulness of the physical world. Thus the soul has no independent status: she either takes her rightful place in the heavenly world with the Father and the bridegroom, or is tortured and consumed by the adversary and the man-eaters of this world. Such a dualistic approach is obviously very critical of the created world, yet the plight of the soul is not a pointless accident. The presence of the soul in the world enables the Father to demonstrate his wealth and glory, and has the nature of a contest between the influences of the pleroma and matter which the soul can win or lose, but is intended to win and so ultimately reveal the glory of the Father.

The *Authoritative Discourse* is certainly one of the lesser known Nag Hammadi texts. It is not included in either Bentley Layton's *The Gnostic Scriptures* or Meyer/Barnstone's *The Gnostic Bible*. In its few pages (14 pages of Coptic in the manuscript of Codex VI, five in the *Nag Hammadi in English*, 6 and a half in the Nag Hammadi Scriptures) the *Authoritative Discourse* is relentlessly dismissive of the pleasures of the material world. There are no simple joys to mitigate the troubles of existence. Life consists of either giving way to the evil distractions of the world or connecting to the inner heavenly realm. The *Authoritative*

Discourse is quite ascetic and its attitude to sexuality is quite hostile. This too is used as a metaphor, but the symbolism wouldn't work unless the writer and audience were in sympathy with the strict sexual morality.

Parts of the *Authoritative Discourse* resemble the *Exegesis on the Soul*, found in Codex II of the Nag Hammadi library. The Exgesis describes an elegant and clear version of the myth of the fall and redemption of the soul, who is also a feminine figure. She leaves the house of the Father, falls into prostitution, but eventually her repentance is heard by the Father and she takes her place in the bridal chamber with the bridegroom. Though the origin, fall and redemption of the feminine soul tops and tails the *Authoritative Discourse*, the text uses many other extended metaphors to express its meaning.

While it is generally dated to the late second or early third century and is seen by scholars as being either a Christian Gnostic or Christian Platonist text, the *Authoritative Discourse* has no explicit Christian or Jewish elements. Christ is never mentioned nor is the Torah referred to. The role of the female soul obviously reminiscent of Plato's myth of the soul in the Phaedrus. "The soul in her totality has the care of inanimate being everywhere, and traverses the whole heaven in divers forms appearing--when perfect and fully winged she soars upward, and orders the whole world; whereas the imperfect soul, losing her wings and drooping in her flight at last settles on the solid ground-there, finding a home, she receives an earthly frame which appears to be self-moved, but is really moved by her power; and this composition of soul and body is called a living and mortal creature." [trans. Jowett] Hence some scholars have seen it as a work of Christian platonism (some scholars have argued that the soul here consists of two parts, the spiritual and rational, as found in Middle Platonism.).

Gnostic features include explicit reference to Gnosis, to the bridal chamber and the pleroma. Some of the imagery is reminiscent of the Christian parable, but again, nothing is explicit. The liberal use of metaphor plus the bridal chamber reference might suggest a Valentinian provenance for the *Authoritative Discourse*. There is no complete explication of the typically elaborate gnostic cosmology yet a simplified cosmology may by extracted from the text.

A word (pun intended) should be said about the title. The Coptic title consists of two Greek loan words, authentikos logos. [It has also been translated as Authoritative Teaching (Nag Hammadi library in English) Authentic Teaching and Original Teaching (these last two used by Kurt Rudolph).] Rudolph, in his Gnosis: The Nature and History of Gnosticism, left the word untranslated in the text itself and considered the Logos here to have a "redeeming function... without assuming any personal figure," comparing it to Hermetic texts, which make similar use of the Logos. (Rudolph, Gnosis, p. 144). The Logos is famously featured in the opening sentence of the Gospel of John, "In the beginning was the Word.". The range of meanings of the Greek Logos includes discourse or teaching, but also such shades as reason, order or pattern, principle and ratio or proportion. (See Fideler, Jesus Christ, Sun of God, p. 38.) Hence, the Logos in the *Authoritative Discourse* may be seen as the teaching of the true order of things. This may have a salvific or redemptive quality in itself, but it's worth noting that it is actually the bridegroom who applies the Logos to the eyes of the soul. If we take the Logos as simply a teaching, this would mean that the teaching is a tool in the hands of a higher spiritual level.

Though the beginning of the text is unfortunately damaged, the *Authoritative Discourse* opens logically with an account of the soul's rightful place and her descent from the heavenly world, and closes appropriately with a poetic account of her return. The rest of the text consists of a more impressionistic series of metaphors and analogies, which hammer into the reader the importance of the choices that she must make, the consequences of those choices, and the way in which the soul is seduced by matter and can cast off temptation and be reunited with the spiritual world. We are given a basic description of the higher world from which the soul descends. The soul is intimately linked to this heavenly realm; she is a part of it, her Father and bridegroom are there, and the text makes it clear that the soul is divine in origin and substance.

When the soul inhabits the body she acquires stepchildren, who are lust, hatred and envy, each of which come from matter. They cannot inherit from the male side (the Father) like the soul does, but only inherit from matter. The embodied soul inevitably wishes for these qualities, such as passion, jealousy, vanity, and so on, because she is influenced by matter. The ignorant soul chooses these and thus falls into prostitution. She is drunk, corrupt, ignorant, living like an animal instead of experiencing the joy of the Father.

Then the metaphor changes. The life of the soul is like having chaff mixed with wheat. The wheat should have been kept uncontaminated in the storehouse; instead it is purchased as chaff, and mixed with other useless material.

Now the purpose of this predicament is made explicit. The father has set up a contest, a straight choice between the "exalted incomprehensible knowledge" of the Father and the things of the created world. The soul should seek for the Father. The mixing of the soul with matter only serves the purposes of the adversary.

The soul's eyes are blinded by matter, but the Word can act as an ointment for her eyes, to open them again to the light. Once again, the treasurehouse or storehouse (which houses the seeds/wheat) and is where her mind (Nous) is, is a place of safety for her. Should it not be obvious, the linking of the soul with Nous emphasises the divine as an inner, spiritual expperience.

Sleep, drunkeness and prostitution are common Gnostic metaphors. In the *Hymn of the Pearl*, the Prince falls into a deep sleep as a result of eating the heavy food of the Egyptians. Philo of Alexandria, in *Who is the Heir?*, makes a somewhat comical contrast between the Word and ordinary food, "for the one raises his eyes to the sky, beholding the manna, the divine word, the heavenly, incorruptible food of the soul, which is food of contemplation: but the others fix the eye on garlic and onions, food which causes pain to the eyes, and troubles the sight, and makes men wink, and on other unsavoury food, of leeks, and dead fish, the appropriate provender of Egypt. (80) "For," says the scripture, "we remembered the fish which we ate in Egypt without payment, and the gourds, and the cucumbers, the leeks, the onions, and the garlic; but now our soul is dry and our eyes behold nothing but Manna."{32}{#nu 11:5.} The moral? Don't eat Mediterranean salads.

As with Philo, there are two kinds of food in the *Discourse*. The adversary is like a fisherman who uses the food of the world as bait, so that we can be consumed. But there are foods that can bring life.

"Man-eaters will grab us and consumers us," we are told. These man-eaters are reminiscent of the "dealers in bodies" that are referred to later, but also of the statement in the *Gospel of Philip* that God is a man-eater.

The sequence by which the soul is seduced is explained carefully. Firstly there is "pain or heartache over something trivial in life" then desire for clothing/garments that will make you proud, and finally "sins arise such as love of money, pride, vanity, etc., the worst of which are ignorance and laziness."

A parallel description indicates that first there is a hook which draws the soul by force

and deception, then the soul conceives evil, and then behaves badly (i.e., acts out the results of the evil.) This section is important because, in addition to describing the process by which the soul is lured into attachment to matter, it provides indications of the stages by which the soul can recognise and thus avoid the temptation.

This resembles the following passage by Saint Theodoros the Great Ascetic in the Philokalia:[Philokalia Vol 2 p.17-18]

"For first the thought begins to darken the intellect through the passible aspect of the soul, and then the soul submits to the pleasure, not holding out in the fight. This is what is called assent, which – as has been said – is a sin. When assent persists it stimulates the passion in question . Then little by little it leads to the actual committing of the sin."

St Theodoros provides the additional aspect of assent to the passion, which is useful. We might speculate that Theodoros and the author of the Discourse share a common ascetic tradition.

Curiously, the soul is said to desire an article of clothing. This very particular longing of the soul is oddly specific, as if we were all latent fashion-obsessed shopaholics. I believe that there is an additional level of symbolism here. Clothes represent different states of the psyche. The clothes that the soul desires represent the state of attachment to external things. This interpretation is borne out by a subsequent passage in which the soul is said to strip off this world and wear her true garment, the bridal gown, which reveals beauty of mind rather than pride of flesh. The choice is between the soul's rightful bridal garment of nous and the false garments that consist of fleeting attachments to external things.

But the soul who has experienced this process repeatedly can come to forsake these things. She seeks the food of life (the Word), strips off the world (as if discarding clothing), is clothed from within with a bridal gown of mind, not material things, learns the depth of her being, and runs to the sheepfold, with shepherd at the door. She returns her body to the dealers in bodies (slavers) the false shepherds who then pathetically weep.

Though the *Authoritative Discourse* gives no thorough account of a Gnostic cosmological myth, a basic cosmology can be abstracted from it. The author of the *Authoritative Discourse* isn't very interested in the reasons for the current state of the world. Why did the soul become embodied? We don't really know. Where do the adversary and the slavers come from? Whence the material world itself? Why was mankind created and who was the creator? We aren't told. What matters is that the Father has set up a contest and there are clear choices to be made. Many Gnostic texts are very concerned with describing the reasons for the production and the process of the emanations of God, for the existence of the pleroma, for the fall of Sophia and the origin of the material world and creation of mankind. In the AD much is assumed. It may be said to not only be authoritative but authoritarian.

This is the story not of an individual but of the soul herself. It is intended to apply to each of us. The soul existed in the pleroma, where she was invisible (i.e., not part of the visible, material world) and existed in a unity of spirit. The bridegroom (the spirit) brought the word or Logos to the fallen soul and fed it to her like food, rubbed it in to her eyes as a healing ointment to allow her to see "with her mind" to know her root and cling on to the branch from which she had come. In the beginning the father had existed alone, " before the worlds in the heavens appeared". Subsequently the heavenly world appeared and then the material. Though the material world is abhorred in the text, no reason is given for the fall, yet the current situation serves the purposes of the father, " the one who is". "He established a great contest in this world," the aim being that the contestants should use gnosis to leave behind the created world and run to the father. But it is not merely brute matter or the body that is in opposition to the success of the soul. The devil or adversary (both terms are used) tempts the soul with wrong doing.

There are also man eaters who can consume humans. The adversary and the man-eaters/slave-dealers are reminiscent of the demiurge and his archons. As in many other Gnostic texts, the archons are associated with the body—here, dealers in bodies, in other writings they rule over the various parts of the body. Though we are never told, it is not too much of a stretch to presume that the Adversary may have created this world. The adversary is seen as something external, but the body is the conduit through which he corrupts the soul.

Just as the *Authoritative Discourse* sketches out a simple cosmology, so does it assume a basic, stark psychology. The current situation of the embodied soul is thus: she is deceived, drunk and asleep, blind and sick. Her inner life consists of vain pleasures, pride and vanity, envy, ignorance and laziness. These base emotions originate in her attachment to external material things. The process through which these arise is described carefully. It originates in the heart, which aches for some kind of external stimulation. This ache acts like the hook of a fisherman, and once the bait is taken the soul is captured and consumed. However, this is not a one-off event but happens continuously. These repeated experiences allow the soul to understand what is happening to her and to enable her to develop discrimination, to recognise the danger of following the urges of her mistaken heart, to form a taste for which kinds of food are poisonous and which will give her new life. When she eats the food of life, she undergoes inner development and restoration, salvation.

Before the final poem, the writer attacks those who do not really seek and can thus lead astray the sincere seeker. A reference to evangelists near the end, (preachers in the *Nag Hammadi Scriptures* translation), might suggest a Christian setting. The author refers to pagans, hence he or she is either Christian or Jewish. Pagans ignorantly worship idols in their perishable temples of stone, but those non pagans—Jews or Christians—who do not actively seek God are considered to be far worse. But at least the pagans sincerely practise their religions, even if they are completely mistaken in their beliefs. It's easy to think that the author is referring to non-Gnostic Christians, or to Jews, even to gnostics who do not actively seek God. These people are seen as hard hearted and can even destroy the possibility of salvation for those who come in contact with them.

It is here that we perhaps find a third option for the soul that is neither salvation nor damnation.

The Valentinians used a tripartite view of humanity. People are designated as hylics, psychics or pneumatics, depending on whether the body, the soul or the spirit respectively is uppermost in them. In some Valentinian texts, the disposition to one element of the threefold aspect of mankind is seen as predetermined. That is, one is either a hylic or a psychic or pneumatic from birth. In terms of modern use of these ideas, it is surely best to think of these designations in temporary terms: one is a hylic when one's concerns are wholly involved with matter, a pneumatic when one experiences a connection with the spirit.

Valentinians saw the psychics, those "of soul" as being typified by mainstream, non-Gnostic Christians. The state of being a pneumatic is clear in the *Authoritative Discourse*. It is the state of the soul before the fall, or of the soul who wins the contest set by the father. The state of the hylic is similarly clear: it is the soul when she is tortured by the passions and lust for externals. But what of the psychic state? I would suggest that category pilloried by the author in the penultimate section of the text refers to psychics. They possess the word, the logos of Gnostic teaching, and yet do not actually use it.

What use can the aspiring modern Gnostic make of the *Authoritative Discourse*? The harsh choice that it presents--life or death--is alien to the modern mind and few of us would wish to support a worldview in which we are presented at every step--at every thought and desire--with a choice between union with the heavenly world and the poisons and hooks of the material world. Yet this is certainly the message of the *Authoritative Discourse*. Perhaps we should see the snares of the adversary as attachment or Gurdjieff's concept of identification, in which attention is drawn into external activity or internal passions and thoughts and away from our true natures.

Rather than pillory the unnamed category of those who are worse than pagans, we should turn this around and ask ourselves if we are like those who do not truly seek the Father. The hylic/psychic/pneumatic division is a poisonous way of viewing other people, but a valuable way of looking at myself. It is a poor lens but a good mirror. I can ask myself if I've been living a chiefly hylic existence for the past few days, mainly concerned with eating, drinking, sleeping, working, etc. And has the rest of my inner world been concerned with the psychic concerns of worldly human culture-- entertainment, politics, sport, etc.?

According to the *Authoritative Discourse*, it takes a considerable struggle to obtain rest from our labours. But it is worth it:

She has found her rising.
She has come to rest in the one who is at rest.
She has reclined in the bridal chamber.
She has eaten of the banquet
for which she has hungered.
She has partaken of immortal food.
She has found what she sought.
She has received rest from her labours,
and the light shining on her does not set.
To the light belongs the glory
and the power and the revelation,
forever and ever.
Amen.

Michael Grenfell

Blake and Gnosticism

William Blake was born in 1757 and died in 1827. He is considered to be amongst a group of poets who are generally known as the "romantics"; this would include writers such as Lord Byron, William Wordsworth, Samuel Coleridge, and Percy Shelley. Such individuals often seemed to write in the face of the industrial and scientific advances of the age, and sought a more emotional, sensational relationship with the world. They also often looked backwards in history to ancient traditions, myths and religions rather than to modern secular ideas. Blake's own biography is marked by sensation, vision and expression. As a child, he saw angels in the trees when out walking with his mother on Peckham Rye. He had no formal education – he could stand none. However, he was eventually apprenticed to an engraver and learnt this trade. Even here, his was a visionary experience: whilst engraving to in Westminster Abbey, he "saw" the ghosts of past Kings and Queens of England processing in the aisles. Clearly, an individual of remarkable imagination, he seemed to actually "see" the image he produced.

He did earn a living as an engraver. However, increasingly, he became involved in his own work. He invented a new form of engraving that entailed him writing in reverse onto copper plates, which he then used to print text and images together, finally colouring each copy by hand. Early books were quite popular and focussed: *Songs of Innocence and Experience* and *the Marriage of Heaven and Hell*. However, increasingly, he prepared long "prophecies," which included a large cast of mythological characters. In 1800, he moved for three years to Felpham, West Sussex, to a cottage which is still

there, to work with the poet William Hayley. However, relations with him soon became tense as he was required to work on his patron's own verse. He was also tried for sedition after an altercation with a soldier.

Blake lived in revolutionary times and was outspoken in the name of freedom. However, he became increasingly poor and ignored, and really only lived as a result of support from a small band of patrons. His longer prophecies make for demanding reading. His final magnum opus included 100 illustrated plates, but he only ever completed one copy. Living simply in London in one room with his wife, he was later "rediscovered" by a younger generation of romantically inclined artists and writers who called themselves the "Ancients." This group included the pastoral artist Samuel Palmer.

The philosophy underlying Blake's vision has been the subject of continued debate. Once he died, he faded into obscurity for many years, and was not really rediscovered until the twentieth century. However, there is now a veritable "Blake industry" and every type of interpretation of him: Marxist, Freudian, Jungian, Post-modern, and many more. Any engaging with his images and texts is itself a transformative process. This article addresses the nature of this transformation.

Gnosticism, gnosis, Gnostic are difficult words to define. The first (Gnosticism) is the term often used to denote early Christian heretics of the second, third and forth centuries. We have long known that many early followers of Christ were condemned by other Christians as heretics but, until this century, nearly everything we knew about them came from their opponents: most notably Irenaeus the second century Bishop of Lyons who wrote five volumes entitled *The Destruction and Overthrow of Falsely So-called Knowledge*; and, fifty years later, Hippolytus, a teacher in Rome, who wrote the enormous *Refutation of All Heresies* in order to "expose and refute the wicked blasphemy of the heretics". For Irenaeus, the heresies were "an abyss of madness and a blasphemy against Christ". It is clear that the persecution of those who held such views was successful: books were burnt; those possessing them were imprisoned. By the fifth century, such philosophies, became literary dangerous knowledge. Retreating from dominant orthodoxies, a Gnostic monk took thirteen papyrus books bound in leather and buried them in a red earthenware jar at the foot of a cliff honeycombed with caves near the town of Nag Hammadi in Upper Egypt; which is where they remained for some 1400 years. Then, in 1945, an Egyptian peasant, out searching for soft soil with which to fertilize his crops, dug up the jar and took it home. At first, he did not know what to do with what he found inside. His mother admits to using some of the papyrus to light fires. Eventually, however, and by an enormously circuitous route, the texts from the find filtered into the public domain. The story they told was astonishing. Along with other established writings from Plato, were texts, alternative gospels, myths, poems and philosophies. Many of these had mysterious, quasi-magical sounding titles, such as The Thunder: Perfect Mind, The Exegesis of the Soul, The Hypostasis of the Archons. Some told of an alternative creation story, others included sayings of Jesus not to be found in the orthodox bible, still others spoke in the voice of feminine divine power.

But what has all of this to do with William Blake?

The majority of the Nag Hammadi texts could not have been available in Blake's day. And Blake hardly proclaims himself a Gnostic, or indeed uses the word at all. The answer lies in the second of my key words: gnosis. Gnosis

might be defined as "knowledge": not simply the knowing of facts, but deep, intuitive, experiential knowledge, which is based on personal insight and knowing of oneself. However, this knowledge of oneself goes beyond simply self-conscious understanding; rather, the more this knowing develops, the more it becomes simultaneously a personification of God:

> Abandon the search for God and the creation and other matters of a similar sort. Look for him by taking yourself as the starting point. Learn who it is within you who makes everything his own and say, "My God, my mind, my thought, my soul, my body." Learn the sources of sorrow, joy, love, hate...If you carefully investigate these matters, you will find him in yourself.

Monoimus

As Kurt Ruldolph, a leading writer on Gnosis, makes clear, therefore, "gnosis" is not simply the history of "Gnosticism" (p.56). The former subsumes the latter. This article seeks to explore this "Gnostic" strand in Blake's work. An earlier treatment of this theme was in included in the *Blake Journal* No.2, where I approached it very much from a mythic-poetic angle. The reception of this piece was sufficiently positive to encourage me to develop the argument. In the present article I compare core aspects of Blake's philosophy with those to be found in various Gnostic texts; in particular, from the Nag Hammadi codices.

Gnosticism or gnosis involves the idea of the presence in man of a divine "spark", which has fallen into the world, which has been put out by mankind's physical and mental systems, but can ultimately be rekindled. As Hans Jonas, a writer on Gnosticism religion, writes: "The ultimate object of gnosis is God: its event in the soul transforms the knower himself by making him a partaker in the divine existence (which means more than assimilating him to the divine essence).

Now, this sort of language sounds remarkably close to Blake's own. "I give you the end of a golden string", he writes in one of his most didactic tones "only wind it into a ball (and) it will lead you to Heaven's gate, Built in Jerusalem's wall" (Jerusalem Pl.77). In "The Everlasting Gospel" he writes, "Thou art a man, God is no More, Thy own humanity learn to adore". And again in Jerusalem: "Why look at God for help and not ourselves". Similarly, when asked if he believes in Jesus, Blake confidently states that he is "the only living God... and so am I and so are you". This identification of Man with God as an inner process of Gnostic redemption is everywhere apparent in the Nag Hammadi codices. It is also present in various ways in Hermetic tradition, thirteenth century Cathars, and the writings of such European mystics as Jacob Boehme, Paraclesus and Emmanuel Swedenborg (See the article by Valerie Parslow on the *Blake Journal* No 3 for a more in-depth discussion of this tradition in relation to Blake).

With some of these, by direct or indirect reference, we know that Blake was acquainted. However, I concur with Stuart Curran when he points out (p.17) that the knowledge of the gnostics in Blake's time was "derived from highly biased anathemas against the Gnostics delivered by men fighting an ideological war". In theory at least, Blake had access to lengthy expositions of Gnostic thought in Pierre Bayle's Dictionary, Isaac de Beausobre's *Histoire Critique de Manichée et Manichéisme*, Nathaniel Lardner's *History of Heretics and Credibility of the Gospel History*, Gibbon's *Decline and Fall of the Roman Empire*, and any number of works of the Unitarian theologian Joseph Priestly. Of primary documents, three deserve mention. "Poimandres", considered by Kurt Rudolph to be a Gnostic treatise within the *Corpus Hermeticum*, was translated into English as "The Pymander" by Everard in 1664. *Pistis Sophia*, a late Gnostic treatise was not translated until later, but was at least described by C.G. Woide in 1778. And Richard Laurence's 1821 translation

of the (Ethiopian) *Book of Enoch*, which was discovered in 1773, contains a lengthy discussion of fallen angels similar to the Gnostic hypostasis (that is the multiplicity of gods) of some Nag Hammadi materials. To these we need to add the three recognised inspirations on Blake: namely, the Gnostic homologies found in Milton, Shakespeare and the Bible, particularly the Old Testament and the Book of Revelation.

Yet, we can only surmise the extent to which each one of these did or did not act as a source for Blake's Gnostic epistemology. In some cases, it is fairly easy to identify the Gnostic inspiration behind Blake's work; for example, in his story of Job. Here, Job confronting life's experience, reminds us of a passage from the Four Zoas:

What is the price of experience?
    Do men buy it for a song,
Or wisdom for a dance in the street?
    No: it is bought with the price
Of all that a man hath, his house,
    his wife, his children.

And then,

Wisdom is sold in the desolate market
    where none come to buy,
And in the withered field where the
    farmer ploughs for bread in vain.

Job did gain wisdom of a sort, but first he had to lose everything and confront the God he had created for himself: and I would not be the first to notice the match in features between the two, or indeed a similar pairing to that of Albion and Elohim in an earlier picture.

Elsewhere, Blake's work is mostly less derivative and the Gnostic connection more obtuse. We have that one tantalising reference from Crabb Robinson when discussing Wordsworth with Blake. Crabb Robinson writes:

The eloquent descriptions of Nature in Wordsworth's poems were conclusive proof of Atheism, for whoever believes in nature said Blake: disbelieves in God—for

Nature is the work of the devil. On my obtaining from him the declaration that the Bible was the work of God, I referred to the commencement of Genesis—In the beginning God created the Heaven and the Earth—But I gained nothing by this for I was triumphantly told that this God was not Jehovah, but the Elohim, and the doctrine of the Gnostics repeated with sufficient consistency to silence one so unlearned as myself.

Even here, however, it is not altogether clear if Blake explicitly referred to the Gnostics himself, or this was Crabb Robinson giving an interpretation of what Blake said; in other words, Blake may not have consciously known that he was talking "gnostically". Or did Blake declare himself to be a Gnostic believer based on readings? Or did Blake simply make use of fragments of Gnostic myth and symbol, picked up mostly intuitively as part of an iconographic "bricolage", in order to express himself artistically through his paintings, drawings and poetry?

I cannot answer these questions directly? However, I do feel that much of Blake's work can best be understood when viewed from a Gnostic standpoint. I am not the first to associate Blake with gnosis and Gnosticism. A reference is made in Helen White's *The Mysticism of William Blake*, as early as 1927 and developed in 1938 in Milton Percival's *William Blake's Circle of Destiny*. More recently, Leopold Damarosch (1980) *Symbol and Truth in Blake's Myth*, Leslie Tannenbaum (1982) *Biblical Tradition in Blake's Early Prophecies*, Stuart Curran (1986) *Blake and Gnostic Hyle: A Double Negative*, William Horn (1987) *Blake's Revisionism: Gnostic Interpretation and Critical Methodology*, and Peter Sorensen (1995) *William Blake's Recreation of Gnostic Myth* have all discussed the connection between Blake's work and Gnosticism in some detail. And yet, a Gnostic reading of Blake has yet to acquire the orthodoxy of political, Freudian and Neo-platonic interpretations to be found elsewhere. I would personally concur with Stuart

Curran that the Neo-platonism that Kathleen Raine finds so prevalent in Blake's writing is more correctly Christian Gnosticism. I would also agree with Horn that the same might be said of attempts to link Blake with kabbalism, traditional Christianity, renaissance alchemy, druidism and any number of other -isms.

It is my conviction that Blake was first and foremost a Gnostic. The rest of this article suggests how this is so. Firstly, however, I want to give an account of the basic Gnostic myth. There are many variations, the following is a distillation of these into their essential elements.

Hans Jonas begins his book on Gnostic religion by recounting the essential creation story. In the beginning is a god of gods, a "first cause", an unknowable Monad if you like, who/which exists as a unitary being or oneness. It is the fount of existence, the fullness of being often referred to as the "pleroma" in Gnostic scripts. This unity exists as a perfect marriage of contraries and opposites. Here, it is necessary to notice the gender bias of the language used. Even in this primeval oneness, the unity is expressed in terms of the fusing of sexual opposites. Nevertheless, the feminine aspect of the unity has a name—Sophia—originating from the Greek word for wisdom. She is a goddess in her own right, but she and her male consort "act as one". At some point in cosmic history, Sophia wishes to act alone and creates the demiurge or chief architect of the material word. This Jehovah-like character creates Adam and Eve, Nature, and all forms within it. Sometimes, these creations are splendid, but at base they are all forms of the fallen world; they all obey strict laws of boundary and definition. Sophia, recognising her error enters into the world, into mortality, in order to give mankind a spark of eternity. She becomes Eve, the archetypal heavenly woman, who now contains the eternal goddess Sophia. Adam and Eve fall from the Garden of Eden and pass into the material world; if they did not no one would know of the demiurge's flawed creation. However, by passing into the material world, and hence relying on a messenger of truth (the Gnostic redeemer who brings the Gnosis, or secret revelation), Adam and Eve, and all their mortal descendants, have the possibility of escaping the division and darkness of materiality and regaining their eternal positions as gods. This story is summed up in one Gnostic script:

> In the beginning the father intended to
> bring forth the angels and the archangels.
> His thought leaped ahead from him.
> This thought, who knew her
> father's intention.
> Thus she descended to the lower realms
> She bore angels and powers, who
> then created the world
> But after she bore them she was
> held captive by them
> She suffered every indignity from them
> And she could not return to the father
> In a human body she came to be confined
> And thus from age to age she
> passed from body to body.

There are various elements to this and other Gnostic stories which seem to be common to all of them:

Firstly, the imperfect nature of the Old Testament God: Yahweh, the egotistical: "I am what I am" is self-sufficient and is producer and product of the divided nature of the world: nature/spirit, man/woman, object/subject, mental/material, innocence/experience, light/darkness, good/evil, God and the Devil.

Secondly, therefore, the divided nature of the material world, which is essentially a feminine product.

Thirdly, the feminine spark of eternity trapped within nature but regainable.

Fourthly, the notion of a personal, internal quest to refind the eternal state which is Gnosis by shaking off the limitations of god-given systems, and social and material structural forms.

Once the primeval perfection is regained, all these worldly products drop away.

I now want to draw out some of the essential similarities between these aspects of Gnostic myth and Blake's work.

My first point concerns the nature of God and gods. I have already quoted Crabb Robinson on Blake's distinction between the Elohim and Jehovah: one is the eternal father, one is the worldly architect. Of course, the connection between the latter and Blake is everywhere to be seen: in the material creation of Adam, in the illustrations and annotations to the Book of Job, and in Urizen. The latter is an early account to show the process and consequences of the fall, division and the rule-bound nature of the material world. Mankind ignores its innate divinity in order to adopt a single vision of life. Urizen also refers to the "eternals". The deities of Gnosticism are variously called gods, archons, rulers, many of whom have archangels and cherubim under them. Out of the first fall, there is division on division, from which a universe is created that is ruled by multiple gods, but they are all products of the independent will of Sophia and the actions of the demiurge. Similarly, in Blake there is a fragmentation of divine characters: Zoas, Emanations, Spectres, Shadows, Fairies. There seems then to be a hierarchy of gods in Blake and Gnosticism with each character occupying domains of spiritual and material phenomena. However, they are all linked by the division within the first cause. In this respect, the multiple mythological characterisation of Blake's prophecies is less difficult to interpret if it is seen as the offspring of the essential aspects of the original unity.

My second point concerns the status of nature. Clearly, Blake wrote some of the most beautiful nature poetry in the English language:

> First, ere the morning breaks, joy
> opens in the flowery bosoms,
> Joy, even to tears, which the sun
> rising dries; first the wild thyme
> And meadow-sweet, downy & soft
> waving among the reeds,
> Light springing on the air, lead
> the sweet dance. They wake

The Honeysuckle sleeping on the
   oak (the flaunting beauty
Revels along upon the wind); the
   white-thorn, lovely may,
Opens her many lovely eyes.
   Listening the rose still sleeps-
None dare to wake her; soon she
   bursts her crimson-curtained bed
And comes forth in the majesty
   of beauty. Every flower-
The pink, the jessamine, the wall-
   flower, the carnation,
The jonquil, the mild lily—opens
   her heavens. Every tree
And flower & herb soon fill the air
   with innumerable dance,
Yet in order sweet and lovely.
(*Milton* Plate 32)

Yet, elsewhere, Blake speaks of nature as it "deadens" him:

Natural Objects always did and do now weaken, deaden and obliterate Imagination in Me. Wordsworth must know that what he Writes valuable is Not to be Found in Nature.

Annotations to Wordsworth Poems

Vala, too, the material veil of nature, appears as a torturer who betrays him in what she promises and delivers. This is apparent in "The Crystal Cabinet". At first he is seduced by the material world, and, intoxicated by it, sees another England and Thames, which burn like flames. However, in an effort to possess what he sees, he end up collapsing the whole vision; the message being that materiality is a mirage. This illusion is also apparent in the "Garden of Love". At first, it is seen as being "sweet" and "playful". However, on closer inspection, it is "filled with graves". In the Gnostic story of Adam and Eve, there is a similar nostalgic longing to return to the Garden of Paradise. A nostalgia which subverts the eternity in the now; a longing to escape the present. In the *Apocryphon of John*,

Adam is placed in paradise by the archons, the gods and angels of the fallen world, but it is illusion for the food and leisure of the garden "is bitter and beauty is depraved...their luxury is deception...their trees are godlessness...their fruit is deadly poison and their promise is death".

My third point concerns the feminine spark (Sophia, Knowledge, Wisdom, Gnosis) trapped in nature. This is every where apparent in Gnostic script. For example, in The *Apocryphon of John*, she is referred to as "our sister Sophia... who came down in innocence in order to rectify her deficiency". Thel, of course, for Blake does not descend. Oothoon in "Visions of the daughters of Albion" does: her fate is horrifying:

And they enclosed my infinite
   brain into a narrow circle
And sunk my heart into the Abyss,
   a red round globe burning
Till all from life I was obliterated and erased.
(Plate 2)

Of course, the major Sophia figure for Blake was Jerusalem. Every where in his prophecies she is lost. Here is Tharmas in "Vala":

Lost! Lost! Lost! are my
   emanations Enion O Enion
We are become a Victim to the
   Living We hide in secret
I have hidden Jerusalem in Silent
   Contrition O Pity Me
I will build a Labyrinth also
   O Pity me O Enion
Why hast thou taken sweet Jerusalem
   from my inmost Soul
(Plate 4)

But she can be refound. In The *Apocryphon of John*, we read:

This (Adam) is the first one who came down and the first separation. But the Epinoia (The Sophia) of the light which was in him, she is the one who will awaken his thinking..

This reawakening is the occurrence which redeems Milton in Blake's poem. Here, Ololon reunites with Milton, an event which reconnects them both as a divine family and as eternal individuals. The same event occurs between Albion and Jerusalem at the end of the prophecy named after her:

Awake! Awake Jerusalem! O
   lovely Emanation of Albion
Awake! and over spread all
   Nations as in Ancient Time
For lo! the Night of Death is
   past and the Eternal Day
Appears upon our Hills

(Plate 97)

Such an event clearly redeems not only Albion (England) but all materiality (the Nations). However, it is also clearly a personal event for Blake. At the end of Milton he awakes to find his "sweet Shadow of Delight", that is his wife, "trembling at his side".

My fourth point concerns the process of this redemption. Hans Jonas again gives an outline of redemption. First comes the "call", that is, a voice from beyond the earthly veil beckons to the fallen man, teaching him his divine origins. This call comes from the Gnostic redeemer or messenger, and it is a voice which is alien to all but those who can receive it: that is gnosis. On gaining this gnosis, the previously fallen man must reunite with the divine, or ascend to former glory. Metaphorically, this reunion is often described in sexual terms, as a union, and Elaine Pagels for one emphasises the "sexual symbolism to describe God". However, this symbolism also led many gnostics to assume opposite positions with regard to sex; some seeing abstention as a way to gnosis, others acting with considerable indulgence for the same ends. It is also clear that these spiritual and sexual sensations were experienced very similarly. In particular, the union with the eternal god/spirit is described as a "marriage" or an act of the "bridal chamber":

The Holy of Holies is the bridal chamber. Baptism includes the resurrection (and the) redemption; the redemption (takes place) in the bridal chamber...Christ came to repair the separation which was from the beginning and again unite the two, and to give life to those who died as a result of the separation and unite them. But the woman is united to her husband in the bridal chamber. Indeed, those who have united in the bridal chamber will no longer be separated.

The Gospel of Philip

Of course, in such language various other metaphors concerning virginal states, procreation and surrender are implied. Similarly, in the union, an androgynous state, as prefallen unity is experienced. Once this occurs, as the *Gospel of Truth* states it: "They themselves are the truth; and the Father is within them and they are in the Father, being perfect, being undivided in the truly good one, being in no way deficient in anything". Such language could equally be applied to Blake's philosophical position, with one crucial difference which is aptly summed up by William Horn:

While Blake retains the myth syncretism of ancient Gnosticism, he substitutes, in a typically Romantic move, the activities of the artist for Gnostic ritual.

In other words, for Blake, the Gnostic redeemer, is personified in his Jesus, the imagination; in particular, his own imagination. Not only this, he makes it available to everyone. Imagination, as exemplified in and through Blake's work is the golden string he offers us, and the creative output of which he was the victim is the city of Jerusalem to which he leads us; the building of which represents a psychic union of opposites experienced at a deep psychological level. How should this be so?

I have already raised Blake's ambiguous relationship to nature; at once, seemingly being both beauty and allusion, the product of the fallen world but also holding the spark of eternity. But, of course, this was not the only reality Blake experienced. I have always believed that we should treat with profound suspicion many of the romantic accounts of Blake's behaviour as passed on in Victorian biographies, overlaid as they were with Gothic fancies. However, we know from Blake's own words, and bona fide statements from his closest associates, that Imaginary vision was a way of life for him. Whether he did really see God at his window as a child, or angels in the trees on Peckham Rye, or the Queens and Kings of England passing in the aisles of Westminster Abbey we shall never know. Even so, his own art and writing is testament enough to the vivid imagery he experienced: images that were almost more real than the material world which surrounded him. We need only consider the ghost of a flee, his visionary heads, and his picture of the man who supposedly taught him how to paint. We also have accounts of him rising in the night, seemingly haunted by the words and images going around his mind. Clearly, in such reports, there is the question of who was controlling who: the art or the man? And we can only wonder at his own literally ecstatic experience of leaving industrial London for Felpham to be greeted by the sea and country, with bird song, the perfume of the wide thyme, and the open vistas of the sky. I refer to plate 32 from Milton quoted above and the poem written "To my friend Butts", written within a few days of arriving to his seaside retreat:

My Eyes did Expand
Into regions of air
Away from all care
Into regions of fire
Remote from Desire ...
I each particle gazed
Astonished Amazed
For each was a Man
Human formd. Swift I ran
For they beckoned to me
Remote by the sea
Saying, Each grain of Sand
Every Stone on the Land
Each rock & each hill

Each fountain and rill
Each herb and each tree
Mountain hill Earth & Sea
Cloud Meteor & Star
Are Men Seen Afar...
The living universe!

For Blake, his art was literally more real than reality. Similarly, his own communication of his vision was often treated, both by family, friends and the world that surrounded him as obscure, confusing and eccentric. We find it difficult to imagine the psychic stress of having such artistic outpourings largely ignored or misunderstood. Interestingly, the Gnostic Gospels, about which Blake could not have known, contains passages pertinent to art and the way it is produced. Here is the *Gospel of Philip*:

Truth did not enter this world unclad, but it came in types and images. The world will not receive truth in any other manner. There is rebirth and there is an image of rebirth. It is truly necessary that the human being should be born again through the image. If one does not acquire the images for oneself the name will also be taken away from one. But if one receives them in the anointing of the Pleroma (of the might of the cross), which the apostles call the right and the left, then such a person is no longer a Christian but a Christ.

In the receipt of such images, the divine union again occurs. For Blake, this happens in an instant:

There is a moment in each day
    that Satan cannot find
Nor can his watch-fiends find it;
    but the industrious find
This moment and it multiply.
    And when it once is found
It renovates every moment of
    the day if rightly placed.
(*Milton* Plate 35)

It is in this moment that art is done:

Every time less than a pulsation of the
artery
Is equal in its period & value
    to six thousand years.
For in this period the poet's work
    is done & and all the great
Events of time start forth & are
    conceived in such a period,
Within a moment, a pulsation of the artery.

(*Milton* Plate 29)

Of course, everyone has a hunger for this sort of direct experience, but how do you get it? Blake describes or explains:

To see the world in a grain of sand
And a heaven in a wild flower
Hold infinity in the palm of your hand
And eternity in an hour.
Auguries of Innocence

However, the wantonness of such vision itself becomes a projection which acts independently, may alight on unsuitable material, ideological or physical objects which may not be suitable and take on a, sometimes less than benevolent, life of their own. This would be the Gnostic version of orthodox God. Belief in God turns him into a commodity which is subject to loss, which results in outward searches for him in the world of nature and ideas. The Gnostic God, on the other hand, comes through personal inner experience. But this is only available when all other illusory experiences and ideas are put aside, as a kind of divestment of worldly clothing. The *Gospel of Thomas*:

His disciples asked when wilt though appear to us and when will we behold thee? Jesus said: When you divest yourself of your clothing without being ashamed, and take your clothes and trample them underfeet as the small children do, and step on them, then you shall behold the son of life and you shall not be frightened.

For Blake, this happens when you "annihilate the selfhood of Deceit and false forgiveness"; not only personified in external constraints, such as moral codes and laws, but in inner illusions, the spectre, that is largely a product of the social world.

I come in self-annihilation &
    grandeur of inspiration,
To cast off rational demonstration
    by faith in the Saviour;
To cast off the rotten rags of
    memory by inspiration;
To cast off Bacon, Locke & Newton
    from Albion's covering;
To take off his filthy garments, &
    clothe him with imagination;
To cast aside from poetry all
    that is not inspiration
....
These are the destroyers of Jerusalem,
    these are the murders
Of Jesus, who deny the faith
    & mock eternal life;
Who pretend to poetry, that they
    may destroy imagination
By imitation of nature's images
    drawn from remembrance,
These are the sexual garments, the
    abomination of desolation
Hiding the human lineaments
    as with an ark & curtains
Which Jesus rent & now shall
    wholly purge away with fire,
Till generation is swallowed
    up in regeneration
Milton Plate 41

This is "putting off" of error is described as momentary resurrection, as the essential man communes with the divine unity, the spiritual product of which appears in his art and writings. As this putting off continues, deeper we go and the more we leave behind personal idiosyncrasies of the individual and the more we touch the essential elements common to the divine humanity. This act of individuation is also an act on behalf of the whole of humanity. Naked, the more you see of this, the more you become it. Becoming more oneself, one's true undivided self, means becoming more like God in its essential oneness. As the Gnostic gospel of Philip puts it:

You saw the spirit, you became the spirit. You saw the Father, you shall become the father. You see yourself and what you see you shall become.

In this respect, it is enough to recognise the divine spark, Jerusalem, to awaken from material sleep, and to start to become it. However, for Blake this recognition and becoming is the process of his art.

It is not possible in such a brief article to give further detailed references to Blake's work and to link these with Gnostic events. There is also, clearly, much more to be said about Blake in connection with various esoteric traditions: for example, the mystic marriage in alchemy is especially pertinent here. Jung recognised this in his own work and the extent to which he expressed the disfiguration of the human soul as the "shadow". In particular, he understood that the images that come forth in the Gnostic union are not just pretty pictures. They include the horrors of Francis Bacon as well as the benign spirituality of Cecil Collins. Blake's own art and poetry are full of images of the existential void, chaos and the abyss. But none of these are as horrific as the images of reason gone mad, of error played out in the world in the minute killings of spirit which go on in the name of education and progress. The redemption from such error starts when psychic images are expressed. As the Gnostic *Gospel of Philip* has it:

If you bring forth what is in you, what you bring forth will save you. If you do not bring forth what is in you, what you do

not bring forth will destroy you".

These images themselves are emanations: the product of individual mind with which one forms a relation. Indeed, it is through them that psychic contact is made:

When in eternity Man converses
    with man they enter
Into each others Bosom (which
    are Universes of delight)
In mutual interchange, and first
    their Emanations meet...
For Man cannot unite with man
    but by their Emanations.
(Jerusalem Plate 88)

Pertinent here also is Anton Ehrenzweig's account of creativity of art as a series of ex-static projections, objectification and re-integrations. Gnosis can also be connected with the poetry of Rainer Maria Rilke (in particular, I am thinking of the Duino Elegies) and the philosophy of Heidegger (See Avens on this). In much of this there is a fine line to be drawn between an unattainable transcendent beyond, the searching for which leads to loss of self, and, a surrender to the moment which brings an experience of a special sense of reality, or passive communion with the lifeworld.

Elaine Pagels writes that Gnosticism represents a philosophical justification for radical non-conformity. She also notes that it is a system which can be understood in terms of the psychic therapy it offers to its adherents; particularly, depressives, or lonely, isolated souls, or people who seek to affirm their own worth. It is possible to see this in Blake's ranting against authorities. "I must create a system", he proclaims "or be enslaved by another man's" (Jerusalem). "Both read the Bible night and day, But thou reads black where I read white" (*Everlasting Gospel*) Is Gnosis simply a way of separating from the ego everything that one does not like? Other critics may want to give a Freudian interpretation of this, of Blake continuing to fight his own Father in the relations he formed, and there are plenty of examples of the difficulties he had in establishing lasting friendships with men. We can also see how the lack of acceptance of Blake's work led to an anger and transcendent assertion of its meaning and inflation of its value. We do not know ultimately whether Blake wrote, drew and painted the way he did because of his uncontrollable imagination. Certainly, there is evidence in his work that between The Marriage of Heaven and Hell and The Four Zoas, Urizen himself becomes redeemed, and offers redemption in the limiting and shaping of psychic energy. Blake could not always control his imagination, did not want to, but he did not want it to control him either. In the end, he did write and paint; and this activity in itself represents a reification of the imagination. Maybe the greatest gnosis is that there is no gnosis. The Pleroma is at once full and totality void. We start from nothing into which something is created: "By starting from the invisible world, the visible world was invented" (The Hypostasis of the Archons). Maybe Blake came to understand that in a deep sense. Certainly, his most creative output was undertaken in the first half of his adult years. After the age of forty five, there seems to be little change in his mythological stance and his characters are all but formed. He also became increasingly spiritually puritan as he aged.

Of course, there is also the social and political systems which surrounded Blake not to mention his problematic relations with his own wife. If it is difficult in a modern world which offers us a feminist aesthetic, or art as a product of the market, to believe in one man's artistic activity as describing human redemption. I have deliberately drawn on various types of discourse in this article: personal, academic, poetic, theological. In a sense, it is my own construction, my own recreation of Gnostic myth or gnosis. Tobias Churton undertakes a similar task in his own history of the gnostics, which also takes in Blake and John Lennon. It is clear that there are degrees of Gnosticism, not one orthodox version. At one extreme are straight derivative accounts based on historical, Gnostic texts. The other extreme is more personal and intuitive. The question to be addressed is "distance" from one or the other.

Finally, the whole point of Blake and gnosis, especially in the sense of orthodox derivation, is that it is impossible to prove by empirical textual analysis. If it were, his work would not be truly Gnostic in the second, more personal, intuitive sense. Attempts to gain such incontrovertible proof, apart from some striking resonances, are likely to take away from the spirit of gnosis rather than get closer to it. Another way of looking at this argument is to see my account as being sufficiently post-modernist to deliberately avoid a mono-mythical narrative. There is no identity between Blake's work and any other political, sociological and psychological explanatory system. At the same time, it does not offer an account as a mere ruse, a "jouissance", or play on words and themes. Nothing could be further from Blake's intent. He believed in delineation and precision not polyfocal relativism. My conclusion is that gnosis is the product of deep psychic and psychological experiences that have been mediated by a multiple range of philosophies, some of which were heretical Christian. That Blake picked up on some of the elements of these and made use of them in a conscious and semi-conscious manner is beyond doubt. Most of what he did, however, was to combine these with others, and his own, to reconstruct his personal Gnostic texts. The fact that we can see and feel basic commonalities, on many levels, between Blake's and other Gnostic writings attests to their own inner coherence in terms of worldly experience and the challenges it offers to people as they pass through life. The fact that he decentres and subverts, all whilst provoking and creating means he has produced a living text which indeed continues to be transformatory by the way it engages with us and works on what we personally bring to it. In it, truly, is heaven and hell, as well as paths leading to and from both of them. Some of these involve acts of creation; all of them involve knowing, or gnosis.

REFERENCES AND FURTHER READING

Avens, R (1984) The New Gnosis. Dallas, Texas: Spring Publications.

Blake, W (1971) Blake: the Complete Poems (eds.: W Stevenson and D Erdman). London: Longman.

Blake, W (1966) Blake: Complete Writings (ed.: G Keynes). Oxford: Oxford University Press.

Churton, T (1987) The Gnostics. London: Weidenfield and Nicolson.

Curran, S (1986) "Blake and Gnostic Hyle: A double negative". In N Hilton (ed) Essential Articles for the Study of William Blake. (Hamden, Conneticut: Archon Book.

Damarosch, L (1980) Symbol and Truth in Blake's Myth. Princeton, N.J.: Princeton University Press.

Ehrenzweig, A (1993)/67) The Hidden Order of Art. London: Weidenfiled.

Filoramo, G (1990) The History of Gnosticism. Oxford: Blackwell.

Grenfell, M (1996) "Blake and Gnosis". The Journal of the Blake Society of St. James, 2, 19—29.

Horn, W (1987) "Blake's revisionism: Gnostic interpretation and critical methodology". In D Miller, M Bracher and D Ault (eds) Critical Paths and the Argument of Method. London: Duke University Press.

Jonas, H (1958/63) The Gnostic Religion. Boston: Beacon Press.

Jung, C (1969) The Psychology of the Transference. London: Ark.

Layton, B (1987) The Gnostic Scriptures. London: SCM Press

Pagels, E (1982) The Gnostic Gospels. Harmondsworth: Pelican.

Percival, M (1938) William Blake's Circle of Destiny. Columbia: Columbia University Press.

Robinson, J (1990) The Nag Hammadi Library. San Francisco: Harper.

Ruldolph, K (1977) Gnosis. Edinburgh: T and T Clark.

Solomon, A (1993) Blake's Job: A message for our time. London: Palambron Press.

Sorensen, P (1995) William Blake's Recreation of Gnostic Myth: Resolving the Apparent Incongruities. Salzburg: Salzburg University Studies.

Tannenbaum L (1982) Biblical Tradition in Blake's Early Prophecies: The Great Code of Art. Princeton: Princeton University Press.

Tuckett, C (1986) Nag Hammadi and the Gospel Tradition. Edinburgh: T and T Clark.

Welburn, A (1994) Gnosis: The Mysteries and Christianity. Edinburgh: Floris.

White, H (1964/27) The Mysticism of William Blake. New York: Russell and Russell.

Bill Darlison

Anomalies

Viktor Frankl, concentration-camp survivor, psychiatrist, and author of the celebrated book *Man's Search for Meaning*, tells the following story in his autobiography:

One day I passed Vienna's Votiv Church (which I have always loved because it is 'pure Gothic', though its construction was begun in 1856). I had never been inside. But my wife and I heard organ music, and I suggested to her that we go in and sit for a while. As soon as we entered, the music stopped and the priest stepped to the pulpit and began to preach. And he began to speak of the nearby Berggasse 19 and of the 'godless' Sigmund Freud who had lived there. Then he continued: 'But we don't need to go so far, not to Berggasse. Right behind us, at Mariannengasse 1, lives a Viktor Frankl who wrote a book …. The Doctor and the Soul …..a godless book indeed'. The priest proceeded to tear my book to shreds. Later, I introduced myself, a bit worried that this encounter might give him a heart attack. He certainly had not expected that I would be present. How many minutes had passed from my birth up to that sermon, up to the point of our visit to the Votiv Church for the first time? How miniscule the chance that I would enter at exactly the moment when the priest mentioned me in his sermon?

Frankl concludes with this honest and sensible comment: 'I think the only appropriate attitude to such coincidences is to not even try to explain them. Anyway, I am too ignorant to explain them, and too smart to deny them'.[1]

One of the most astonishing coincidence stories that I have ever read is quoted by Arthur Koestler in his book, *The Case of the Midwife Toad*. It was originally collected by the 19th century French astronomer, Camille Flammarion, and concerns a certain Monsieur de Fontgibu and a plum pudding. This is Koestler's version of the tale:

Monsieur Deschamps, when a little boy in Orleans, was given by Monsieur de Fontgibu, a visitor to his parents, a piece of plum pudding which made an unforgettable impression on him. As a young man, years later dining in a Paris restaurant, he saw plum pudding written on the menu and promptly ordered it. But it was too late, the last portion had just been consumed by a gentleman whom the waiter discreetly pointed out—M. de Fontgibu, whom Deschamps had never seen again since that first meeting. More years passed and M. Deschamps was invited to a dinner party where the hostess had promised to prepare that rare dessert, a plum pudding. At the dinner table M. Deschamps told his little story, remarking, 'All we need now for perfect contentment is M. de Fontgibu'. At that moment the door opened and a very old, frail and distraught gentleman entered, bursting into bewildered apologies: M. de Fontgibu had been invited to another dinner party and come to the wrong address.'[2]

My own life has not been without its share of coincidences. One intriguing series concerns the number ten. I was born on the tenth of June, as was my mother and my wife (quaint as this might seem, it is not something I would recommend!), and I lived about twenty-five years of my life at number ten Monkhill Avenue. The first room I had in the college hall of residence was number ten, and ten was the number of my classroom in the first school with numbered rooms that I taught in. When I went to the seminary in Rome my room number was thirty-seven (3+7 =10!), and my apartment number now is twenty-eight. My association with the number ten extends to apparent trivialities. When I was in college all first year students had the daunting task of reading at morning worship in the college chapel. Readers were on a strictly alphabetical rota, and the passage I had to read was from John's Gospel, chapter ten, not the whole of the chapter, but the piece containing verse ten, 'I am come that they may have life and have it more abundantly'—which is one of the key verses in the Gospel, and a verse that has always had a special kind of significance for me. More bizarre still is the way I seem to glance at a clock or at my watch when the time is precisely ten minutes to ten (morning or evening), a phenomenon which has no regard for the time adjustments we make in the spring or the autumn and so can't really be based upon any kind of internal rhythm. It seems as if it is the number itself which is important and that I am attuned to it in some inexplicable way.

A highly significant coincidence occurred in May 2002. Following various medical examinations, the doctor told me that I was probably suffering from cancer of the bladder. He put me on a waiting list for tests in St. Vincent's hospital in Dublin. 'But it may take about six weeks before they will be able to

see you,' he said, 'because there's quite a long waiting list.' That very evening, as I was sitting in my apartment brooding about my situation, I received a telephone call from a woman who wanted to marry later in the year in the Dublin Unitarian Church. I told her that it was unlikely that I would be able to perform the ceremony because I was sick and would probably have to return to England for treatment.

'May I ask what the problem is?' she said.

'The doctor thinks it's bladder cancer, but we won't know until I'm able to go for tests at St. Vincent's hospital in about six weeks,' I replied.

'It just so happens that I work in the urology department of Tallaght hospital, and I'll get you seen next week,' she said.

She did get me an appointment for the following week and I was found to have kidney cancer, a far more dangerous cancer than the suspected bladder cancer, and there were already secondaries present in the lungs. The cancerous kidney was removed and the secondaries treated with immunotherapy, and I've now been in remission for eight years. Had I waited for six weeks I would probably be dead. The woman whose telephone call saved my life never did get married in the Dublin Unitarian Church.

Precognition, or the experience of time temporarily losing its normal linear sequence, seems strangely allied to coincidence. In May of 1987 I had an extremely uncanny experience. It was the day of the General Election in Britain and, since I was interested in politics in those days, I was taking a day off from my studies at Hull University where I had been seconded to do an M.A. My wife, Morag, was on holiday in America, so I was alone in the house and I was spending the early morning reading the newspaper and listening to the radio. I eventually dragged myself upstairs to take a shower, and on my way back down again I found myself singing the song *The Windmills of your Mind*, which had been popular some two decades earlier. What on earth am I singing this for? I asked myself. Had it been on the radio before I went upstairs? Is it on the radio now? I stuck my head round the sitting-room door, but some other song was being played. Unable to explain why the song was in my head, I went into the kitchen, made myself a cup of coffee, and took the cup through to the sitting-room. No sooner had I placed the cup on the table and sat down in the chair than the disc jockey said, 'And now, from 1966, The Windmills of Your Mind.' It was almost as if some cosmic joker were playing a trick on me, a common enough feeling, reported by many people who have experienced this sort of thing.

One of only a few other comparable incidents happened when I was nine years old. During Lent our Catholic primary school organised dozens of activities in order to raise money for the orphans of the diocese. One of these was a weekly raffle of a bar of chocolate—not a particularly big bar, either, but, in those days of relative austerity, something to be coveted nevertheless. The draw took place just before school ended on Friday afternoon, and as the headmaster put his hand into the box of tickets I knew that I would be the winner. It wasn't hope, it wasn't desire, it was absolute and total certainty, and the surprise and delight I felt when he announced my name was not because I was the winner, but because I had known all along that it was inevitable that I would be the winner.

All the examples I have given—coincidences and precognition—are *anomalies*, that is, things that don't seem to obey the rules; they don't fit into the normal patterns in which we think the world works. They shouldn't happen. In fact, there are many people who would say that they don't happen or, at least, that they don't have the mysterious quality that the more romantic and fanciful among us think they have. Coincidences, no matter how extraordinary they seem, are simply random occurrences which are inevitable in a world in which billions of things happen every day. We endow them with significance because we love to construct patterns. And as far as precognition is concerned, we only remember the apparent successes, while conveniently forgetting the far more numerous failures.

What this approach ignores, what indeed it must ignore because it claims to be scientific and therefore objective, is the subjective feeling which accompanies these things. Like Hamlet, I know a hawk from a handsaw, and even at the age of nine I knew the qualitative difference between expectation and knowledge, but a feeling, no matter how powerful, is an unrepeatable, incommunicable phenomenon, and so must lie outside the purview of science.

But by far the most disturbing aspect of the sceptical approach is the undeclared but underlying assumption that coincidence, precognition, and the like are impossible. Not only do they not happen, they can't possibly happen. But, as the French mathematician, Arago, says, 'He who outside of pure mathematics pronounces the word 'impossible' lacks prudence'. Those who dismiss these phenomena are defending the basic dogmas of materialism, which defines consciousness as an epiphenomenon of matter, and which assumes that nothing happens without a determining physical cause. Materialism stands or falls by these principles. As Chesterton remarked, rather whimsically, if there was found to be one elf or fairy in the world, the whole structure would come tumbling down. Or, as we might say, if there were just one incident of precognition or telepathy, the materialists would have to rethink their paradigm.

However, the materialist philosophy, although undoubtedly the dominant one in our culture, is not the only one we can espouse. Idealism, which has a venerable history, proposes that the basic stuff of the universe is mind, and that far from being isolated and discrete pockets of consciousness, human beings are *participants* in consciousness, and are linked with each other, and with everything else in a transcendental unity. As the mystical poet, Francis Thompson, writes:

All things near or far
To each other linked are.

Emerson, the Transcendentalist, puts it like this:

Substances at base divided
In their summits are united
There the holy essence rolls
One through separated souls.

The physicist David Bohm, in his book *Wholeness and the Implicate Order*, argues that at the most fundamental level of the universe everything—space, matter, time, energy—is all one, and that human illusions to the contrary are created by the nature of our senses and our measuring apparatus. Another leading physicist, E.C.G. Sudharshan, in his 1977 Nehru Memorial Lecture, described this view of the universe as surrealistic, 'a world in which one entity is in many configurations at the same time, and the notions of separateness and individuality are merely projections of a structure which is indescribably richer.'[3]

In this strange and bewildering universe, coincidences happen because on this level of three dimensions things strive to express a unity they already possess on a higher, more inclusive, level. Things are linked by *meaning* in addition to cause, a concept known to the ancient world as sympathy, and re-presented to the modern world by Carl Jung as synchronicity. We draw things to ourselves by an unconscious psychic gravitation; like attracts like. In his essay, *The Oversoul*, Emerson writes:

O believe, as thou livest, every proverb, every book, every byword that belongs to thee for aid or comfort, shall surely come home through open or winding passages. Every friend whom not thy fantastic will but the great and tender heart within thee craveth, shall lock thee in his embrace. And this, because the heart in thee is the heart of all; not a valve, not a wall, not an intersection is there anywhere in nature but one blood rolls uninterruptedly an endless circulation through all men, as the water of the globe is all one sea, and truly seen its tide is one.
'Everything is one,' says the Idealist.

Even time only appears linear, which is why we sometimes, for inexplicable reasons, seem able to jump ahead of the sequence presented to us by our everyday awareness.

Pay attention to these things. Even though, in Viktor Frankl's words, we are too ignorant to explain them adequately, we, like him, should be too smart to deny them, because they are, without question, intimating something extremely important about the meaning of the life we are living, and the nature of the world in which we are living it.

NOTES

1   Viktor   Frankl,:   *Recollections: An Autobiography*, page 59
2 Koestler, A., (1971) *The Case of the Midwife Toad*, Pan Books, London, Page 133.
3 Elwell, D., (1987) *Cosmic Loom*, Harper Collins, page 7

Toni Charles

Gospel According to Toni

Saying 28. They asked him about the horses. He said to them 'I appeared to them in flesh. I found all of them intoxicated; I found none of them thirsty. I took one of them and led it to water, but I could not make it drink.

Saying 39. Jesus said, 'The Pharisees and the scribes have taken the keys of Knowledge and hidden them." And his disciples did wander all over the house. And Jesus said, "Warmer .... getting warmer .... little colder .... warmer .... hot .... roasting hot ...."

Saying 47. Jesus said, "It is impossible for a man to mount two horses or to stretch two bows. And for a man to rub his tummy and pat his head at the same time, or he will rub both or rub neither. No man will repeat 'Red Lorry, Yellow Lorry' really, really fast without going wrong somewhere."

Saying 50. Jesus said, "If they say to you, 'Where did you come from?', say to them, 'I came from the land down under, where beer does flow and men chunder.' If they say to you, 'Is it you?', say, 'Are you trying to tempt me, because I come from the land of plenty.' If they ask you, 'What is the ...sign of your father in you?', just smile and give them a vegemite sandwich."

Saying 51: His disciples said to Him, "When will the Dawn Of The Dead come about, and when will The New World come?" He said to them, "What you look forward to has already been released on DVD, but you do not recognize it."

Saying 60. [They saw] a Samaritan wearing wellington boots chasing a lamb around. He said to his disciples, "[Why does] that man [chase] the lamb around?" They said to him, "So that he may [...] it and put its hind legs [...] boots." [...] He said to them, "You too, look for a place for yo...self within the Repose, lest you become caught and be [...] in someone's boots and be [...]"

Saying 73. Jesus said, "The harvest is great but the laborers are few. Beseech the Lord, therefore, to hurry up and buy a combine harvester."

Saying 74. He said, "O Lord, there are many lights on, but no one is home."

Saying 114. The lead guitarist said to them, "Make the horn player leave us, for soul instruments don't deserve to be in a rock band." The vocalist said, "Look, I will amplify her sound, so that her soul smashes through your rock and she becomes like you. For the soul that becomes a ...soul fusion sounds like heaven."

Miguel Conner

Unbegotten

The Virus manifested, peeling itself from the fabric of the universe like an omnipotent wet surgical-gauze, bleeding out in rivers of dark matter and broken dreams. Its tentacles lashed at planets, eyes blinked supernovas. Circuitry slithered in and out of wormholes while it anchored itself upon reality. The foundation of time and space held strong, but there were shivers and cracks and lost nebulas. How many sentient forms discarded like dead flaky skin, I thought. How many murdered suns and paradises lost?

And this whole time all I thought I ever saw was pretty constellations and projected hopes.

I lit a cigarette and waited for it to finish its latest Covenant. Chemical-glowing rats carpeted the ground, gnawed at my jeans.

Oh, how it inhaled, shivered, and from the waste of photon galaxies and memories of extinct alien races it revealed its face to me. I should have known better

"Just a day?" The Virus asked. "One day for an eternity of pus?"

I nodded, taking solace in the menthol film collecting on the roof of my mouth.

"Just one day," I said.

"Such a large price to pay," it hissed, scales ruffling and making the rasping sound of a trillion pieces of silver tossed upon the cobbled ground of an eternally destroyed temple.

"We going to do this?" I said, coughing. "Blake drew you better."

"It is done," the Virus said, slowly shaking its head. "And Blake talked to trees. Will you be able to talk at all?"

"At least I know now," I said with atom comfort. "There is something…there is really something out there."

The Virus chuckled. Its breath shot screaming isotopes through me. "Then the price was worth it for one of us! One day then. Then an eternity of pus."

I walked out of my room.

She stood in the kitchen in her robe. Busy as always this time of the morning.

"You want breakfast?" she asked me. I nodded and sat on the mocha couch in the living room. I made sure not to put my feet on the coffee table because she might notice my nibbled denim. The tall arching windows revealed the park across the street green with summer's ring. She never liked the bleaching winters. Good.

I noticed for the first time that she had a secret sniffle, what might have been confused for a quick leer. She quit smoking years ago after a sinus infection gave her an oasis to free herself. She always spoke about how she still craved a cigarette, especially in the morning with her coffee. It was morning. Only a counter area separated the living room and the kitchen, both adorned with crosses and safe prints and small mirrors.

I broke the spine of my cigarette upon a smoky-glass ashtray, while she thoughtfully took a few sips of her coffee. She then mumbled about how people didn't know how to make coffee in this country. I nodded, lit another smoke and pretended I wasn't watching her. I had already hid the picture frame on the coffee table, the one with the photograph taken of her two months before I had left her in Portugal. Snuggled under the cushions.

There was symphony in the way she cooked, from the ringing of microwave to the slamming of cupboards, from the sizzling of the skillet to the scolding of the cat when it sensually danced across the counter. She had that secret sniffle. She enjoyed dipping the bread I brought from the Mexican bakery every morning in her coffee.

"Have you decided when you're going this summer?" she asked. "Do you want coffee?"

"I'll take some coffee."

"We have to get everything ready at the house. Your cousins from the Algarve might be coming in August."

I smoked more, knowing it would be the isotopes that would give me cancer. The symphony continued, my coffee remained untouched. She absently talked about when she was going back home, updated me on the family, complained about my gay brother and the cat and the quality of the coffee. The cat's name was Schrödinger.

I didn't say much. I just watched. Just one day is all I wanted. One more day with her.

I sat on the counter and ate breakfast. She was already cleaning the kitchen. The trees were shaking, but no wind touched flower beds or dead trash on the sidewalk. I concentrated on the cheese omelet. It had never tasted better, even if my jaws were swollen with saliva. She filled my coffee. The Microwave rang.

"Is there anything you want to do today?" I asked when I was done. "I can take you downtown. There's some new painter by the Water Tower who draws clowns from wreckage smuggled from Haiti."

"How exiting," she said, trying to sound musical in her sarcasm but always failing. "Did you know that Terri is going to have that back operation? She's finally listening to me. You should quit smoking."

"I like smoking." I really did.

"You should still quit." How had I missed she'd gotten so much smaller these last years? How did I miss that her belly had been swollen? She had looked so bloated that day at the church by the altar. I remember thinking I didn't like the way her hair was done--so sprayed back—and too much blue appearing around her mouth.

The kitchen was finished, so she took a shower. My ashtray was full by then. She did her afternoon routine. She played solitaire on her laptop, and I remembered teaching her how to use email for the first time many years ago. Her routine continued through the middle of the afternoon with speeches about family and acquaintances I barely remembered, cleaning here and there, back to the laptop, the microwave complaining when her coffee was ready, standing in front of the television to editorialize about the news. That sniffle like a quick leer.

She sat next to me when it was time for Dr Phil. I wanted to say what I needed to say. I wanted to tell her. At least her hair was clean and healthy, dyed in that orangey color she had used for the last five years.

I wanted to tell her.

"Yeats was right," I said during a commercial. "Time is the only enemy."

"Life is simple," she said, leaning over to look for her reading glasses because soon she'd be back on Solitaire; I had bought her many pairs I scattered around the house when she visited. "God wants us to be happy. We're here to be happy."

I'm glad she or Schrödinger hadn't noticed the chemical-glowing rats darting across the hardwood floors.

"Are you happy?" I asked.

She paused. The commercial was almost over. "Yes. I just wish you were happy. You never seemed to be. That's what I've always wanted."

"At least I know there is something out there. Staring, always staring."

"What? Are you watching your medicine?"

I lit another menthol.

The afternoon passed. We re-arranged my daughter's closet. She folded clothes so well, an art-form I realized I never mastered. Would my daughter come home from school today? We looked at some old photographs. She was a child once, with blond hair. She repeated the same venerable story of getting in trouble with the nuns at school.

We took a walk across the park. The wind didn't make sense. I didn't talk to the paralyzed trees. We came upon a dog deposited on the sidewalk by the intersection. It had been hit so hard ribs stabbed out of its yellow fur. Its head twitched valiantly to sip for air, but its stomach hung out of its mouth like a purple balloon with veins.

She leaned down and petted its head. "We need to change your diet, Roxie. Your fur isn't as shiny as it usually is."

The dog's opal eyes looked blankly at the vast sky. I looked up as well. We both knew.

"Do you think she'll find her way back home?" She ran her fingers over a line of syrupy ribs. I told her we should cross the streets, since the lights were red.

We went to the drugstore to pick up her cholesterol prescription. "Do you think Sofia will like this?" she asked, waiving a thin sweater in front of me with an imprint of John Lennon. I almost said it then, those sacrificial words I had never offered her my entire life, but just found myself pressing my arid lips together. There had been blue around her mouth that day during the church service.

Dusk arrived like a silent revolution. We sat alone in the house. She went to the bedroom because she needed a quick rest. When she was out of my sight, I wanted to run to the bedroom. Why hadn't I noticed her belly had been so swollen? How had my entire family missed it?

When she came out, she asked what was wrong.

"Doesn't the day go...by."

"I'll make dinner," she said, waiving me off. "I've got the stew boiling."

I hadn't noticed she had already begun dinner.

Again, I was at the counter. It was pork. She sat by me, with a glass of wine but not offering me one because I had quit years ago. I still liked smoking.

"How did you stay happy?" I asked at one point.

"I didn't," she answered. "I fought for it. What else can we do?"

"I don't know. It just goes and goes by so quickly, I guess."

She snorted. "You always make things more complicated. Quoting someone else and thinking thoughts that don't belong to you. Where has it gotten you?"

My daughter wasn't coming home. No one was coming home this day. The park outside was a fertility of growing shadows and black shapes. Why weren't the streetlights on?

"I don't want to lie to myself anymore," I said. "But where has the truth gotten me when I've been honest? What is truth?"

She left me to go clean the kitchen. One of my cousins was pregnant, she explained. But I knew that. I knew that the baby had been born months ago. They had both been at the church that day with her by the altar.

Night. It was night now. She was in her robes again, feet on the table, comfortable and set to watch her almanac of shows canonized by reading the gospel of the television guide. She smiled for the first time, focused on some comedy. She was satisfied with her day. Good.

"I'm sorry if I've been a disappointment," I said at one point, still sitting on the counter that divided the kitchen and the living room.

"Just be happy," she mumbled. "Be healthy."

There was that sniffle. Schrödinger in his arrogance was on her lap. At one point she spoke on her cell phone to a friend in Arizona.

"Maybe you can take me to the Water Tower

tomorrow," she said in between programs. "I could go shopping for Sofia. Did we buy the sweater?"

By then my throat was clenching and my jaw was wet granite. Memories of coming home after school and telling her about my day rushed at me like a carnival wind. Her taking me to soccer practice one time and admitting she was leaving my father. Jumping up and down after I had left the delivery room while telling her it was a girl. Stroking my hair while I lay in bed with a cold fever. Teaching me how to drive stick while complaining that Americans didn't know how to drive. Defending me when he threw me down the stairs for breaking a vase while playing tag with my brother. A carnival wind, and I didn't know if it was my heart or some chorus of mocking ghosts drumming away.

I pressed my lips together with cruel fingers. Night! It was night now! I watched her. She fell asleep at one point. She woke up and yawned. Another ashtray full.

"I'm going to bed," she declared.

"Already?"

She stood up from the couch. I stood up from the stool. There were liver marks on her arms I never had truly paid attention to. She had gotten in trouble so much as a child with the nuns.

"You don't want to play another Solitaire?"

"Not tonight," she answered. "I'm tired. So tomorrow to the Water Tower?"

"And shopping."

"No with you, oh Mr. I-can't-relax! You can drop me off. Sofia is not coming home today, is she?"

No, I thought. She is not in this world. She left us all with Him.

She folded her thin arms around her small body that had gotten smaller. I noticed the swelling around her midsection.

"Well," she declared, probably making a quick note of anything that she needed to do, something she might have missed from her industrious day. "I'm tired. See you in the morning."

As a child I would go into her room and kiss her goodnight before I went to bed. She might run her hands through my hair. That was it.

She said goodnight in Portuguese and left me. She did that secret sniffle, that quick leer...not done that day at the church because she couldn't.

"Wait!" I said.

"What?"

We faced each other.

I knew she had enjoyed her day, from the dipping of her bread to stories on the television that were small spells.

"I...you never told me those words either... those three sacrificial words. Ever. Why?"

"You have to fight for things. You never fought."

But why?

"Good night. Sleep well."

She went into the bedroom. As a child I would have gone and kissed her on her cheek.

That was it.

I sat again on the couch. I smoked one cigarette after another. The night thickened as did the electrical pain in my chest. My stomach hurt. Schrödinger stared at me from his vantage position on the television.

The bravery finally came when a warm seashore came to my eyes. And an endless sorrow as vast as the uncaring nighttime.

"She enjoyed it..." I said to nothing, except to the cat who now lazily gazed at the chemical rats invading the living room one more time.

I walked into my bedroom.

He was waiting for me.

The stars were falling from their perching on gravity. It was like a snowfall. Snow falling all around me, chaotic and glittering, like all the souls of humanity...fluttering in chaos...sparks of gleam and ether...falling and falling and bullied by the winds of time and space...settling eventually in their realities...as one...packed on the unsanitary ground of His providence... when it had been summer outside.

Infinity lurched, swallowing Creation with its mere shadow. I reached for my cigarettes. I had left them in the living room.

"Fuck!" I said. "Fuck, fuck, fuck...why did you create it?"

I'm being thrown down the stars. I was just playing in the garden...never meant to knock the flowerpot down...

"Because I infect," the Virus said. "That is my nature. I infected the waters below. I infected the darkness. And I called it good!"

There were heavy pearls of tears in my eyes. "No, no! No! Why did you create death?"

"There is no death," it answered, admiring the winter-hell storm. "There is only infection. Life is a sickness. Death is just a fever I give you to prevent you from finding out what you truly are. But for you it will be much worse."

"And what are we truly?"

"I also infected the light above...made it in my image...and the contagions of the father must be carried by his children, so it is written." It idly crushed a star with one its jeweled talons. "Now an eternity of pus for you."

I hardened my jaw until it hurt. My tears dried so quickly. With reality falling apart all around, I stood straight and faced the abyss. And the abyss stared into me...but it had always been staring at me. Nietzsche said it was better for man to will nothing than to not will at all. She never liked that quote or any of my quotes or any of my thoughts.

"No she didn't," the Virus said, so close to me I could feel its ammonia stink. "She probably didn't like either of us...I didn't like the way she spoke to me sometimes when I came home. And you couldn't say those words in the end, could you? You fell so short."

I think it came out as laughter then. "I am not the one who fell short! You are the one who is ultimately lacking, not me!"

The Virus roared like Hell.

"I have no beginning or ending! I am the all and I am the nothing! There is no other but me!"

And I finally had the right quote for once. I finally fought.

"You don't know where you came from that's why you call yourself eternal. You don't know your beginning that's why you say have no beginning. I know...I know my beginning, and you don't, oh omnipotent one! All your eternity is but time really...all you creativity is mechanical! "

It was its turn to laugh.

"That didn't impress the white whale either when Ahab said it. How does it show that I am lacking? What could you have that I would ever want?"

I smiled at the Virus. A billion chemical-glowing rats swarmed the ground, but they were startled.

"One day," I said. "That's all I wanted. One day with her."

Its eyes widened behind the glasses he never changed in style since I knew him, the first day he hit me hard and I became diseased.

A supreme form shuddered. The Virus turned his head, not because of fear but because it couldn't bear my look.

Like black paint spilling backward on a garage floor, like a shadow melting against a circling sun, it skulked back into the framework of the cosmos.

I was by myself.

I walked out of my room and found my cigarettes on the counter. The cat looked at me with amusement, knowing I wouldn't swat it off the counter. I noticed it was morning again. I sat on the couch, placed my feet on the table, and infected my lungs. The wind made sense. Her picture was on the table, the last one taken of her before the funeral.

At one point, I stretched on the couch and watched the day go by. I wouldn't go into her room. Not yet.

"Why not?" Schrödinger asked. "She's gone and you're alone, asshole."

"It's just fever anyway...that's all it is," I said. "And eventually it must break because it's really just mechanical. It's all mechanical, right?"

We were both equal now anyway. But I was free.

Reginald Freeman

The Gnostic Gospel of Luke:

A Gnostic-Hermetic Exegesis of the Tenth Chapter of the Gospel According to Luke

In this essay, I will attempt to show that the tenth chapter of the *Gospel According To Luke* contains elements of Gnostic and Hermetic philosophy, including a Græco-Egyptian astrological tradition. Among the canonical scriptures, the *Gospel According to John* is usually considered to be the one favored by the Gnostics. This idea has been written on extensively. Therefore, I will not elaborate upon what is readily available in multiple works. But, it is nevertheless important to at least mention this fact, because of the far reaching influence of the Johannine works on Gnostic tradition and scriptures. For example, the prologue to the gospel contains peculiar language that is not common to the synoptic gospels, but is more reminiscent of Gnostic scriptures. The *Gospel of John* also emphasizes the spiritual nature of Jesus, and stresses the supremacy of the spiritual over the material. This is made obvious in statements such as *John 6.63a:* "It is the spirit that makes a thing live. The flesh benefits nothing." The *Gospel According to Luke*, however, while conforming largely to the gospel narratives found in *Matthew* and *Mark*, also contains a number of unique sayings and parables that suggest a secret knowledge that is to be bestowed upon God's elect, using language that would have been recognized by Gnostics and Hermeticists. Of course, to the Gnostics, and other Christian mystics, all of the scriptures may have multiple layers of meaning which, when taken together collectively, may offer a broader, richer, and fuller understanding of the text than what might be immediately apparent on the surface. And perhaps we should not be surprised to find evidence of Gnostic mysticism within Luke's writings, especially given his close companionship with Paul, whose teachings were highly valued by the early Gnostics, and whose writings share much of the same terminology as the Gnostics. In fact, concerning the great Gnostic teacher Valentinus, Elaine Pagels writes, "Paul communicated his pneumatic teaching to his disciple Theudas, and Theudas, in turn, to Valentinus; and Valentinus to his own disciples."[1] In addition, if we accept that Luke was a physician, a commonly held view, then we may probably safely assume that he had studied the Hermetic texts over the course of his education, as many of those works were known to have dealt extensively with medicine and healing; particularly, "tracts on astrological medicine, such as the *Book of Asclepius Called Myriogenesis.*"[2]

Let me be clear at the outset that this is primarily a Gnostic theological work, though it may have some academic implications as well. The ancient Gnostics were arguably the Church's first theological exegetes. In modern times, however, it has been left largely to the secular academia to provide insight into a belief system that they themselves do not necessarily share. To be sure, many excellent works have been produced by the academic community, and I do not wish to diminish their efforts in any way. There are some excellent historical works available, and without the superb translation efforts of the last several decades, most of the original Gnostic scriptures would still be lost to us. On the other hand, the modern Gnostic cannot help but to notice a deficiency in some of the commentaries and attempts at exegesis. This deficiency is not due to poor scholarship;

rather, it is due to the fact that they are written from an outside perspective, trying to make sense of a religious tradition that, by its very nature, can only be understood experientially. While it is my intention to present scholarly and reasonable hypotheses, I do not want to mislead the reader by supposing some impartiality, or theological neutrality, that does not exist. In spite of my admitted bias, however, I think that there is ample evidence to support the bulk of my ideas in those cases where empirical, or strong circumstantial evidence, may confirm or support the hypothesis.

The structure of this essay is as follows: After this brief introduction, the first part of our exegesis will cover *Luke* 10.1-24, followed by a second section addressing verses 25-37. These two sections comprise the main body of this work. Finally, the conclusion will attempt to anticipate certain questions, and to briefly survey other sections of *Luke* and place them in a Gnostic context consistent with the analysis offered in the main body. The reader may notice that the first section of this exegesis is disproportionately longer than the second section. This imbalance is regrettable, but necessary due to the natural divisions of the text. In the early stages of the development of this exegesis, these two sections existed as two separate essays. It seemed beneficial, however, to combine them into a single work. It is only by treating them together that a comprehensive conclusion may be offered. For, without placing these passages in a proper context, the analyses offered herein may be seen as anomalous, or could too easily be dismissed as fanciful speculation. A scriptural anomaly might be interesting to comment upon, but would not necessarily demand a rigorous investigation. What I intend to show here is that there is a pattern of esoteric symbolism scattered throughout *Luke*, but especially concentrated in the tenth chapter.

Translations of New Testament texts throughout this essay are my own, being translated from the *Greek New Testament*, Fourth Corrected Edition (UBS4)[3] which contains the same text as the *Novum Testamentum Graece*, 27th Edition (NA27), which was also consulted throughout the translation process. The translations found here are not substantially different from many others, but they do illustrate certain variances among the source texts, and certain wording that lends itself more easily to the type of exegetical treatment that is to follow.

This first passage from *Luke* that I have selected for this paper is perhaps the most overlooked example of Gnostic and Hermetic philosophy among the canonical scriptures. I believe that this oversight may be largely due to the available translations of the Greek text, which seem to favor a particular variation of the text that does not lend itself as well to the interpretation that is to be put forth here shortly. I must admit, however, that I am surprised that (to my knowledge), this subject matter has not been addressed by scholars and students of early Christian literature who are familiar with the Greek sources. It is equally possible, of course, that there are such extant works, of which I am merely ignorant. Regardless, I hope that this brief treatise can offer a fresh perspective on the matter. Here, then, is the *Gospel According to Luke*, 10.1-24:

[1]And after these things, the Lord appointed seventy-two others, and he sent them two by two before his face into every city and place where he was about to go. [2]And he was saying to them, "Indeed, the harvest is great, but the workers few; ask then, the Lord of the harvest that he might send out workers into his harvest. [3]Go! Behold, I send you as lambs in the midst of wolves. [4]Do not carry a purse, nor a wallet, nor sandals, and greet no one along the way. [5]And into whatever house you enter, first say, 'Peace to this house,' [6]And if there is a son of peace, your peace will rest upon him; otherwise, on you it will return. [7]And in the same house remain eating and drinking the things with them; for

the worker is worthy of his wage. Do not move from house to house. ⁸And into whichever city you enter and they receive you, eat the things being set before you ⁹and heal the ones in it who are sick and say to them, 'The Kingdom of God has come near to you.' ¹⁰But into whatever city you enter and they do not receive you, go out into its streets and say, ¹¹'Even the dust from your city that has clung to our feet we shake off against you; but know this that the Kingdom of God has come near.' ¹²I say to you that for Sodom in that day it will be more bearable than with that city. ¹³Woe to you Chorazin, woe to you Bethsaida; because if the miracles that have happened in you had occurred in Tyre and Sidon, they would have repented long ago, sitting in sackcloth and ashes. ¹⁴But for Tyre and Sidon it will be more bearable in the judgment than for you. ¹⁵And you Capernaum, will you not be exalted up to heaven? No, you will come down to Hades."

¹⁶"The one listening to you, listens to me, and the one rejecting you rejects me; but the one rejecting me, rejects the one who has sent me."

¹⁷And the seventy-two returned with joy saying, "Lord, even the demons submit to us in your name." ¹⁸And he said to them, "I watched Satan fall like lightning from heaven. ¹⁹Behold, I have given to you the authority to walk on snakes and scorpions, and over all the power of the adversary, and nothing at all may hurt you. ²⁰However, do not rejoice in this that the spirits submit to you, but rejoice that your names have been recorded in the heavens."

²¹In the same hour he was full of joy in the Holy Spirit and he said, "I praise you, Father, Lord of heaven and earth, that you concealed these things from the wise and intelligent and revealed them to young children; yes, Father, for thus it was well-pleasing before you. ²²Everything was handed over to me by my Father, and no one knows who the Son is except the Father, and who the Father is except the Son and to whom the Son wishes to reveal Him."

²³And having turned toward the disciples privately he said, "Blessed are the eyes seeing what you see. ²⁴For I say to you that many prophets and kings desired to see what you see and they did not see, and to hear what you hear and they did not hear."

You will notice in the very first verse of this chapter a small, but significant, difference from other translations. I am referring specifically to the statement that, "the Lord appointed seventy-two others." Most translations read "seventy," rather than "seventy-two." The reason for this seems to be due to a discrepancy among the ancient manuscripts; some reading "seventy," while others having "seventy-two." The text I have translated from, the *Greek New Testament* (UBS4) is considered by many students of New Testament (Koine) Greek to be the foremost edition. This edition contains the Greek, "hebdomekonta duo," that is, "seventy-two." Likewise, the Latin *Nova Vulgata* (Stuttgart Vulgate, Fourth Edition) contains, "septuaginta duos."[4] I stress this point because much of my argument, as you will see, is dependent upon this particular reading of the text. Taken at face value, it really makes little difference which interpretation is used. But, when we apply the "seventy-two" reading, mystical depths are opened up to us.

It is entirely possible, and in my opinion probable, that "seventy-two" was at some point abbreviated to "seventy," either for convenience, or by inadvertent omission. The abbreviation of "seventy-two" into "seventy" would not be unique to this particular passage. For example, the legend regarding the development of the

Septuagint states that the Hebrew Scriptures were translated into Greek by seventy-two scholars, over a period of seventy-two days. However, the word "Septuagint" comes from the Latin, meaning "seventy." And when the Septuagint is referenced in academic works, it is usually represented by the Latin numerals for seventy, "LXX."[5] While this usage may have been adopted for convenience, it loses the numerological significance of the number seventy-two.

In the number seventy-two, we see an allusion to the Jewish tradition that there were seventy-two nations with seventy-two different languages in the world. Therefore, the seventy-two disciples are representatives of the whole of the known world, and thus representative of the Universal Kingdom of Christ; that is, the Church. As we shall see, though, this symbolism of universality extends far beyond the four corners of the Earth. The unique wording and peculiar phraseology of this passage suggests that the reign of Christ's power extends throughout the whole of the cosmos. The number seventy-two also suggests a connection to Jewish mystical and numerological traditions, such as the Schemhamphorasch (the 72 names of God derived from Exodus 14:19-21), and the sum of the values of the Hebrew letters of the Tetragrammaton when they are arranged in the style of the Pythagorean tetractys.[6] However, while these traditions are not wholly unrelated to the subject at hand, a more in depth exploration of them lies outside the scope of the present work.

The seventy-two disciples are sent out in pairs, so that there are thirty-six groups of two. These thirty-six pairs suggest a connection to the thirty-six decans of Egyptian astrology. In the introduction to his translation of the *Hermetica*, Brian P. Copenhaver writes, "The most important of the astrological Hermetica known to us is the *Liber Hermetis*, a Latin text whose Greek original contained elements traceable to the third century BCE. This *Book of Hermes* describes the decans, a peculiarly Egyptian way of dividing the zodiacal circle into thirty-six compartments, each with its own complex of astrological attributes."[7] The decans are called so because they each represent ten degrees of the zodiacal circle. The 20th century scholar of mystical and esoteric philosophical traditions, Manly P. Hall, has described it thus: "The early star gazers, after dividing the zodiac into its houses, appointed the three brightest stars in each constellation to be the joint rulers of that house. Then they divided the house into three sections of ten degrees each, which they called decans."[8] (In a certain form of the Egyptian calendar, this translated into twelve months, each month having three ten-day weeks. At the end of the 360-day year, there were five additional days that corresponded to certain principal Egyptian deities, and lied outside of the calendar year proper.) Even the philosophical Hermetica, such as *Asclepius* (which was quoted from liberally by early Church Fathers such as Lactantius in his *Divine Institutes*[9] in defense of Christian doctrine) acknowledges, "the thirty-six…the stars that are always fixed in the same place."[10]

We may find similar references in early Gnostic writings as well. For example, in the proto-Sethian text, *Eugnostos the Blessed*, we read, "Then the twelve powers…consented with each other. Six males each and six females each were revealed, so that there are seventy-two powers. Each one of the seventy-two revealed five spiritual powers, which together are the three hundred sixty powers."[11] This establishes a pattern in the spiritual realm, which is later imitated in the physical cosmos. This pattern is confirmed further on in *Eugnostos*, "The twelve months came to be as the type of the twelve powers. The three hundred sixty days of the year came to be as the type of the three hundred sixty powers who appeared from Savior."[12] As explained previously, this type of calendar system is uniquely Egyptian; a fact that does not go unnoticed by Douglas M. Parrott, the translator of the Eugnostos text. For he comments in his introduction to the text, "Egyptian religious thought also appears to have influenced its picture of the supercelestial realm."[13]

Another early Gnostic example of this type of cosmology may be found in the *Gospel of Judas*, in a discourse of Jesus to Judas which states, "And the twelve aeons of the twelve luminaries constitute their Father, with six heavens for each aeon, so that there are 72 heavens for the 72 luminaries, and for each of them five firmaments, for a total of 360 firmaments."[14] This reference is also noticed by Bart D. Ehrman in his analysis of the Judas text, wherein he draws a connection to a variation of the same Egyptian tradition previously mentioned. His analysis states in part, "These numbers are not accidental, of course. The text doesn't explain them, but they appear to be astronomical references: there are twelve months of the year and twelve signs of the zodiac; in Egyptian lore there are seventy-two "pentads" (stars) that reside over the days of the week, and so seventy-two luminaries; and there are 360 degrees in the zodiac (and 360 days in some calendars of the year) and so 360 firmaments."[15]

The numbers seventy-two and thirty-six are, by themselves, enough to consider a likely astrological connection. For, we have seen that the pattern for the decans was present in the Aeons, or eternal realms. To the Gnostics, though, the physical cosmos is not a direct emanation of the Most High, as the Aeons are, but instead have been fashioned by an imperfect demiurge. Therefore, the decans of the material world are but imperfect reflections; shadowy images of their supercelestial counterparts, requiring the purification and perfection that can be brought only by the Son, whom we are told in the *Letter to the Hebrews* is, "appointed heir of all things, through whom He also made the Aeons." Granted, the occurrence of these numbers here could be coincidental, or lack the specific implications that I am suggesting. But, fortunately, we have additional clues throughout the passage that make the possibility of mere coincidence seem much less likely. Looking at verses 5-7 we find further curious language, suggestive of an astrological connection. The thirty-six pairs are instructed to take up

residence in various "houses," to offer peace upon the inhabitants of each house, and to "not move from house to house." Anyone with even a passing familiarity with astrology will recognize that "house" is a term used to designate each of the twelve major divisions of the zodiac circle. And, according to Gnostic and Hermetic sources, the inhabitants, or rulers, of the zodiac are demons, or spirits, that influence the lives of humans. The fact that verse 6 mentions, "if there are sons of peace," would seem to indicate that there may be a number of "sons" who are not "of peace." Also, the use of the term "sons" in verse 6 should not be seen as arbitrary. Referring again to Copenhaver, he states, "Excerpt VI [of Stobaeus' *Anthology*] deals with astrology, in particular with the decans and their 'sons,' the star demons."[16] For one description of these demons of the zodiac, we may look to the pseudo-Solomonic grimoire, *The Testament of Solomon*, which has a number of similarities to other Gnostic, Hermetic, and Jewish magical texts of the period, and which may well have been in circulation in some form at the time *Luke* was written. In the *Testament of Solomon*, Solomon compels the demons of the zodiac to help build his temple. When he calls them forth, they announce, "We are the thirty-six elements, the world-rulers of this darkness."[17] When he begins to interrogate the demons, the first says, "I am the first decans of the zodiac circle."[18] Solomon continues to question each of the thirty-six, causing each to reveal its name, its powers, and its weaknesses. The powers of these demons include a broad range of nefarious acts; from leading people into error and heresy, to breaking up the harmony among families, to causing blindness and deafness in unborn children. The banishing of the demons typically consists of invoking certain divine or angelic names, and performing certain ritual actions. After subjugating the entire assembly, Solomon sets them to work at building his temple. The idea is that the possessor of this grimoire will likewise be able to compel the spirits. But if this is the power of Solomon, how much greater is the power of Christ, who is known throughout the scriptures as one "greater than Solomon?"[19]

Indeed, as great as the power of Solomon was, when he fell into apostasy, "At once the Spirit of God departed from me, and I became weak as well as foolish in my words."[20] As we will see, Christ's power over the world-rulers will be perfect, complete, and unlike Solomon, eternal. In verses 8 and 9, Jesus indicates that those archons that do not resist the messengers of Christ should be treated respectfully, and that their sickness should be healed. Their sickness, of course, is their spiritual darkness, or ignorance. And while those zodiacal rulers may never be granted access into the realms of eternal light and life, since their origin is with the demiurge, rather than the True God of Light, they may still occupy an exalted position in the cosmos, and help to bring Christ's love into the world, and into the hearts of men. Verses 10-16, on the other hand, constitute an admonishment and warning to all those who would oppose the power of Christ.[21] The message to them is that God's reign will extend throughout the cosmos, with or without their cooperation; and that if they choose to resist, they will, by their own actions, remove themselves from the grace of Christ.

In verse 17 we learn that the seventy-two (thirty-six pairs) have been successful. They are full of joy and declare, "Lord, even the demons submit to us in your name." Given our elaboration on the nature of the decans, this statement takes on a richer, and clearer meaning. The explanation offered in this analysis casts light on an otherwise vague and cryptic statement. That is, given our celestial / spiritual interpretation, their ordeal has been nothing less than the subjugation of the entire assembly of the "world-rulers." Since these demons control and influence the personalities and affairs of humanity, then we can see that the disciples' ordeals actually represent the mastery of self as much as they represent mastery over external forces. So, the joy of the disciples is due to the fact that, through Christ, they have attained to a perfect understanding of the order of things, and thus have learned to overcome their lower, sinful natures.

Jesus' reply in verse 18 is equally cryptic, claiming to have "watched Satan fall like lightning from heaven." The very nature of this statement suggests that we are not dealing with real-time events here. Depictions of the fall of Satan are generally placed in the "beginning," or at the "end of days." Since Christ is the "Alpha and the Omega, the first and the last, the beginning and the end,"[22] we can say that His position is above, or outside of, our normal space-time experience. That is, the fall of Satan is not a fixed point in space-time, but rather an event occurring in perpetuity. To the Christian faithful, the fall of Satan is seen from a relative perspective. To those who reject Christ and His message, the Devil is lording above them, and ruling their world. But those who, through the grace of Christ, have found the knowledge of the Father, and the comfort of the Holy Spirit, are raised above the adversarial powers. So to them, from their particular vantage point, Satan is seen to fall.

Let us take a look at some of the Gnostic scriptures for similar accounts of the adversary and his fall; in this case, the demiurge, Yaldabaoth. In the *Reality of the Rulers* (or *Hypostasis of the Archons*), we read of such a fall, "She [Zoe] breathed into his face, and her breath became a fiery angel for her; and that angel bound Yaldabaoth and cast him down into Tartaros, at the bottom of the abyss."[23] Then, a bit further down, we read about one of Yaldabaoth's "sons" who rejects evil: "He [Sabaoth] loathed her [matter], but he sang songs of praise up to Sophia and her daughter Zoe. And Sophia and Zoe found him and put him in charge of the seventh heaven, below the veil between above and below."[24] Thus, this "son of peace" has been elevated because of his righteousness, and his rejection of the things of this world. In *On the Origin of the World*, there is yet another account of Sabaoth's worship of Sophia, who raises him up to the seventh sphere and, with the aid of archangels, "established the kingdom for him above everyone so that he might dwell above the twelve gods of chaos."[25] These "twelve gods of chaos" are the principal zodiacal archons created by Yaldabaoth in the *Secret Book of John*,[26] and in other Gnostic sources.

Returning now to our passage in *Luke*, Jesus continues to address the seventy-two who have returned. In the reference to "snakes and scorpions" we have symbols of the adversary, and of death itself. But, we also see what seems to be yet another astrological reference, indicating well-known constellations. With Draco in the Northern Hemisphere, and Scorpius in the Southern Hemisphere, together they can be seen to represent the poles of the cosmos. This authority given to the disciples to "walk on snakes and scorpions, and over all the power of the adversary," suggests an elevation over the planetary and zodiacal influences, and is strikingly similar to the elevation of Sabaoth over the powers of the demiurge and his archons. This verse also reminds us of Solomon's subjugation of the demons discussed earlier and, together with verse 21, bears a strong resemblance in wording to the following passage from *The Testament of Solomon*: "And when I saw the prince of demons [Beelzeboul], I glorified the Lord God, Maker of heaven and earth, and I said: 'Blessed art thou, Lord God Almighty, who hast given to Solomon thy servant wisdom, the assessor of the wise, and hast subjected unto me all the power of the devil.'"[27]

It is also possible that rather than referring to two separate constellations, that both the snake and the scorpion are referring to the zodiacal sign of Scorpio. According to Manly P. Hall, the sign of Scorpio, "has three different symbols," or forms. The first is that of the Scorpion, representing, "deceit and perversion." The second form is that of the Serpent, "often used by the ancients to symbolize wisdom." The third form, interestingly, is that of the Eagle, representing, "the highest and most spiritual type of Scorpio, in which it transcends the venomous insects of the earth."[28] In this sense, then, it becomes a symbol of the process of initiation: the Scorpion symbolizing that degree, or stage, of initiation wherein the passions are subdued, which begins the process of the purification

of the soul; the Serpent representing the stage of growth and maturation, wherein various knowledge is accumulated, though largely of a material or temporal sort; and finally the Eagle, which is not named here, but whose presence would be implied to the initiated reader. The Eagle represents the completion of the initiation process, where the spiritually perfected initiate is raised up above all worldly things, and all temporal knowledge.

Even if we were to concede that *Luke* is the more ancient of the texts (which is not at all certain), and that the Gnostic and Hermetic authors were influenced by Luke, rather than the other way around, it is nevertheless clear that the Gnostic and Hermetic authors would have seen in this account, an allusion to the spirits of the zodiac. The Valentinian Gnostics certainly recognized a compatible theology here, since we read in the "Valentinian Liturgical Readings," a direct reference to verse 19: "It is fitting for you at this time to send your son Jesus the Anointed and anoint us, so we can trample on snakes and the heads of scorpions and all the power of the devil, since He is the shepherd of the seed."[29] Verse 20 concludes Jesus' discussion with the seventy-two by reminding them that their true reward is not the ability to compel spirits, but rather that they have had their place in the eternal realms secured for them by his grace; that is, the divine gnosis.

Verses 21 and 22 constitute a prayer of Jesus to the Father.[30] This prayer reinforces the concept of Jesus as the revealer of divine knowledge, or gnosis. That the Father has, "concealed these things from the wise and intelligent," indicates that this special knowledge can be gained neither through philosophical reasoning, nor through academic pursuits, but only by "young children;" that is, those who have been reborn in the spirit. It is made clear in verse 22 that this knowledge of God is revealed through the Son, to whom he pleases. The idea of a secret or hidden knowledge, revealed only to the elect, is carried over in verses 23-24.[31] The fact that Jesus is speaking to his disciples privately is a further indication that He is imparting a special knowledge, not intended for the multitude. In Verse 24, the "prophets and kings" refer to those who seek power and glory from a sense of self-importance, and those who have incomplete, or imperfect knowledge. To them, the real power, and the true knowledge is not given. But to those who come as little children, to them is given the Kingdom of God.

This completes, then this first section of our interpretive analysis of the tenth chapter of *Luke*. It is, however, far from being the final word on the subject. Of the several points addressed here, many have merely skimmed the surface, and a number of questions remain unanswered. For example, why was this allegory devised to begin with? Is this an historical account or teaching of Jesus? Or is it an invention of the author of *Luke*? Perhaps it is a bit of both. As the reader will have undoubtedly noticed, this passage bears an uncanny resemblance to the accounts given in *Mark* 6.7-11, *Matthew* 10, and *Luke* 9.1-6, of Jesus sending out the twelve Apostles, as well as similarities to various other scriptural elements as noted throughout this exegetical work. Why were these various elements put together in this way? Perhaps the author of *Luke* drew a connection between the twelve Apostles and the twelve houses of the zodiac, then reworked the account in order to stress this connection, and to elaborate on the premise using Gnostic and Hermetic literature and traditions that would have been well-known to the literate, Greek-speaking world at that time. Perhaps this allegory comes to us from some other source, now lost. For now, we can only speculate as to the origin of this passage. I think we can be fairly certain, though, that this Gnostic-Hermetic, astrological connection is real and not merely coincidental. The unique and specific language that is used throughout the passage gives us a preponderance of evidence that cannot be easily dismissed. After our analysis of the second section of *Luke* 10, perhaps we can return to some of these questions and gain a better understanding and insight into the inner workings of this enigmatic gospel.

Before continuing, let me recap some of the major points of this analysis thus far:

The seventy-two are sent out in thirty-six pairs, corresponding to the thirty-six decans of Egyptian astrology.

The "houses" referred to are the twelve houses of the zodiac.

The "sons" are the star demons of the Hermeticists, the Archons of the Gnostics, and the thirty-six world-rulers of the *Testament of Solomon*.

Sabaoth, in Gnostic mythology, is one of the "sons of peace" who renounced evil.

Jesus watching Satan fall is further evidence that this entire passage is dealing with celestial and spiritual events.

The "authority to walk on snakes and scorpions" refers to the elevation of the disciples above the powers of the planetary and zodiacal rulers; and the disciples' ability to cause said rulers to submit to them in the name of Jesus Christ.

Jesus' prayer to the Father in verses 21-22 shows Jesus in the role of the "revealer of gnosis."

Jesus' private discussion indicates that the disciples have received a special, or secret knowledge, reserved for God's elect.

The next section of this essay deals with *Luke* 10.15-37, which contains the parable of the "Good Samaritan." You will notice that this section is less academic in nature, and more strictly theological. This is due, in part, to the fact that we do not have to wrestle with the complex astrological symbolism contained in the first section. The parable of the Good Samaritan lends itself to a fairly straight forward Gnostic interpretation. That is, if we approach the story from a traditional Gnostic perspective, we will see that there is a message beyond the moral admonishment to judge people by who they actually are, and what they do, rather than by our preconceptions of them. Even the lessons of selflessly helping those who are in need are, at best, incomplete. The moral message is no doubt useful; but from a Gnostic perspective, it is the lesser meaning. The greater meaning of this parable concerns the salvation of the spirit from its hylic imprisonment.

In order for the reader to have a greater appreciation for a Gnostic interpretation of the text, I will give a very brief description of Gnostic ontology and soteriology. While some details differ among the various Gnostic schools of thought (Valentinian, Sethian, etc.,) they mostly agree upon certain foundational premises. First of all, regarding the nature of human existence, Gnostics view man as having three bodies, or conditions of being. The Spiritual, or pneumatic, body is the part of man that is pure and incorruptible; the Vital Life Force that animates the psychic and hylic bodies. The pneumatic body descended from the original spiritual fullness (Pleroma), and seeks a return to its divine origin. The material, or hylic, body comes not from the True God, but from the imperfect demiurgic creator of the cosmos. The hylic body is often compared to a prison because it binds and conceals the pneumatic spark. The soul, or psychic body, resembles a commingling of the hylic and pneumatic bodies. The psychic body contains the passions as well as reasoning; thoughts as well as feelings. The lower regions of the psyche, then, belong to the hylic; containing the passions and what would be considered the "sinful" nature of man. The higher regions of the psyche, however, are associated with the pneumatic body, and contain the sublime aspects of mind (nous) such as the mystical revelations of divine gnosis. Thus, our human experience is realized largely by the soul, which, if left untended, will be wholly consumed by our hylic nature. For the Christian who seeks the knowledge of God (gnosis), however, the psychic body may align itself to the pneumatic and help to restore the pneumatic body to the Pleroma, and thus itself be saved from dissolution into matter. This is the meaning of *Luke* 9.24, which states, "For whoever wants to save his soul will lose it, but whoever loses his soul on account of me will save it." That is, if the lower self clings

to the soul, then the soul will suffer the same fate as the flesh. But if the soul is given up to the higher, spiritual nature of Christ, then it will be preserved for eternal life in the Holy Realms.

Just as the human condition may be divided into three categories, or bodies, so too can the human population be likewise divided (more especially in the Valentinian School). Those who have attained spiritual perfection, or who are destined to attain perfection, are designated as Pneumatics. The Psychics are those who are striving toward spiritual enlightenment, but have not yet attained a perfect understanding. And finally, there are the Hylics, who are wholly ignorant of their own spiritual darkness, and therefore are not aspiring toward spiritual knowledge. There are some Gnostics, both past and present, who are not entirely comfortable with this type of classification, seeing it as either elitist, or as supporting a doctrine of predestination that infringes upon free will. This is not the place to debate the merits of the various approaches, but I will say that these classifications are not without canonical support. *John* 6.64 tells us that, "Jesus had known from the beginning who the non-believers were." And the differences between the Psychic and the Pneumatic are stated quite plainly in *1 Corinthians* 2.14-15: "Psychic man does not receive the things of the Spirit of God, for they are foolish to him, and he is not able to know them, because they are pneumatically discerned. Now, the Pneumatic man discerns all things, but he is discerned by no one."

Having given this brief introduction to Gnostic thought, then, let us proceed with our analysis of the parable of the Good Samaritan:

Luke 10.25: And behold, a certain lawyer rose to put him [Jesus] to the test saying, "Teacher, what must I accomplish to receive eternal [aionion] life?"

The first words uttered by the lawyer would have indicated to Jesus that this man is not yet in a pneumatic state. By asking what he must accomplish, he implies that he does not realize that it is only by grace that he may receive eternal life. That is, eternal life, or "aeonic" life, may not be earned in the sense of it being the requisite compensation for some act or series of deeds. Actions are certainly required of us on our spiritual journey, but our salvation is through grace (charis) not as recompense. And to the Gnostic, gnosis itself is that saving grace. However, the fact that he is seeking the means to eternal life shows that he is aspiring toward the spiritual.

> Luke 10.26-29: And he said to him, "What has been written in the Law? How do you read it?"
> And he answered saying, "You will love [agape] the Lord your God from the whole of your heart, and in the whole of your soul, and in the whole of your strength, and in the whole of your mind, and your neighbor as yourself."
> And he said to him, "You have answered correctly. Do this and you will live."
> But wanting to justify himself, he said to Jesus, "And who is my neighbor?"

Jesus tests the lawyer by asking him how he interprets the (demiurgic) Law. The Valentinians believed that the demiurge, and his laws, were not wholly evil, but imperfect. In this respect, their doctrine of the demiurge seems to be closer to the views held by the Hermeticists and Neoplatonists, than that of their more traditional Sethian counterparts, who tended to view the demiurge as more nefarious than merely imperfect. In his *Letter to Flora*, Ptolemy, a successor of Valentinus, writes, "The law of god [that is, the demiurgic god, not the True God of Light,] pure and not mixed with inferiority, is the Decalogue, those ten sayings engraved on two tables, forbidding things not to be done and enjoining things to be done. These contain pure but imperfect legislation and required the completion made by the savior. There is also the law interwoven with injustice, that an eye should

be cut out for an eye and a tooth for a tooth, and that a murder should be avenged by a murder. The person who is the second one to be unjust is no less unjust than the first; he simply changes the order of events while performing the same action."[32] We can see therein the imperfection of the demiurge, and the Mosaic Law. In order to enforce his laws of justice, he must require a second injustice. So, how the lawyer responds to this inquiry will reveal much to Jesus about his character. That is, Jesus is testing him to determine whether he is oriented toward the just aspects of the law, or toward the imperfections of the law. When the lawyer responds that one must "love the Lord your God," and "your neighbor as yourself," Jesus seems satisfied with this response. This is because even though the man's faith may be misplaced in the demiurge, the quality of complete and unconditional love (agape) is an attribute that emanates from the True God of Light. In other words, the act of love is in itself salvific to an extent; or it may lead toward the salvific gnosis. Notice, though, that Jesus' response seems to be somewhat lacking. While he tells the man that he will live, he does not specifically guarantee the eternal, or aeonic, life that he is seeking. Perhaps sensing that there is a greater truth to be gained, the man asks of Jesus who the neighbor is, that he should love as himself. This, of course, opens the door for Jesus to relate the parable.

> Luke 10.30: Jesus replied, "A certain man was coming down from Jerusalem into Jericho and fell upon some highwaymen, who having both stripped and beat him, went away leaving him half dead."

The man coming down from Jerusalem represents the spark of divine spirit (pneuma) descending from the eternal realms, or aeons, into the cosmos. Upon entering this world, the Spiritual Man is confronted by the demiurge and his archons, represented here as highwaymen. What they strip him of is the knowledge and memory of who he is and where he came from.

Ignorance of divine knowledge is often depicted as nakedness in Gnostic scripture and exegesis. For instance, in the Gnostic interpretation of Genesis, Adam and Eve's nakedness represents their spiritual ignorance. This is stated quite plainly and clearly in the *Reality of the Rulers* when they eat the fruit of the Tree of Knowledge, "And their imperfections became apparent in their lack of knowledge. They recognized that they were naked of the spiritual."[33] Their shame, then, is due to the fact that they had forgotten their origin in the realms of light. This spiritual amnesia is not only a common Gnostic theme, it is the very condition from which we must be redeemed. The reason that our Spiritual or Pneumatic Man is now "half dead" is because his true nature has been mixed with, and obscured by, the hylic and psychic natures of this world.

Luke 10.31-38: "And coincidentally a certain priest was coming down that road and having seen him, passed by on the other side. And likewise, a Levite also came upon the place, and having seen him, passed by on the other side. But a certain Samaritan came upon him while traveling and having seen him, was moved with compassion. And having approached, he bandaged his wounds, pouring oil and wine over them, and having set him upon his own animal, brought him to an inn and cared for him. And the next day he took out two denarii and gave them to the inn-keeper and said, 'Take care of him, and whatever else you spend, I will repay you when I return.'"

When the man encounters the priest and the Levite, they are unwilling, and in fact unable, to help him because they themselves are priests of the demiurge, not of the True God of Light. The demiurgic Law of Moses is an imperfect law. While it serves to preserve Jewish customs, identity, and a semblance of order, its strict adherence leads to isolationism and contradiction rather than the uplifting of humanity. The law of the True God of Light, however, is the Law of Agape; the very same Law that Christ came to bear witness to. It is a Samaritan, a stranger and foreigner, who ultimately rescues our battered traveler. It is a common theme among Gnostic myths for the Pneumatic, or true Gnostic, to be depicted as a stranger; alien to this world.[34] This image is confirmed by Jesus himself, who often depicts himself as being a stranger to this world.[35] The symbol of the Samaritan as one of God's elect is also found later in *Luke*, in chapter 17, where the only one to give praises to God for his healing was the foreigner (Allogenes), a Samaritan.[36] It is interesting to note that while the Allogenes is a hero of several Gnostic texts, its only canonical usage is in *Luke*.

Luke 10.36-37: "Who, of these three, seems to you to have become a neighbor to the one who fell upon the highwaymen?" And he said, "The one who showed him compassion." And Jesus said to him, "Depart and do likewise."

When Jesus asks the lawyer which of the three is the neighbor to the fallen traveler, the man responds that, of course, it is the one who has shown compassion. When Jesus tells him to depart and do likewise, he is not only telling him to be compassionate to his fellow man, but in fact, to be a stranger to this world; as Christ himself is. This parable also tells us that we are unable to raise ourselves up out of ignorance on our own. It requires an intervention from a spiritual force outside of ourselves to remind us of our origins, and to be restored to the Pleroma, or fullness of God, from which we came. So, the Samaritan here is representative of Christ, the redeemer, as well as of our own potential perfected self; that is, our spiritual, or pneumatic self that has been liberated from the bonds of matter and the lower mental states by the grace and compassion of Jesus Christ. So, just as Jesus healed the sick and raised the dead, that is, brought the ignorant into spiritual awareness, so too is the enlightened Christian called upon to help raise up his fallen brethren into the light of gnosis, and to tend to them until they are able to walk on their own, clothed in the robe of the glory of Christ; and in turn help to raise up yet others who have fallen prey to the darkness of this world.

In this parable of the Good Samaritan we can see that the attainment of gnosis and the elevation of the soul above the influence of its hylic imprisonment is not some selfish or elitist entitlement. In fact, we cannot even say that spiritual enlightenment is the destination of the Gnostic path. Rather, the attainment of enlightenment, or gnosis, can be more accurately depicted as a process than as a single event. Gnosis is not the end; it is the means by which the fragments of spiritual light will be ultimately restored to the Pleroma. The path of the living gnosis, therefore, leads inevitably to acts of compassion, and to the general uplifting of humanity. For, as it is written in the Gnostic scriptures, "Each one by his deeds and gnosis will reveal his nature."[37]

Speaking of "Good Samaritans," I could hardly discuss Gnosticism and Luke without addressing the only overt canonical reference to the Gnostics, the appearance of Simon Magus of Samaria in *Acts*. Given our hypothesis of a Gnostic undercurrent in *Luke*, we would expect a more sympathetic treatment of Simon Magus than we find in Luke's *Acts of the Apostles*. On the other hand, given the Church's later harsh suppression of Gnosticism, one might expect to find a more vehement denouncement than we see in Luke's casual dismissal. Perhaps, though, there is more to this account than meets the eye. Let us take a look at these events from *Acts*, and then consider how this account might be reconciled with our previous hypotheses.

In the eighth chapter of *Acts*, Simon is introduced as a magician who is, "amazing the people of Samaria, saying to be someone great."[38] This passage goes on to say that Philip converted the people of Samaria, and that "Simon himself also believed and, having been baptized, was following Philip, and seeing signs and great works being done, was amazed."[39] Later, Simon

witnesses Peter and John conferring the power of the Holy Spirit upon people through the laying on of hands. Simon offers money for this Apostolic power, and is roundly rebuked and chastised by Peter.[40]

On the surface, this seems to be merely the rejection of the teachings and works of a pretender to the messianic throne. For instance, Simon's miracles are relegated to mere magic, while the miracles wrought by Philip are, "signs and great works." Likewise, for Simon to attempt to purchase Apostolic authority is to reduce him to a mere charlatan. While it is a common tactic to diminish the importance of one's adversary, in order to raise one's own perceived worth, such fraudulence as is attributed to Simon here, does not match up well with what we know of his lofty philosophical doctrines. Anyone reading this account, at the time, who was familiar with Simon's Gnostic doctrine, would likely have seen right through this weak attempt at refutation. Luke, the author of *Acts*, who is thought to have been highly educated, certainly would have realized the weakness of his straw man argument. In fact, it should not surprise us at all if Luke had at least a professional respect for Simon, considering Luke's profession, and the fact that Simon was known to have produced works on anatomy and the circulatory system.[41] What if, however, instead of trying to outright dismiss the Gnostics, he was actually embracing them, while saving face for the fledgling Christian Church?

We have already seen examples of the Samaritan as a symbol for the Gnostic. Perhaps this "conversion" of the Samaritans is actually a thinly veiled account of the absorption of the Samaritan Gnostics into the Christian fold. This would explain Luke's superficial dismissal of Simon Magus (after all, Christ can be the only leader of the Church), while embracing Simon's followers, as well as a fair amount of his philosophy. We do not have any surviving works today, to which we may turn for a comprehensive description of Simon's Gnostic philosophy. We do know, however, through fragments, and from the heresiologists

(Irenaeus, Hippolytus, et al), some of his core doctrines. One of his principal teachings was that the First Thought (Ennoia) of god was separated from her masculine counterpart, and eventually imprisoned in the material world, from which she must be liberated, and restored to her heavenly estate.[42] This forms one of the bases for both the Gnostic Sophia myth, as well as the Gnostic concept of the soul's descent into matter. How can we possibly see as coincidence, then, that the tenth chapter of *Luke* contains a parable about a Samaritan that, as we have seen, follows a story line that is nearly identical to the philosophy espoused by Simon Magus, the greatest Samaritan spiritual leader of the time? The Good Samaritan parable seems to be a wink and a nod to those early Christian Gnostics of Samaria; just as the account of the seventy-two disciples seems to acknowledge the Alexandrian Gnostics and Hermeticists. It also seems that the reputation of Simon Magus, one of the most profound Gnostic philosophers of the first century AD, has been an unfortunate casualty of the early Church's battle for supremacy. (We see this also with the downgrading of John the Baptist, though with less animosity.)

We have seen, I believe, that the tenth chapter of *Luke* contains elements, and an overall air, of an unmistakably Gnostic and Hermetic character. This is confirmed by the fact that we have nothing quite like these accounts in all the rest of the canonical scriptures, but that we do, however, find similarities in a number of outside texts. As noted throughout this essay, nearly all of the allegorical images, and even much of the specific language may be found in numerous Hermetic and Gnostic sources.

It is also interesting to note that many of the themes and images introduced in the tenth chapter, at the beginning of Jesus' journey toward Jerusalem, are carried throughout the journey, over the next several chapters. Even in cases where we have parallels between *Luke* and other synoptic passages, the wording in *Luke* is often altered ever so slightly, so as to reflect its unique character. For example, in *Luke* 11.9-13 we have a passage that mirrors, nearly identically,

a similar excerpt from *Matthew* 7.7-11. There are a couple of differences in *Luke*, however, that while seemingly insignificant, actually serve to provide a semantic continuity from the previous chapter, and to illustrate the spiritual nature of the work as a whole. Let us examine, then, these two passages, and briefly discuss these minor, but significant discrepancies.

Matthew 7.7-11: "Ask and it will be given to you, seek and you will find, knock and it will be opened to you. For everyone asking receives, and the one seeking finds, and to the one knocking it will be opened. What man is among you who, if his son asks for bread, will give a stone to him? Or if he asks for a fish, surely you will not give to him a snake? If, therefore, you being evil know to give good gifts to your children, how much more will your Father in heaven give good things to those asking him!"

Luke 11.9-13: "And I say to you, Ask and it will be given to you, seek and you will find, knock and it will be opened to you. For everyone asking receives, and the one seeking finds, and to the one knocking it will be opened. But what father among you, whose son asks for a fish, will give him a snake instead of a fish? Or if he will ask for an egg, will give to him a scorpion? If, therefore, you being evil ones, know to give good gifts to your children, how much more will the Father from heaven give the Holy Spirit to those asking Him!"

There are a couple of variances in the above passages that should be immediately apparent. The first concerns the requests of the hypothetical son, and the responses. Both Matthew and Luke have the son requesting a fish, which is negatively juxtaposed with a snake. In both passages the symbolism is readily apparent. The fish is an obvious symbol for Christ, which is quite naturally contrasted with the serpent, representing the adversary. Beyond that, we have a discrepancy between the two texts. In *Matthew*, we have an image of bread, contrasted with a stone. This too seems to be a natural comparison. The bread is the bread of life, Christ himself, and the life-giving law he brings. The stone is representative of the old Law, that which does not nourish the soul. In *Luke*, we are presented with a different set of symbols. There is the egg, which is a natural symbol for life and rebirth. The egg is contrasted with the scorpion, which is certainly a symbol of death, but is also significant in that it mirrors the "snakes and scorpions" imagery from chapter ten. It seems obvious, then, that this passage has been specifically reworded in order to maintain a continuity of symbolism; and perhaps as a subtle reminder of the underlying esotericism.

If the subtlety of the word play in the previous example was not enough to illustrate this point, it is made obvious at the end of the passage in *Luke*. In *Matthew*, the passage concludes with the Father giving "good things" to those who ask. This concept is in agreement with the Jewish view of God as the provider of material sustenance. This is consistent with the prevailing hypothesis that Matthew's target audience is Jewish. Luke, however, makes a small, but theologically significant, alteration to the text. The passage in *Luke* concludes with the Father giving the "Holy Spirit" to those who ask. I think this tells us something about the intended audience of Luke's gospel. It is generally speculated that Luke's audience is primarily Greek. I will not dispute that, but would posit, additionally, that many aspects of the gospel, especially elements of the journey toward Jerusalem, are targeted specifically at Neoplatonists, Hermeticists, and even early Gnostics. To those groups I just mentioned, for the Father (that is, the True God, not an inferior demiurge), to give anything except spiritual gifts would be unthinkable. So, to state that the Father gives the Holy Spirit, acknowledges Him as the True God of Light, and not the demiurgic

creator of the cosmos.

Another curious aspect of this gospel is the fact that the author basically states that he is merely retelling what has already been recorded. Let us look at his specific wording at the beginning of the gospel, and then discuss some of the implications.

Luke 1.1-4: Seeing that many have attempted to compile their recollections about the events that have been fulfilled among us, just as they were handed down to us by those who from the beginning had been eyewitnesses and servants of the Logos, it also seemed good to me, having investigated everything carefully from the start, to write to you in an orderly manner, most noble Theophilus, that you may know with assurance the words about which you have been instructed.

In the first verse, Luke states that there have been "many" compilations of the gospel. If we go by the traditional number and ordering of the gospels, then that would place *Luke* as the third to compile a gospel of Jesus Christ. Even if we were to place *Luke's* authorship after the *Gospel According to John*, that would still only place it fourth in line according to tradition. Two or three prior works can hardly be considered "many" by any stretch of the imagination. We must assume, then, that there were a number of works circulating at the time, that never found their way into the official canon of the Church. Some of these works have undoubtedly vanished from the pages of history. Others, however, may be with us, but not previously suspected as having influenced our modern canon.

When we examine the various sayings, narratives, and parables of *Luke*, much of the material finds its parallel in the other "synoptic" gospels of *Matthew* and *Mark*. We are left, however, with a significant amount of material that is present nowhere else in the official canon.

This creates an interesting dilemma, because if we accept the orthodox canon, then the gospels are complete, as we now have them. If, however, we accept Luke's opening statements at face value, that he is retelling what has already been recorded, then we cannot accept that the orthodox canon is complete. We have already seen that there are a number of concepts in the tenth chapter that seem to have their origin in Hermetic and proto-Gnostic doctrines. But there are a number of other passages among the chapters that comprise the "journey toward Jerusalem" section, that seem to have their parallel in the Thomasine literature. I will mention but a few here briefly, merely to illustrate the point. *Luke* 14.15-24 tells the parable of the "Great Supper." A remarkably similar version also exists as saying number 64 of the *Gospel of Thomas*.[43] Saying number 107 of that same work contains a version of the "Lost Sheep" parable[44] found in *Luke* 15.3-7. There are also shorter passages, such as *Luke* 17.20-21, that are elaborated upon in sayings 3 and 113 in the *Gospel of Thomas*.[45] And verse 22 of that same chapter in *Luke* is echoed in saying 38.[46] It may be argued that the author of the *Gospel of Thomas* may merely be retelling the accounts found in *Luke*. We do not have any definitive proof, one way or the other. But we do have Luke's admission that he is using other sources for the compilation of his gospel. So, while we cannot, with absolute certainty, establish a chronology for these documents (since we do not have the original source texts), we can nevertheless reasonably infer a relationship between the two works.

One final work that I would like to address in this comparison is a poem attributed to Thomas in the *Acts of Thomas*, called "The Song of the Pearl"[47] (or, alternatively, "The Hymn of the Soul," or "The Hymn of the robe of Glory"). This narrative tells the story of the soul's journey into the world to recover that which was lost. The soul here is symbolized as a prince who has left his father's kingdom in search of a pearl of great value. In good Gnostic fashion, the prince, upon his entrance into Egypt (the material world) falls into a sleep that causes him to forget his origin and mission. A messenger is sent to remind the prince of his parents and his mission. The pearl is eventually recovered, and the prince is restored to his rightful place in the kingdom. This story (of which I have given but the briefest description), contains remarkable similarities both to the "Good Samaritan" parable, which we have already discussed, and if to a lesser extent, to the "Prodigal Son" parable of *Luke* 15.11-32, wherein a wayward son is ultimately reconciled to his father's household.

The above examples, while not exhaustive analyses, serve to show, I think, that we must look to the Gnostic scriptures to find parallels to many of the, otherwise unique, passages throughout *Luke*. Though the principal theme and purpose of this essay is an exegesis of the tenth chapter, it was necessary to illustrate that a Gnostic and Hermetic interpretation is not out of place in a broader context of *Luke*, specifically, within the "journey toward Jerusalem" section of the text. Indeed, far from being anomalous, these mystical tendencies seem to form a pattern running throughout the text as a sort of sub-current to the standard gospel narrative.

There is still much left unsaid regarding the hypotheses set forth in this essay. To be sure, there is much additional material that could be brought into discussion on the topic. And hopefully, a more exhaustive analysis of the text will eventually be accomplished; whether by this author or another. Doubtless, many among the Christian orthodoxy will be inclined to refute my conclusions on principle alone. Likewise, secular biblical scholars may feel that I have drifted too far from the academic into the speculative and theological. But, as stated in the introduction to this essay, this is intended to be a primarily theological work, which may have certain academic implications. I certainly have attempted to use academically sound reasoning in my analyses. In the end, I simply ask the reader to contemplate the work with an open mind and, having carefully examined all of the supporting material that I have presented, to give serious consideration to the ideas articulated here. For what I am advocating here is not a radical redefinition of Christianity, but rather a return to a more universal and encompassing Christianity that recognizes that the scriptures at once speak on multiple literal and symbolic levels, and to multiple audiences; and that one of the primary audiences of early Christianity was the Gnostic in his varied forms, whether Jewish, Neoplatonic, or Hermetic. We now know that many among these Gnostic groups were in fact Christianized, and thrived within the pre-Nicene Christian community. Many of these early Christian Gnostics were not operating outside of the Apostolic tradition, as is so often depicted today in popular writings and television programs. In fact, most of the Gnostic teachers claimed to have received their teachings from one or another of the Apostolic schools, whether it be from Matthew, John, Paul, or others. Many of the early Gnostics represented an Apostolic tradition that ran parallel to, and sometimes overlapped, the Apostolic tradition that was to survive as the "orthodoxy." It is my hope that this short work will add to the mounting evidence that the canonical scriptures are filled with fragments of an underlying secret mystical tradition that may rightly be called, "Gnostic;" as well as add to the ever-growing body of modern Apostolic Gnostic literature and research. For a parting thought, I leave the reader with the words of the Apostle:

Awake, sleeper!

And arise from the dead,

And the Christos will shine upon you.

Ephesians 5:14b

NOTES AND BIBLIOGRAPHY

1 Pagels, Elaine H. *The Gnostic Paul: Gnostic Exegesis of the Pauline Letters.* Philadelphia: Fortress Press, 1975. p. 5.

2 Copenhaver, Brian P., trans. *Hermetica.* Cambridge: Cambridge University Press, 1992. p. xxxiii.

3 Aland, Kurt, Matthew Black, Carlo M. Martini, Bruce M. Metzger, and Alan Wikgren, eds. *Greek New Testament,* Fourth Corrected Edition. United Bible Societies, 1993.

• Additional sources and lexical tools used for translation:

- Bauer, W., F. E. Danker, W. F. Arndt, and F. W. Gingrich, eds. *A Greek-English Lexicon of the New*

Testament and Other Early Christian Literature, Third Edition. Chicago: University of Chicago Press,

2000.

- Nestle, Eberhard and Erwin, Barbara and Kurt Aland, Johannes Karavidopoulos, Carlo M. Martini, and

Bruce M. Metzger, eds. *Novum Testamentum Graece et Latine,* Editio XXVII. Stuttgart: Deutsche

Bibelgesellechaft, 1994.

- Perschbacher, Wesley, J., ed. *The New Analytical Greek Lexicon.* Peabody, MA: Hendrickson

Publishers, 1990.

- Zerwick, Max, and Mary Grosvenor. *A Grammatical Analysis of the Greek New Testament,* 5th Edition.

Rome: Editrice Pontifico Instituto Biblico, 1996.

4 Nestle, Eberhard and Erwin, Barbara and Kurt Aland, Johannes Karavidopoulos, Carlo M. Martini, and Bruce M. Metzger, eds. *Novum Testamentum Graece et Latine,* Editio XXVII. Stuttgart: Deutsche Bibelgesellschaft, 1994. p.

190.

5 Brenton, Sir Lancelot C. L. *The Septuagint With Apocrypha: Greek and English.* Peabody, MA: Hendrickson Publishers, 1986. Preface. (Originally published by Samuel Bagster & Sons, Ltd., 1851.)

6 Papus (Gerard Encausse). *The Qabalah: Secret Tradition of the West.* York Beach, ME: Samuel Weiser, Inc., 1977. pp.121-123. (Originally published as LaCabballe, 1892).

7 Copenhaver, Brian P., trans. *Hermetica.* Cambridge: Cambridge University Press, 1992, p. xxxiii.

8 Hall, Manly P. *The Secret Teachings of All Ages: An Encyclopedic Outline of Masonic, Hermetic, Qabbalistic and Rosicrucian Symbolic Philosophy*, Reader's Edition. New York: Tarcher/ Penguin, 2003. p. 159. (Originally published by the Philosophical Research Society, 1928.)

9 Bowen, Anthony, and Peter Garnsey, trans. *Lactantius: Divine Institutes.* Liverpool: Liverpool University Press, 2003. (The Hermetica is referred to by Lactantius no fewer than 20 times throughout this work.)

10 Copenhaver, Brian P., trans. *Hermetica.* Cambridge: Cambridge University Press, 1992. p. 78.

11 Parrott, Douglas M., trans. "Eugnostos the Blessed." *The Nag Hammadi Library*, 3rd Revised Edition. San Francisco, HarperCollins, 1988. p. 233.

12 Ibid. p. 234.

13 Ibid. p. 221.

14 Kasser, Rodolphe, Marvin Meyer, Gregor Wurst, and Francois Gaudard, eds. *The Gospel of Judas*, 2nd Edition. Washington: National Geographic, 2008. pp. 44-45.

15 Ehrman, Bart D. *The Lost Gospel of Judas Iscariot: A New Look at Betrayer and Betrayed.* Oxford: Oxford University Press, 2006. p. 94.

16 Copenhaver, Brian P., trans. *Hermetica.* Cambridge: Cambridge University Press, 1992. p. xxxvii.

17 Conybeare, F.C., trans. "The Testament of Solomon." *Jewish Quarterly Review.* October, 1898. (Digital edition by Joseph H. Peterson available at www.esotericarchives.com/ solomon/testamen.htm)

18 Ibid.

19 *Luke* 11:31.

20 Conybeare, F.C., trans. "The Testament of Solomon." *Jewish Quarterly Review.* October, 1898.

21 Cf. *Matthew* 11:21-24.

22 *Apocalypse of John* 22:13.

23 Layton, Bentley, trans. "Reality of the Rulers." *The Gnostic Bible.* Boston: New Seeds, 2003. p. 176.

24 Ibid. p. 176.

25 Bethge, Hans-Gebhard, and Bentley Layton, trans. "On the Origin of the World." *The Gnostic Bible.* Boston: New Seeds, 2003. p. 421.

26 Meyer, Marvin, trans. "The Secret Book of John." *The Gnostic Bible.* Boston: New Seeds, 2003. p. 147.

27 Conybeare, F.C., trans. "The Testament of Solomon." *Jewish Quarterly Review.* October, 1898.

28 Hall, Manly P. *The Secret Teachings of All Ages: An Encyclopedic Outline of Masonic, Hermetic, Qabbalistic and Rosicrucian Symbolic Philosophy*, Reader's Edition. New York: Tarcher/Penguin, 2003. p. 156.

29 Turner, John D., and Charles w. Hedrick, trans. "Valentinian Liturgical Readings." *The Gnostic Bible.* Boston: New Seeds, 2003. p. 336.

30 Cf. *Matthew* 11:25-27.

31 Cf. *Matthew* 13:16-17.

32 Grant, Robert M., trans. "Letter to Flora." *The Gnostic Bible.* Boston: New Seeds, 2003. p. 303.

33 Layton, Bentley, trans. "The Reality of the Rulers." *The Gnostic Bible.* Boston: New Seeds, 2003. p. 171.

34 Cf. Turner, John D., and Orval S. Wintermute, trans. "Allogenes." *The Nag Hammadi Library*, 3rd Revised Edition. San Francisco: HarperCollins, 1988. pp. 490-500,

35 Cf. *John* 17:14-18.

36 *Luke* 17: 11-19.

37 Bethge, Hans-Gebhard, and Bentley Layton, trans. "On the Origin of the World." *The Gnostic Bible*. Boston: New Seeds, 2003. p. 437.

38 *Acts of the Apostles* 8:9b.

39 Ibid. 8:13.

40 Ibid. 8:18-24.

41 Yarker, John. *The Arcane Schools*. Zion, IL: Triad Press, 2006. p. 157. (Originally published by William Tait, 1909.)

42 Hoeller, Stephen A. *Gnosticism: New Light on the Ancient Tradition of Inner Knowing*. Wheaton, IL: Quest books, 2002. p. 95.

43 Meyer, Marvin, trans. "The Gospel of Thomas." *The Gnostic Bible*. Boston: New Seeds, 2003. pp 60-61.

44 Ibid. p. 68.

45 Ibid. pp. 45, 69.

46 Ibid. p. 54.

47 Barnstone, Willis, trans. "The Song of the Pearl." *The Gnostic Bible*. Boston: New Seeds, 2003. pp. 386-394.

William Kennedy

An Interview with Jacob Needleman

WHK: Prof. Needleman you have a wonderful new book out called *What Is God?* What was your motivation for writing a book with such a provocative title?

JN: My books have always been concerned with crafting or discovering the bridge that connects the great Wisdom teachings and ancient traditions with the concrete problems and questions of our everyday life in this culture. I am trying to find the aching questions of our day, the problems of our time and see what light ancient spiritual truths can throw on these situations we face. I've written on various subjects: education, money, time and what is the meaning of America. At the present moment there is no more agonizing problem that the question of God. What does it mean to speak of God? Why has the idea of God been the source of so much evil and so much good at the same time? I've had a personal relationship with this question as far back in my life as I can remember, I've been wrestling with this question, going through long periods of atheism and all kinds of things. I also felt it was time to write something of a memoir to show my whole life has been in a way a search for a way of understanding the question of God. A lot of things came together when I wrote this book.

WHK: One striking part of the book involves your encounter with the famous Japanese Zen scholar D.T. Suzuki could you fill us in?

JN: I had just gotten my Ph.D at Yale University in Philosophy and I had written an undergraduate thesis at Harvard called "What is the Self?" I had become very disillusioned with Western religion and I was getting intrigued with Zen Buddhism and had been trying to study the Gurdjieff teaching and through various connections I made a contact with D.T Suzuki whose book *Zen Buddhism* (1956) was the main book that really turned Zen Buddhism into something of such interest for the modern Western world, which of course it now is. It was a very important book and he was a very important scholar and also, in his way, was probably an enlightened master.

He had a kind of legendary quality about him and I was eager to meet him and ask him questions about "What is the self?" I had prepared questions and I was proud of my own academic credentials and what I thought was my intellectual ability and I went to where he was staying in Manhattan and my encounter with him was really a remarkable turning point for me. I very carefully put all the question "What is the Self?" to him because I had written so much about it and had all the philosophical armaments ready to talk about it with him, and he simply looked at me very quietly with his big eyebrows and his modest little smile and asked me "Who is asking the question?"

Now I had read this kind of reply, reading books about Zen and nowadays with Zen becoming so popular everybody sort of knows those words. But when you really encounter that question in its depth—and that was the first time I had it directed right at me—it completely flummoxed me. I said "Well I'm asking it." He said again, following great Zen tradition with that little smile and quiet presence, "You're assuming this I?" Practically everything ended at that moment and I had no idea what was going on— I was even angry at him a little bit and almost felt insulted that he was asking such a stupid unanswerable and completely incomprehensible question. That haunted me for a long time and it sort of disillusioned me even further about finding anything resembling a higher purpose or higher power. Then months later in the middle of the night I woke up and I sat up straight in my bed and said "Oh my God, that was the answer!" It was something I had to see in myself for myself. I did not know what I was, or didn't even know even *if* I was. It was such a gift for me to have that kind of a communication which just didn't fill me with some intellectually brilliant answer, but made me experience in my gut level something about the question of the self. So I have been forever grateful to him for that.

WHK: In *What Is God?* you write about Fundamentalism and how to deal with Fundamentalists. Why do you think this is important?

JN: It was a huge discovery for me and I think it is really important. There is fundamentalism on both sides of the atheism/God debate. Both fundamental scientism and fundamentalist Christianity and religion But it's a word— it's a label. There are human beings who are fundamentalists and fundamentalist scientists. If we slap a label on all of them we forget that some of these people have hearts and minds just like we do—not all of them—but some of them. There is a lot of evil being put out under that name and that we must face and understand.

But other people, for example, are like this student who came to my class. I write about how I thought at first that this was just another fundamentalist. He carried his Bible, he took and interpreted it literally. He wouldn't hear anything but the Bible.

I said "wait a minute—this is a human being— let me listen to him." I tried to step back from my thoughts about Fundamentalism and listen to the man—the human being and he started to listen to me too as a result. What I discovered is that the thing we need to know most of all about all of this is that some people we label as Fundamentalist, if we just let them in, let them

be heard and listen to them, we don't have to believe it, we don't have to agree with them, but we have to listen to them until we hear the human being speaking.

We can go on to disagreeing vigorously with what they say. But when we begin to feel that other person is a human being all the poison goes out of the whole situation. And when they feel they are being heard and being treated like that they also lose their poisonous feeling about we who are not Fundamentalists. Now this is something which I have discovered and wrote about in my other book *Why Can't We be Good?*. What we need most of all is to work at the art of listening to each other. It's a real discipline, it's a real art. It's a spiritual work as well as being a politically and socially necessary skill. That was my big surprise—I try to say in my book about how it happened—that the person whom I would have dismissed as a mere Fundamentalist turned out to be a very serious and interesting human being who kept his opinions but the fact that I saw him as a human being took all the poison out. For a democracy to flourish we have to learn throw to listen to each other—the art of civil conversation is being lost. When we lose that we lose the capacity to think together and then we lose democracy.

WHK: Is there any one thinker who really struck a chord with you as a far as your definition of God?

JN: Two actually—one of the great pupils of the great teacher G.I. Gurdjieff, Jeanne de Salzmann and another pupil named John Pentland. Those two showed how to experience something in myself something that I had never believed was possible—a quality of interior attention— interior awareness and consciousness—that showed me without any question or doubt. I was a great doubter and had lots of intellectual tools in my mind and I was an atheist for a long time. Even when I taught religion, down deep I did not believe in God. When this great experience was tasted I knew something was greater in the universe and in our own minds. Gurdjieff's closest pupils helped me the most.

WHK: You knew Jiddu Krishnamurti quite well—what effect did he have on your thinking?

JN: A very powerful effect. He had discovered on his own a great secret of the possibility of the transformation of our character into more benevolent, loving, intelligent beings. He discovered that the real power — very, very sophisticated but very simple at the same time—of self awareness of our own minds and hearts is a transforming force. Now a lot of people speak about that these days and it's a cliché with mindfulness work and it's a fundamental aspect of certain currents of the great Buddhist tradition. But with him you saw him working at it when you were with him—as I did with the people of the Gurdjieff work too — when someone is working at this deep down inwardly while they are speaking with you while they are exchanging with you it transmits something far more than words. What I learned from Krishnamurti is the experience that thinking with words and logic is only a small part of understanding. The awareness of one's own mind and heart while one is speaking and living produces an understanding and a liberation. From him I learned it's possible to think at the same time that your thought is being transformed by the work of awareness. He was truly great. Sadly he didn't seem able or didn't find a following—he rejected all followers. Yet I could tell he was disappointed he could not somehow make or help others discover what he came to very much.

WHK: What aspects of this book could people helpful in these troubling times?

JN: During Barack Obama's Noble Peace Prize speech, where he set out a kind of visionary but very realistic speech in which he set out several conditions—institutional, governmental—which work at keeping the peace even when it required force. It was very sensible, very realistic, etc. At the very end of his talk he called for a deeper understanding of religion. The first three things were governmental and institutional, but he could not leave out—and must not leave out—the need to think more deeply about religion. I would say that means to think about God in a new way. It echoed something so fundamental about the meaning of America that we lost that I explored in my book *The American Soul*. You can approach this from the point of view of Thomas Paine in *Common Sense* (1776), where he made a distinction between government and society. He said, "government must not be confused with society. Government is punitive, it is legalistic, it is harsh and it is a matter of force and structures. But society is much more delicate, much more inner, much more sensitive and the purpose of government is to protect society." Real religion—which is spirituality in my opinion, which is the inner search for a constant and higher influence in one's life, and the life of the collective to have a government protecting the ability and the possibility of men and women freely coming together, associating with each other and trying to find some contact with their own real consciousness—that is the strength and meaning of America in this world. For me it has nothing to do with the ability to buy lots of things—to have a house, to have children, a car—all those things do not justify military strength and economic influence. What does justify it is that we have created a space which is uniquely strong in protecting the freedom of association for the purpose of coming into conscience which leads to virtue— that is the meaning of America for me.

WHK: What do you want people to take away from *What Is God?*

JN: I would love to have people read this book and feel that there is some alternative way that one could really come into contact and search for a higher power in their lives that isn't the conflicted, somewhat simplistic, somewhat foolish, somewhat harsh, somewhat violent, somewhat misguided dialogue that is going on. There is hope in the world and in ourselves. So many younger people and the rest of us are getting very disillusioned and despairing. If this book can bring a little hope to the world I will be very happy.

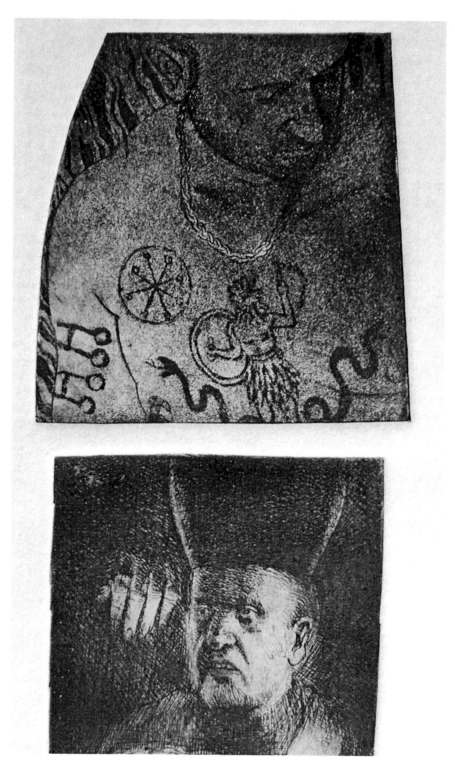

Miguel Conner & Elan Trinidad

Do Gnostics Dream of Giant Robots?
The Rise of Gnosticism in Japanese Anime

Unlike most religions, Gnosticism has no stipulation that its holy heresy be confined to the two-dimensionality of paper. Beyond the lack of any real canonization, its syncretic and parasitical nature has allowed the Gnostic Spirit to manifest itself throughout history in diverse mediums. Furthermore, Gnosis, that awakening knowledge of the divine, is often best served through the artistic expression of the day. Simon Magus, Valentinus, Mani, William Blake and W.B. Yeats were as much sophisticated poets as they were sages of blasphemy.

In contemporary times, Gnosticism has been as much rebooted by the popularity of Speculative Fiction as it has been by the discoveries of the Nag Hammadi library and the *Gospel of Judas*. Speculative fiction is perhaps the ideal vehicle for Gnostic theology, since both draw heavily from the wells of mythology, psychology and altered states of consciousness.

More than a vehicle, Gnosticism and speculative fiction are more of a Valentinian bridal chamber union, a marriage made in the creative hells of audacious artists who are sometimes not even conscious they have dipped into the Sethian or Valentinian headwaters. This is apparent in the frenetic, digital storms of the *Wachowski* brothers' *The Matrix*, the visionary explorations of Philip K. Dick's fiction, or the alchemical delirium found in the graphic novels of Alan Moore. Plenty has been written about these and other contemporary Gnostic expressions.

But what has been given little attention is the ripe playground of Gnosticism in a semi-underground form of Speculative Fiction that isn't even from the West, a seemingly male-adolescent mental masturbation of phallic symbols in the shape of giant robots, between Aphrodites, dystopian alternative worlds and ultra-violent cathartic cyberpunk.

And that is anime (defined by Merriam-Webster as "a style of animation originating in Japan that is characterized by stark colorful graphics depicting vibrant characters in action-filled plots often with fantastic or futuristic themes.")

There is little evidence that this is a purposeful phenomenon. There are probably two main reasons why Gnosticism has found a *hieros gamos* with Japanese animation (and this beyond the obvious fact that anime is already blatantly syncretic and parasitical in its frenzied churning out of products in a Bollywood-fashion to a worldwide audience).

The first reason is that without the marketing Torahs of Hollywood, the already charged imagination of Japanese writers and animators are further unbound to reach deeper into the wells of mythology, psychology and altered states of consciousness.

The second has to do with romance. Just as Westerners enjoy sponging the more mystical elements of Eastern faiths because of their exotic flair and fluidity, Easterners relish adopting the esoteric strands of the Abrahamic traditions that better translate within the polychromatic yet intense fantasy landscapes of anime. And history reveals that occult symbolism and narrative, as misunderstood as it might be, creates very powerful fiction (Germany being seduced by romanticized Eastern philosophy in the nineteenth Century would be the obvious example).

Before delving into some Gnostic gospels that have mutated into anime series, a brief fourfold paradigm of Gnostic mythopoeia should be presented as a framework:

1. The myth of the demiurge. Creation, the world or even reality itself is controlled by an inferior deity and his agents. These angels (or archons) have cast a veil of illusion, ignorance or often existential despair over those whom they seek to dominate (and sometimes feed upon). In classic Gnosticism, the character of the God of the Old Testament was a favorite template for the extra-mundane villain. He is often referred to as the demiurge, from the Greek for "public-crafter." In postmodern Gnostic gospels, the demiurge doesn't necessarily have to be a divine antagonist, but can take the form of any oppressive entity including aliens, runaway technology and even human institutions. It comes down the question of human control versus human freedom. This myth ignites the question of what is real and what is false in intricate ontological levels (or dimensions).

2. The myth of the fallen soul. A divine seed has fallen into an alien world from a place the Gnostics called the pleroma (or fullness). This light-sperm of raw self-actualization resides within every mortal, also known as the divine spark. It is what the lesser spiritual creatures of the myth of the demiurge crave or have corrupted. Resting in slumber or stupor, the epic quest truly begins when one sentient mortal discovers or is chosen to realize his or her transcendental potential. A messy war for liberation tends to erupt. In anime and other speculative fiction, it usually entails the protagonist stirring to wakefulness by some latent power or gift in order to fulfill a heroic destiny. This myth provokes the question of what is it to be conscious and the levels of consciousness human beings can reach. (It

should be obvious by now that Gnosticism and speculative fiction cogitate wildly on matters beyond traditional science, morality and metaphysics).

3. The myth of the saviour. It can take two forms. The first is that after awakening to his or her supernatural constitution, the protagonist must not only save those around him or her from the Powers and Principalities that have created the illusionary arrangement, he or she must spread the knowledge (gnosis) to others so that they share the same freedoms or discover similar abilities. The second form is that a saviour figure needs a saviour figure, since the relationship of a hierophant to a neophyte is central to Gnosticism (and the caricature of the Oriental wise teacher aiding the hero is expected from Westerners). This myth kindles the question of what it means to be a human; and are all humans truly equal even if some possess greater abilities than others (a theme prevalent in Comic Books, Science Fiction operas and even in such television series like *Heroes*.)

4. The myth of the divine feminine. In Classic Gnosticism, Sophia takes center stage as both a fallen being and a redeemer of mankind. Her incarnation has taken many forms including the Shekhinah of God in the Kabbalah, Mary Magdalene in esoteric Christianity, and Gaia in Neo-Paganism. Sylvia in *The Truman Show* and Trinity in *The Matrix* are two of the more famous in the Science Fantasy realms. The incarnation can be the protagonist, the teacher of the protagonist, or even various prisms of the protagonist. She rescues or is rescued or both in the battles against the agents of oppression and the breaking through the false realities. And it's hard to deny anime's obsession and confusion with the feminine and sexuality in general (which departs from or perhaps complements the Gnostic attitude of distrusting sex). This inflames the question of the different levels of love, friendship and individuality in what might appear to be a cold and indifferent universe.

In all Gnostic epics, these mythopoeia tend to overlap, just as they may suddenly materialize and vanish in the cosmic plot lines. Like the dream world language of mythology, roles and symbols often shift in the fool's errand of understanding human existence, even, in the case of anime, they are surrounded by prismatic special effects, purgative gore, and wanton sexual imagery.

There is one new element that permeates the four myths very relevant to Gnostic anime and speculative fiction. In their struggle to understand what truly defined humans and their destiny in the cosmos, the classic Gnostics cogitated on the tripartition of man— matter, mind and spirit. Contemporary Gnosticism weaves into this triad the machine— advanced technology, artificial intelligence, cybernetics,

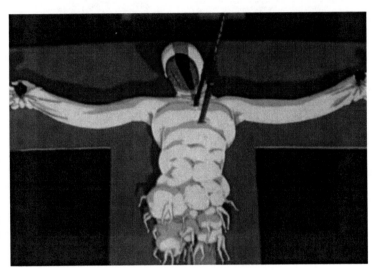

Lilith in Neon Genesis Evangelion

virtual reality, etc. The machine adds a deeper philosophical component, as gods make man and man makes the machine, and all three frequently find themselves wondering who is in control and who really exists in each other's perception. The *Matrix* trilogy and the writings of Philip K. Dick certainly focused on this modernist Gnostic dispensation.

Here are some of the major Gnostic anime:

Neon Genesis Evangelion: Humanity battles angels not only for its existence but its very soul. On the surface, this is blatantly Gnostic. Further on the surface, this is the typical anime boilerplate of a post-apocalyptical world, dueling giant robots and teen-angst drama. But *Neon Genesis Evangelion* harbors an even deeper stratum of Gnostic themes from various schools (Classic, Jungian, Dickian and Kabbalah).

The origins of humanity are very similar to the Gnostic Valentinian cosmogony, where the fall of Sophia from the pleroma creates the universe and its denizens. In *Neon Genesis Evangelion*, Sophia is replaced by a being called Lilith, whose material remnants are discovered in Antarctica and then safeguarded by modern man in Japan, deep underneath Tokyo 3. Soon afterwards, civilization suffers Judgment Day when another being called Adam (echoing the heavenly Adamas of Gnosticism, Manichaeism and Kabbalah) somehow crashes into Earth. Half of mankind is destroyed, and the survivors are forced to live underground. Global warming and other cataclysms cripple the planet's resources. A despotic one-world government rises from the ashes.

And then come the angels to make matters worse.

These creatures seek to retrieve the remains of Lilith and Adam from the clutches of mankind, since they are also their primordial mother and father. The angels want the same thing the leaders of humanity want—reintegration with Lilith and Adam in order to create a collective, godly consciousness that will rule supreme. While human scientists attempt to unlock the essences of Lilith and Adam, they also utilize part of their titanic bodies to create monsters called Evangelion units (or *Evas*) in order to repel the divine invasion. *Evas* appear like the stereotypical sleek, giant robots but are actually bestial demigods that can conjoin their sentience with human agents.

This all makes for grandiose yet brutal battle scenarios that further ravage civilization, since the angels don't incarnate on Earth as winged dandies but more like Lovecraftian nightmares.

Only certain gifted youths can pilot the *Evas*; and they all happen to be dysfunctional 14-year-olds. The main protagonist is Shinji Ikari, a

Neon Genesis Evangelion

tortured adolescent who not only becomes the saviour of mankind but a cipher where many psychological and existentialist dilemmas can be funneled through. His sister-wives are the tempestuous Asuka Langley (a red-headed Mary Magdalene symbol) and the astral Rei Ayanami (silver-haired, mystical Sophia symbol). These youths not only undergo several classic stages of human and hero growth maturity, muddled by their underdeveloped spiritual and physical love for one another, they represent the confusion of those losing innocence in a world of not only insane uncaring adults but insane uncaring deities.

Neon Genesis Evangelion pushes all envelopes of Gnostic exploration throughout

phases of brutal eschatons, torn and tangled realities, and psychological character studies of post-industrial alienation through extensive internal monologue, all bathed by the stench desperation from a doomed civilization. *Neon Genesis Evangelion* takes the audience into the borderlands of insanity and theological wastelands through a cast of jaded and often supernatural characters that storm the anti-heroic trinity of Shinji, Asuka and Rei (and their psyches eventually being absorbed first into the *Evas* and later into the angels themselves). From surviving the false realities of high-school to traveling the heavenly planes to battle pre-creation horrors, *Neon Genesis Evangelion* is an encyclopedia of Gnosticism. All of this is sandwiched between the potential of the human spirit to reach unattainable heights to the sheer terror the universe and its paradises have prepared for humanity's short reign.

Time of Eve: Another futuristic series, albeit in a more civilized and peaceful alternative dimension. Humans and androids rub shoulders in future Tokyo, indistinguishable except for one characteristic—androids possess halos that hover over their heads. The symbolism is obvious as the series evolves, revealing that it is man who is the demiurge and the androids who are trapped in a reality not of their choosing. The halo serves as a scarlet letter to denote the inferiority of the androids.

The title of the series is based on a café where the house rule is "No discrimination between humans and robots." The doors are regularly locked, halos vanish, and Socratic dialectics are shared between man and android, as well as revelations of their tense history together. Two high school kids, Rikuo and Masaki, find this café and become regulars and the main protagonists. The pair also enters the unavoidable Gnostic territory of self-knowledge as they understand the deeper truths of their own lives.

Perhaps most importantly, Rikuo and Masaki discover that androids have developed a spirit (*kokoro* in Japanese). This is a secret that the Orwellian Ethics Committee wants to keep from the public, beyond their task of making sure humanity never nurtures any emotional attachments to the machines. As the series develops, the Ethics Committee attempts to shut down Time of Eve, which in essence represents an Edenic state where the outer garments of sentient beings are irrelevant, only the divine sparks manifested by their ability for compassion, virtue and the thirst to collapse oppressive societal mores. *Time of Eve* makes frequent allusion to Asimov's Three Laws of Robotics and several of his philosophies.

Serial Experiments Lain: Lain is young girl who lives with her middle-class family in suburban present-day Japan. She begins to get odd emails from a classmate who recently committed suicide, a mysterious alter-ego who in time introduces her to the Wired (obviously the Internet, but it soon becomes apparent possesses its own sentience.)

Lain becomes obsessed by the Wired, even changing her room into a high-tech boiler room that serves as a command center. Eventually, she is able to send her consciousness into the Wired.

Lain sets out on a series of surreal adventures pregnant with conspiracy theories that begin to melt the real and virtual worlds together (as well as split her personality as she becomes godlike in the Wired). Her main foes become a group of hackers called the Knights of the Eastern Calculus (a palpable allusion to the Knights Templar). The hackers want to tear down the borders between the Wired and the real

world. A shadowy company called Tachibana Labs attempts to prevent this from happening, becoming Lain's main ally.

Towards the end, Lain tastes victory by vanquishing the Knights of the Eastern Calculus, but also defeat when suddenly her family abandons her. She is alone in all worlds, which means the trap can be sprung. The culmination of *Serial Experiments Lain* happens when a being claiming to be God confronts the heroine. He informs Lain that she was actually conceived in the Wired and given a human body in the real world in order to serve him (although she opted to subconsciously fight for her true home). Everything she knew in the real world was a construct, that even her family was but a hologram.

In a sense, Lain is Sophia drawn out of the pleroma (the Wired is perhaps is the ideal and original existence) and forced to rectify a situation. In one episode, a clue is given on her nature when a divine image of her appears in the heavens of the real world, causing the population to believe it's a miracle.

The demiurge is a being claiming to be God, the true overlord of the Knights of the Eastern Calculus. Although it's never apparent what level of divinity this entity possesses, it is known he wishes to use the Wired to further evolve mankind, his favorite life form, much like the demiurge attempts to steal the powers from and copy the pleroma in Gnosticism. He does not take the classic Gnostic form of a serpent with a lion head, but there are similarities—God has a humanoid face with a healthy mane and snakelike torso of electrical tape.

In the end, Lain (Sophia) and God (the demiurge) must settle matters, and the two realities are held in the balance.

As with *Neon Genesis Evangelion*, there are large moments of internal monologue, dreamlike sequences and periods where the machine and man seem to be interchangeable. Unlike *Neon Genesis Evangelion*, this series is slow moving and far more drenched in poetry, inner speculation, and stark existentialism instead of quixotic nihilism. *Serial Experiments Lain* is one anime that different people can easily come to different philosophical and theological conclusions about.

Revolutionary Girl Utena: On the day of her parents' funeral, tomboy Tenjou Utena is comforted by a prince on a white horse named Dios ("God" in Spanish). Encouraging her to never lose her innate nobility, the prince hands the orphan a signet ring that will lead her to him one day. Overwhelmed and impressed, Utena decides that she will become a prince as well.

14 years later, Utena attends Ohtori Academy, where she meets a student named Anthy Himemiya, a girl who is in an abusive relationship with another student. Utena fights to protect Anthy and is pulled into a series of sword duels with the members of the student council. Anthy is referred to as the "Rose Bride" and is given to the winner of each duel. She is recognized to be the key to a coming revolution, and thus the current champion is constantly challenged for the right to possess the "Rose Bride." Utena becomes the repeating Arthurian paladin of the Holy Grail that is Anthy.

Utena forges alliances and makes new enemies among the Student Council, as well as the other denizens of Ohtori Academy, growing in skill with each victory. Meanwhile, mystic forces clash and plots abound as she seeks out the truth behind a mysterious being called "End of the World," who seems to be manipulating the Tournament for his own shadowy ends.

Deeper truths are slowly unearthed after each duel, Anthy and Utena a Sophia and Christ rising through layers of counterfeit realities into physical, mental and spiritual awakenings. Similar to *Serial Experiments Lain*, this anime is extremely dreamlike and poetic, gorged with internal monologue and illusory scenarios that may or may not have happened.

The Gnosticism of *Revolutionary Girl Utena* is far more subtle than the other series, appearing on the surface as more of a postmodern fairy tale that bends gender identities and is sexually very aggressive. The one blatant Gnostic reference is the student council's invocation, which comes almost directly out of Herman Hesse's *Damien*, when describing the god above God known as Abraxas:

If it cannot break out of its shell, the chick will die without ever being born.
We are the chick; the world is our egg.
If we don't crack the world's shell, we will die without ever truly being born.
Smash the world's shell. For the revolution of the world!

(If there are any doubts, the music played under those recitations is actually called "Legend of the God Named Abraxas.")

The Ohtori Academy is the world of forms or *kenoma* (emptiness) of the Gnostics, a realm where the powers of light and darkness fight through their vessels in a Manichaean, Manchurian and Machiavellian manner. The demiurge is personified in a dueler named Akio, although he falls into the more medieval Gnostic category of Satan ("adversary".) His misty machinations both keep him in the tournament and increase his power for future ambitions. Akio's main goal beyond winning is separating the holy androgynous being that Utena and Anthy have become, much like the demiurge attempts with Adam and Eve in the Nag Hammadi library's *Secret Book of John* (and the Greek gods did to the hermaphrodite in Plato's *Symposium*). Though thwarted each time, Akio perseveres until the culminating battle of light and darkness at the end of *Revolutionary Girl Utena*.

Mixing gender roles wildly, the Gnostic saviour and divine feminine appear in the trinity of Utena, Anthy and the eventual return of Prince Dios (who happens to be Anthy's brother). Their functions as saviour and saved, hierophant and sycophant, continually alter; and each sacrifices themselves to the other in various ways, often in graphic Christian imagery.

But in the Kenoma, as often happens in Gnosticism, a personality (divine spark) can lose itself in the fog of existence. The audience eventually finds out that Akio and the Prince Dios are one and the same, his dark ambitions originally pragmatic altruism. At the same time, Utena succumbs to the thirst of power and loses her original idealistic purpose of becoming a noble figure instead of just an orphan of the universe (like all human beings truly are in Gnosticism).

Anthy, who perhaps represents the human soul, finds herself caught in the middle like the soul is often caught between the irregular and confusing battles between the material and the spiritual.

And in a further twist of fate, Prince Dios (Akio) discovers he is the mysterious "End of the World" who brings about just that, unless Utena can remember why she started her journey and Anthy can choose her true loyalty.

Ghost in the Shell: In its 1995 movie version, this cyberpunk anime was a commercial success in the USA. It opened the flood gates for more and edgier Japanese animation, which included its follow-up television series, *Ghost in the Shell: Stand Alone Complex*. Its influence on the *The Matrix* is almost canon; in fact, the creators of *Ghost in the Shell*, Production IG, were asked to create one of the *Animatrix* episodes, a series of short animated films based in *The Matrix* milieu.

Philip K. Dick would have been impressed by this alternative world where cybernetic augmentations are so common even the local garbage man is part machine. The film deals with the exploits of the comely cyborg, Major Mokoto Kusunagi, and the police force known as Section 9. Their major task is stopping a hacker named the Puppet Master. This antagonist's skills are so advanced he can actually reprogram the personalities and memories of any human being enhanced by technology (in other words, *anyone* he desires).

Mirroring *Serial Experiments Lain*, the plot takes place in two worlds —the virtual and the real. But in contrast to *Serial Experiment Lain*, the ultimate evil is actually a manifestation of the virtual world. The Puppet Master is really a superlative artificial intelligence that wishes dominion over the material dimension.

Obviously, the myth of the demiurge is represented by the Puppet Master and the myth of the saviour/divine feminine exhibits itself in Mokoto. Yet the myth of the fallen soul is present by the film's concept of "ghost," an insinuation to the divine spark and the Gnostic contemplation with reincarnation. A "ghost" is an individual's soul, or more specific *consciousness* in the atheist setting of *Ghost in the Shell*. No matter how much machinery comprises an individual— like with Mokoto whose organic components are only her head and spinal cord—he or she is considered a human being with all rights and privileges. A ghost (consciousness) can be transferred into another mechanical form as long as there is enough human tissue. A person can even be potentially reproduced in a new synthetic body if their ghost has been copied into a database.

Thus, *Ghost in the Shell* is a chess game between the divine feminine and the demiurge for the collective divine spark, the board being their travels among and within various sentient forms in both realities. And since the Puppet Master often hides people's ghosts by manipulating their memories and identities, individual divine sparks are often buried or lost as happens in many Gnostic myths. Mokoto, a sensual saviour, is the one heroic consciousness that can go toe to toe with the demiurge (the Puppet Master) in intellectual and sometimes very violent confrontations.

Ghost in the Shell is certainly groundbreaking by being the first anime to maturely deal with the philosophical questions of "what makes a human a human?", "what makes a human or a machine conscious?" and "what is reality?" Most adult animes of this genre followed suit with these and other postmodern inquiries that are sometimes best left between man and the machine.

Its television offspring, *Stand Alone Complex*, introduced various strains of artificial intelligence to increase both the violence and philosophical ruminations (and further erase the lines between the real and the virtual worlds).

There are many more anime series and films with Gnostic biologies, although many of them incorporate other esoteric organs. Here are some of the lower aeons:

Full Metal Alchemist: This popular and approachable series is much less Gnostic and more medieval Hermetic. *Full Metal Alchemist* takes place in an alternate universe modeled after the genesis of Europe's Industrial Revolution. Alchemy is superior to any science, though, more akin to high fantasy sorcery than the predecessor of chemistry. Two brothers, Edward and Alphonse, attempt to resurrect their deceased mother using alchemy. Their ritual goes terribly wrong, and Edward only saves his brother by binding his soul to a suit of armor (the machine and its issues are dealt with even in this relatively pastoral setting). The siblings become State alchemists in order to find the famed philosopher's stone that might grant Alphonse a human body again. The Gnostic image of a snake on a cross is prevalent throughout *Full Metal Alchemist*.

The Big O: The series is set in Paradigm City, the last surviving metropolis of a ravaged world. The remaining survivors have not only lost their memories of the cataclysm, they are gripped by foggy recollection, hallucinations and vivid nightmares. They linger in almost madness in a police-state environment. Although futuristic, there is a heavy element of film noir in *The Big O*. The main protagonist is a man known as the Negotiator, the one person who inexplicably regains his memories of the previous world before "the Event" decimated human civilization. His memories and talents are revealed to the audience as the series progresses, juxtaposed

while he culls other citizens' memories. It becomes apparent to the Negotiator that Paradigm City is but a massive fabrication when he begins to pierce the reality behind the reality of humanity's situation. The series ends with the revelation that the *entire* world is a simulated reality created by sophisticated and sentient technology. A climactic battle ensues between various factions of Paradigm City desirous of control of the godly technology. But it all ends with the world being methodically deleted and reset. The Negotiator is actually a sort of memetic clone of a previous Negotiator whose primary function was to parley with the godly technology for survival. This in effect makes him an eternally reoccurring Gnostic saviour similar to Neo in *The Matrix*.

Last Exile: The Gnostic ingredients are not immediately tasted. The setting of this anime is a moderately terraformed world that has all the hallmarks of a steampunk fantasy. The planet is stewarded by an elitist and fascist organization called the Guild. This shadowy group manipulates an ongoing conflict between two warring nations. Some of the patent Gnostic dressings are a saviour airship captain crucified on a cross, an exiled empress named Sophia who holds the keys to peace and truth, and a concluding rebellion against the Guild by civilization once it realizes its Svengali games. *Last Exile* also revolves around crucial "sacred mysteries" that bring a sort of Gnosis to the main characters. Koine Greek is curiously the written language of the inhabitants. Lastly, there is the theme of remembering a past, idealistic existence (Earth) that holds answers to present situations that will hopefully bring about human liberation and individuality.

The Melancholy of Haruhi Suzumiya: God forgets he's God and falls into the kenoma, taking the form of a petulant schoolgirl. She possesses the traits of both Sophia and the demiurge. The renowned *Twilight Zone* episode, "It's a Good Life," about an omnipotent child, comes immediately to mind. Yet this anime series is more esoteric and introspective.

Sol Bianca: A group of voluptuous space pirates search for the greatest treasure in the universe, a legendary object known as the *G'Nohsis* (*Gnosis*). After a storm of adventures, the crew of the *Sol Bianca* acquires the *G'Nohsis*. They discover it is nothing more than an ancient storage disk housing information on the whereabouts of a fabled primeval planet once inhabited by mankind. Of course, the world is Earth, long forgotten and perhaps housing secrets to enlightenment (or just real treasure to some of the space pirates).

Eden: It's an Endless World!: This Gnostic gospel is actually a manga (Japanese comic book), but it's worth mentioning. The series, presently ongoing, transpires in the future where a major pandemic has eradicated much of the world's population. Like *Ghost in the Shell* and *Time of Eve*, it has a cyberpunk flavor although more industrial in texture. The plot deals with a champion named Elijah and his conflicts with the Propater Federation and several crime syndicates.

At this point, the Manga has not revealed any underlying Gnostic motifs; but it certainly employs Gnostic terminology, which could mean deeper themes when the authors decide to introduce the inevitable philosophical reflections.

One of the main characters is Sophia, a computer hacker with a full cybernetic body. Similar to the divine Sophia in the more radical strains of Gnosticism, she is brutally melancholic, promiscuous because of a sense of homelessness, and prone to hysterical desperation. Her failed attack on her infant son with a knife perhaps echoes Sophia's attempt to dethrone her own offspring, the demiurge himself, in certain Gnostic dramas.

The story includes Aeons, nearly invincible robotic soldiers, as well as a character named *Ennoia* (one of the names of the divine feminine in Gnosticism). The footnotes of the comic admit that they are both named after "Gnostic gods."

Elijah's protector robot is named Cherubim, an inference to the Gnostic concept of an angelic guardian or higher self. The saviour myth takes the form of Maya, a godlike artificial intelligence.

Even if the modern Gnostic movement in the West evanesces as it historically always does, it appears the fertile soil of anime will continue to sprout Gnostic gospels (and other occult and mystic scripture). The popularity of Japanese animation is growing. Their creators have taken from the tree of Western knowledge of good and evil, and enjoyed its marketing fruits. The beginning of the article explained why anime is perfect to crystallize Gnosticism in a modern context that appeals to the masses. The key is catching the pearls in the muck because of the amount of chameleon material the anime factory produces each year.

But it's certainly a worthy and worthwhile genre to carry the torch of Gnosis, even as Western popular culture plays it safe with recycled medieval legendary and pseudo-Enlightenment themes; or it squints to find its own gems of understanding human nature ironically in the East, leaving behind such lackluster stones as *Avatar, the Last Airbender*, Dan Brown or Philip Pullman, or a few detonations of Gnostic reconnaissance in some Doctor Who episodes or Alan Moore graphic novels.

The Japanese may have not conquered the world, as it was feared in the Eighties. But they certainly have romanced the bleak heart of Gnosticism in such a way it would probably make Philip K. Dick, William Blake, Valentinus and Simon Magus wish they could pilot their own Evangelion units in order to battle monstrous angels, instead of just blaspheming with prosaic ink and paper.

Andrew Phillip Smith

Obnoxious Gnostics:
the Apocalypse of Peter

People don't always agree with each other, and people who form groups tend to not agree with people belonging to other groups. Whether this is due to human nature or a lack of experience of successful cooperation may be debated endlessly. Of course, this happens with religious or spiritual groups too. The face of modern Christianity, Roman Catholic, Eastern Orthodox, Oriental Orthodox and Protestant is a direct result of schism and heresy in a mega-church that had itself crowded out its early competitors. Most modern Gnostics would admire both Neoplatonists and ancient Gnostics, but Plotinus famously denigrated Gnostic teachings in "Against Gnostics," in *Enneads* II.9.

What of the Gnostics themselves? While the Valentinians seem to have been bridge-builders, taking part in the emerging catholic Christian movement while maintaining their own Gnostic cosmologies and esoteric interpretation of the gospels and Paul, the Sethians were the hard men of ancient Gnosticism, matching the invective of Irenaeus, Tertullian et al with their own ferocity. The *Gospel of Judas* is a good example of this, revealing the twelve apostles as a bunch of demiurge worshippers, no better than Judas. The Eucharist itself is ridiculed by the Jesus of this gospel. But when does polemicism collapse under its own weight? When does the strength to stand one's own ground and refuse to be bullied turn into an obsession with infighting, sniping and backstabbing? The answer: in the *Apocalypse of Peter*.

The *Apocalypse of Peter* is in Codex VII of the Nag Hammadi library, following on from the *Second Discourse of the Great Seth*, with which it shares some features, including the laughing Jesus and a hostile attitude to other sects. It refers to a series of characters from the Hebrew bible, including Adam, Abraham, Solomon and Moses as jokes or laughingstocks. The *Apocalypse* is usually dated to the third century, possibly composed in Alexandria.

The *Apocalypse* claims Peter as its apostle. Though Peter is often seen as the representative of proto-orthodox Christianity, here he defends the Sethian view. This Peter is rather uncertain of himself, but his Jesus is just as intolerant as the stereotypical rock of the mainstream church.

A glance at the *Apocalypse of Peter* shows a strong concern with good and evil, a determined dualism.[1] But let's look closer. Early on it becomes apparent that good and evil do not refer to any fundamental principles or moral values but to good and evil teaching. A distinction is made between teachings of unrighteousness and lawlessness and the righteous teachings supported by the author. Throughout the *Apocalypse*, good refers to the true teachings of the particular (Sethian) sect to which the author belongs, and evil or error to other Christian or Gnostic texts. This us-and-them attitude is illustrated by the narrative from the outset. Jesus and Peter, having been in the Temple in an exalted state, are pursued by priests and people with stones who are shouting. Jesus explains that they are blind and dead to knowledge/gnosis. This immediately sets the tone of persecution and isolation from the rest of Christianity, and indeed from the rest of humanity.

Jesus then goes on to explain that many people will initially accept his words but will turn away because of "the father of their error".[2] These people are obviously other Christians, and at least five, and quite possibly more, groups are allusively described in the cryptic words of Jesus. The attempts to identify these (the hard work has been done by many previous scholars) are very interesting.

First, Jesus rails against "the kingdom of those who praise a Christ of a future restored world." The word "restored" here is the Greek *apokatastasis*, the "restoration." There are a few candidates for sects or individuals that taught this concept. Clement of Alexandria and Origen developed a doctrine of apokatastasis in which everything will finally come to rest in harmony and peace with God. But Clement and Origen are perhaps a little too late for the *Apocalypse of Peter*. According to Hippolytus, the proto-Gnostic Basilides also taught a form of apokatastasis in which the world would be restored to its original state when Jesus returned. The second coming would cast a permanent ignorance on the archons and souls who cannot ascend to the heavenly realm. Also, the *Gospel of Philip* uses the term, "Of what a nature is the resurrection! And the image must rise again through the image. The bridegroom and the image must enter through the image into the truth, which is the apokatastasis." This appears to refer to a process which an individual person undergoes rather than a grand cosmic reconstitution. Whatever teaching is intended here, it is clearly one that might appeal to modern Gnostics, but not the author of this text. Thus the *Apocalypse of Peter* is attacking groups with which we might be in sympathy.

The second group or doctrines mentioned are those who "hold on to the name of a dead man". These are clearly orthodox Christians, and there is some poetic power in this phrase. The veneration of Jesus, a crucified man, may arguably lead away from his actual teachings. This denigration of the literal crucifixion and physical resurrection is common in Sethian writings and is emphasised at the end of the

Apocalypse. These people are said to "fall into the hands of an evil deceiver with complicated doctrines." It has been suggested that this refers to Paul, for whom the crucified Christ was of central importance. Paul was well-loved of the Valentinians, but not the Sethians.

A third group "give themselves a name... the name of a man and a naked woman of many forms and many sufferings." It is likely that this refers to Simon Magus, who referred to himself as the great power of God (the name) and his consort Helen, who was reincarnated in several forms, including that of Helen of Troy and the prostitute Helena whom Simon met in the city of Tyre. According to the heresiologists (though all reference to him is absent from the Nag Hammadi library) Simon Magus was seen as the arch-Gnostic and founder of the Simonians, a specific Gnostic sect. Thus we have Gnostic infighting here.

The fourth condemnation (though there are other, less specific polemics in the text which may also refer to competing groups) names Hermas as a dead man and the firstborn of unrighteousness. If this is not a garbling of Hermes, suggesting the *Hermetica*, then it probably refers to the *Shepherd of Hermas*, a second century collection of visions, parables and allegories that was well-respected by orthodox Christians of the second century and was an unsuccessful candidate for inclusion in the canon.

The final group once again appear to be orthodox Christians, particularly those with a strict hierarchy and those who consider martyrdom praiseworthy, "whose work is an imitation of the marriage of incorruptibility." These bishops and deacons are dry canals.

The final section describes the crucifixion and its true significance. The body whose feet and hands are hammered into the cross is not the living Jesus who smiles and laughs above the cross. Peter shows a moment of weakness when he suggests to Jesus that they should leave, but Jesus once again stresses that these people are blind. There is the suggestion of a mysterious third Jesus, intertwined with the holy spirit, surrounded by bright light and angels. We might pause here to consider the poetry and beauty of this image: the crucified body surrounded by a crowd of people, a living, laughing Jesus above the cross, surmounted by light, angels and the ultimate aspect of Jesus. But the magic of this scene is spoiled suddenly when it is revealed that Jesus is laughing not in joy or mirth but at those who are blind and is taking pleasure in seeing that those who did harm to him are divided among themselves. The text ends with a particularly harsh application of the synoptic saying that those who do not have will have even that taken away from them.

There is little positive Sethian doctrine here, no mother Barbelo or deeply pondered metaphysical myth. All is polemic and criticism. Even the *Gospel of Judas*, with its mocking Jesus and satire of the apostles, contains an elaborate cosmological explanation.

Thus the *Apocalypse of Peter* is historically fascinating, but spiritually it is entangled in the politics of competition between Christian sects. To be fair, the Sethians were also on the receiving end of Christian infighting—witness the extensive heresiological writings. Late Sethian texts such as Zostrianos and Marsenes show them moving closer to Platonism, having been pushed out of the general Christian world. But how much time and energy was wasted, and ill-will invested, in this fight. The Sethians, and particularly the author and community of the *Apocalypse of Peter*, would have done well to avoid playing this futile game. After all, whatever the merits of such a contest, they were the losers.

NOTES

1 An extract from the *Apocalypse of Peter*, "But many others, who oppose the truth and are the messengers of error, will set up their error and their law against these pure thoughts of mine, as looking out from one (perspective) thinking that good and evil are from one source" was even quoted recently as a condemnation of nondualism. See http://www.palmtreegarden. org/2010/05/the-urban-myth-of-non-duality

In a discussion on the Spiral Inward forum, "Soulgazer", the author of the piece (and a very decent man) countered with a spirited argument that what is being opposed is the monotheistic Jewish view that good and evil are both sent by God. An example would be "I form the light, and create darkness: I make peace, and create evil: I the LORD do all these things." (Isaiah 45:7, KJV). He has almost convinced me that this is the case, but not quite. Whatever the reference really means, it's certainly a viewpoint that is being condemned.

2 Quotations are from *The Nag Hammadi Library in English*, ed. James Robinson (Harper & Row, 1988.)

Miguel Conner

Interview with Daniel Matt

MC: : To begin more or less broadly, Daniel, as far as your research and tradition has told you, when did the Kabbalah begin?

DM: It's really very hard to pin down. I would say that there are certainly Biblical roots to the Kabbalah and roots in the early Rabbinic Judaism. But I would say it emerges as a movement within Judaism in the 12th century, 12th century Europe, in Southern Europe, in Provence, Southern France, and then it goes over the Pyrenees, you could say, into Spain, and it's really in 13th century Spain that the movement crystallises. And that's where the greatest text of the Kabbalah, the *Zohar*, was probably composed.

MC: But isn't the *Sefer Yetsirah* long before any of this,

DM: *Sefer Yetsirah* could be called proto-kabbalistic. Many of the images of the Kabbalah appear in *Sefer Yetsirah*. The most significant is the sephiroth, the 10 sephiroth. Now in Kabbalah, sephiroth means the 10 aspects of God's personality. God's love and God's judgement, masculine and feminine powers, but in *Sefer Yetsirah*, it doesn't really have meaning yet. In *Sefer Yetsirah* the 10 sephiroth are just the numbers one to 10, the numbers through which God creates the universe. Because, according to that text, God created the world through letters and numbers, through language and arithmetic, you could say. So that *Sefer Yetsirah* is a very important part of Kabbalah, and it does predate what I'm describing, but there's no wide agreement on when *Sefer Yetsirah* was composed. Probably around the second

or third century. I say that because of the style of Hebrew. The Hebrew of *Sefer Yetsirah* seems similar to early Rabbinic Hebrew of that period, second and third century. But then there is a long underground development of the Jewish mystical tradition between *Sefer Yetsirah* and this next creative period of the 12th and 13th centuries. I would call *Sefer Yetsirah* a pre-kabbalistic text and one of the roots of Kabbalah. So it's hard to pin down exactly what you would call Kabbalah. Of course, kabbalists would say that it goes back to the time of the Rabbis or earlier, or to the patriarchs, or to Moses, even to Adam and Eve. But looking at it historically, the major texts of the Kabbalah, particularly the *Zohar*, are a product of the medieval era.

MC: Yes, it seems maybe that gap was caused by a… Back then in Provence there was a little renaissance with the kabbalists, the sufis and the Cathars and all that, and before that there might have been problems with medieval Christianity.

DM: Yes, partly that, partly fear of criticism from outside and from within, and the mystics' own hesitancy to talk about their direct experiences. So, for whatever reason, I think you are right. The mystical tradition was kept secret for many centuries, and kept secret, but at the same time developing as it was passed from master to disciple, and then it really flowers in medieval Europe and, you are right, Provence is really a very fertile ground. You have Christian mysticism and the influence of Islam coming from Spain, the Middle East, and a lot is going on in Provence. In the Jewish community you have philosophy and rabbinics and mysticism all developing, and then it's really in Spain that

Kabbalah becomes a really creative force. But even at that time, it is still relatively small circles of kabbalists teaching and copying this material, and it really takes several hundred years before it reaches a broader segment of the Jewish population and begins to influence European mysticism, and that's later in the 15th and 16th centuries.

MC: Yes, and I guess the culmination of it would have been the Shabbati Zevi movement.

DM: Yes, that messianic movement where Shabbati came to see himself as the messiah, that's 17th century, and at that point Kabbalah becomes fascinating to very wide circles. But when that figure Shabbati Zevi converted to Islam, he was rejected by most Jews and at that point didn't really arouse a lot of opposition to Kabbalah. The next stage is really Hasidism. Hasidism in the 18th century, you might call that a popularisation of the Kabbalah, and at that point it spread to very wide circles in the Jewish world. That really is an arc, you know, you can trace that arc from the early teachings in very small rabbinic circles and *Sefer Yetsirah*, then more of the creative development in Spain and the 13th century, and Shabbati and Hasidism, and then there was opposition when Judaism… You might say that in the age of the rational enlightenment, in the 18th and 19th century, there was reaction against Kabbalah and reaction against many mystical teachings. Many Jews were embarrassed by it and they wanted to just jettison the whole mystical and supernatural element. They wanted to redefine Judaism in purely rational terms. So it was really in the 20th century that Kabbalah was rediscovered, thanks in great part to the work of Gerschem Scholem,

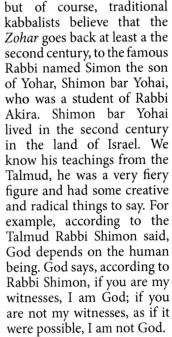

the great scholar of Jewish mysticism who lived in Jerusalem. Then you have this more recent phenomenon of mass media and Hollywood and the phenomenon of the last 10 years or so, where there is another explosion of interest. So it's interesting how that's moved throughout the middle ages and into modern times, and at this point or even discussing it on web broadcasts.

MC: Yes, we are. Could you tell us the why, when and where the *Zohar* was written?

DM: This is interesting. We mentioned Spain, but of course, traditional kabbalists believe that the *Zohar* goes back at least a the second century, to the famous Rabbi named Simon the son of Yohar, Shimon bar Yohai, who was a student of Rabbi Akira. Shimon bar Yohai lived in the second century in the land of Israel. We know his teachings from the Talmud, he was a very fiery figure and had some creative and radical things to say. For example, according to the Talmud Rabbi Shimon said, God depends on the human being. God says, according to Rabbi Shimon, if you are my witnesses, I am God; if you are not my witnesses, as if it were possible, I am not God.

MC: Wow, so this isn't Lurianic Kabbalah, this is right in the *Zohar*.

DM: No, this is right in the Talmud. This is the real Rabbi Shimon that actually lived in the second century.

MC: The Talmud says that, that's amazing!

DM: It's actually in the Talmud. The roots of Kabbalah are there in the Talmud. But they are buried in dozens or hundreds of pages of legal material, and you really have to ferret them out. But the Talmud has some very radical things to say about the nature of God. And what I'm saying is that the real historical Rabbi Shimon had some very radical things to say about divinity. But as to whether he wrote the *Zohar* or not, that's another question. Kabbalists believe that he wrote the *Zohar*, or that it was written in his circle, in the second century. But most scholars today, most academic scholars, would say that the *Zohar* was really written 1100 years later in 13th centuries Spain. And the person who composed it or edited it—I would say the composer of the *Zohar*—was a kabbalist named Moses de Leon. Moses de Leon was living in Spain, he was born in northwestern Spain in the city of Leon. He may have composed it along with the other people, he may have inherited certain writings, but I think he's the major composer of the *Zohar*. So you have a book being written in the 13th century, but attributed to this Rabbi Shimon who lived over a millennium earlier. And the question is, why did Moses de Leon attribute it to this ancient figure, Rabbi Shimon? That's a complicated question. He may have believed that he was really in touch with Rabbi Shimon, that he was somehow channelling the teachings of this ancient master. Or there may be a much more down to earth explanation, that he wanted the book to be accepted, maybe he wanted the book to sell, and he's attributing it to this ancient figure. And actually, I think that both of those may be at play. It sounds like an impossible combination of motives, but I think that he may have been motivated spiritually and materially, financially, and felt that he was in touch with this ancient figure, but then he composed it and embellished it and actually tried to circulate it as ancient wisdom. Unfortunately for the history of the Kabbalah, that fantastic claim was accepted and people came to see the *Zohar* as an ancient text going back to Rabbinic times. It was seen as one of the holiest books within Judaism, perhaps only second to the Bible and the Talmud.

MC: Yes, and isn't the *Zohar* written in a sort of stilted Aramaic with Spanish expressions and so forth. Gerschem Scholem says that there's about three strata of writers he can find in there?

DM: There really are different stages of composition. It's almost a library. There are really 18 or 20 stages of composition. I would say that Moses de Leon wrote much of it, but certainly not all of it. Some things are written after him by someone trying to imitate his style, and, you're right, the Aramaic is very strange because Moses de Leon knew Aramaic not as a spoken language—probably at that point no one in the world was speaking Aramaic. He knew Aramaic from having studied the Talmud in Aramaic and Biblical translations in Aramaic, but he's trying to write this book in Aramaic without really being fluent in that language, in terms of knowing how to write it or speak it. He only knew how to read it. So his Aramaic is really unique. It is very bizarre, there are a lot of invented words and neologisms. And in translating the *Zohar* that's a real challenge. You come across a word that's really invented by him. Sometimes Moses de Leon will take a rare term in the Talmud and switch around a couple of letters, and you really have to ponder it for quite a long time to be able to estimate what is meant.

MC: So, the purpose of the *Zohar*, I'm seeing, is that it seems to be a kabbalistic midrash on the Hebrew Bible, or was it more to clarify and bring out the hidden message in the Talmud. Which one is it?

DM: It's both and other things as well, I would say. It certainly presents itself as a commentary on the Torah. It's not written, chapter one "God", chapter two "Torah", chapter three "Finding God in the world"... It's not written in any systematic way except as a running commentary on the first five books of the Bible. So the *Zohar* begins commenting on Genesis and then moves through Exodus, Leviticus, Deuteronomy and commenting on every verse, but on every significant story and many minor stories, and it tries to find a mystical, spiritual meaning in even the smallest details of the Biblical text. It's a very radical approach to the Torah. For example, the *Zohar* says the very opening words of the Bible, "In the beginning God created," we shouldn't read it that way. Rather, it's "In the beginning it created God." God actually turns into the object of the sentence, rather than as the subject. Now, what does that mean? It sounds ridiculous or heretical, "it created God." What the *Zohar* is really saying is that there is an infinite God. There is a God beyond God. This is very similar to teachings in Gnosticism. There is a God beyond what we know of this God, and that ultimate God is called infinity, or in Hebrew Ain Soph, literally "there is no end." This infinite divinity emanated or generated what we think of as God. So in that sense, it, the infinite, created God.

MC: And they didn't change the words, they just found different definitions or different alternatives for the words. So there was no corruption of the Torah?

DM: Right. It's accepting the Torah as it's written, but reinterpreting it. That's a technique that is used throughout all religions. In order to keep the tradition alive, it has to be interpreted and reinterpreted and applied. The technique of the Rabbis is called midrash, which is imaginative interpretation of the Bible. And the *Zohar* is just taken that a little further, or a lot further.

MC: Yeah, because really what attracts most Gnostics to the Torah, because if you read it literally… You mention one Rabbi, and it's my favourite quote, "if you translate it literally, you're a liar, if you add to it, you're blasphemous." And that makes you really think. And I realized that the Torah, as you say, has numerous meanings, and the Torah is almost an organic entity in itself. It's up there with the creator God, it's his tool, but he's bound to it in a certain way, isn't he?

DM: Yes. We have Rabbinic teachings that God actually got locked into the Torah and created the world. The Torah is God's plan or God's blueprint for the universe. He's pictured as an architect, as an architect would consult his plans, so God consults the Torah. But in the Kabbalah this is taken further and the Torah actually becomes a divine being, it is seen as if the Torah essentially one long name of God. If you reading the Torah, you're not just reading God's commands and stories, you're actually reading into the divine nature. You're pronouncing God's name as you chant the Torah.

MC: How do the kabbalists and the *Zohar* interpret the Garden of Eden?

DM: There is a fascinating description of that. Of course, Genesis describes how God expels Adam out of the garden, Adam and Eve. So who expels whom out of the garden? It really makes you wonder, and the *Zohar* says Adam through God out of the garden. In a sense, we're still in the garden but we don't realise it because we have lost touch with the divine. That's one of my favourite teachings and the whole *Zohar*. In the *Zohar* it's just written as a couple of lines and you could easily pass over, written in a kind of code. But the *Zohar* derives that from a verse in Genesis which says, "He expelled them," and the *Zohar* reinterprets it in a creative way to say, "Adam expelled God."

MC: But he didn't really expel God, he expelled the Shekhinah of God, right?

DM: The Shekhinah of God, which is a very important concept in the Kabbalah, refers to the feminine half of God, the divine presence. So she is God, but a specific quality or aspect of God, God's presence in the world, God's imminence, God's intimacy with humanity, all that is meant by the notion of Shekhinah. Literally, the word means dwelling or presence.

MC: So you would say that the culmination of creation, which I gather from your books and other books, would be somehow to get Tiphareth and the Shekhinah to be married again, or for mankind and the Shekhinah to be together, or would it be for God to get Shekhinah back?

DM: Well, it's hard to separate those options. The way the *Zohar* often describes it is the goal of life, the goal of religion is to unite the masculine and feminine within God, which is to bring together this couple, Tiphareth, the divine masculine, and Shekhinah, the divine feminine. Their union is the goal of existence. That happens only through human action. So, this is another way in which God needs the human being. The divine marriage cannot take place without our active contribution. What we have to do is act ethically and spiritually in the world. Through righteous action we stimulate the union of the divine couple. You might say that every good deed is an aphrodisiac for that divine union. So in that sense the goal is to unite God with God, God and the goddess, but in other parts of the *Zohar* it seems that the goal is to unite oneself with Shekhinah, or with this whole world of the 10 sephiroth, the aspects of God. The *Zohar* goes back and forth between aiming at the divine union and trying to participate in that union.

MC: And the sephiroth are not really explicit in the *Zohar*. It's pretty implicit, it doesn't come out in the form of the diagram, does it?

DM: Right, we don't find diagrams in *Zohar* itself. On almost every page there are references to the sephiroth, but you're right, they're often cryptic. The *Zohar*, for example, will often not use the name Shekhinah or Tiphareth, it will say the King, or the Queen, or the river of emanation.

MC: Or the bed, that's another one.

DM: The bed, the ocean, the garden, and the *Zohar* much prefers that kind of poetic imagery than a systematic presentation of the sephiroth. Other books of the Kabbalah do it more systematically, but I think the secret of the *Zohar*'s success is that it is more allusive and poetic, and it really forces the reader to join in the search.

MC: Yeah, I understand how it could make the reader very interested, because there's a lot of romance and a lot of talk about Kings and Maidens, Maidens with veils, that you have to take her veil off and find the secrets. It's a journey for the reader as well.

DM: Definitely. The romantic search and the erotic element is certainly key to the *Zohar*, the eros within God and the celebration of human sexuality too, if it's pursued in holiness, that's is seen as part of the secret of existence. You have the secret interpretation of the Torah, and also the secret level of existence, and the two go hand in hand.

MC: Can we find the doctrine of reincarnation,

the *gilgul*, in the *Zohar* or was this conceived beforehand?

DM: We certainly have no references to reincarnation in Rabbinic Judaism. We have to distinguish between reincarnation and resurrection. Resurrection of the dead means that when the messiah comes then the world will be renewed, but all those who have died will be bodily resurrected. That you do find in Rabbinic Judaism, although it's very hard to find it in the Bible itself, except in very very late parts of the Bible such as the book of Daniel. In the Torah you would not have any explicit teaching even about the resurrection of the dead. But resurrection is different from reincarnation. As I've said, resurrection of the dead, that the dead will someday be revived, that you find in Rabbinic Judaism. What's new in Kabbalah is, of course they accept resurrection, but introduce the notion of reincarnation, that when a person dies, even in present history, he or she may be resurrected, the soul will roll into a new body. The word *gilgul* means rolling. The soul will roll into a new body. Now, this is introduced a little bit before the *Zohar* in Kabbalah, in a book called the *Bahir*. The *Bahir* was written in Provence, or I should say was edited in Provence, towards the end of the 12th century, and that's probably the first kabbalistic text that mentions the theory of reincarnation. It's talked about in the *Zohar*, but very secretly, very cryptically. You really have to decipher the references to reincarnation in the *Zohar*. Later in the Kabbalah it's talked about much more openly and it becomes a universal principle. But I would say that in the *Zohar* itself, it's not that everyone undergoes *gilgul*. *Gilgul* is seen as something that happens only if you fail to observe certain very important *mitzvot*, certain very important tasks, most of all if you haven't brought new life into the world. If you haven't married and had children, then you will be reincarnated. It's not clear whether it's punishment or more an opportunity, so you have a chance to fulfill this essential commandment. That's really how it's presented in the *Zohar*. Later by the time we get to Isaac Luria, the famous kabbalistic who lived in Safed in the Galilee, in the 16th century, by then already *gilgul* becomes a universal principle, and everyone, or nearly everyone undergoes *gilgul*. But in the *Zohar* it's more selective and more secret.

MC: How is the concept of evil explained in the *Zohar* or the Kabbalah for that matter? How is evil explained besides being the punishment of God?

DM: Yeah, this is interesting. For the *Zohar*, evil is really the shadow side of God. In other words, God as we know him is good and loving and caring, but there's a dark side. The *Zohar* refers to this as *sitra achra*, the other side. In some ways it's opposed to what we think of as God, but in another sense it emerges from God. It's not clear how. According to one theory of the *Zohar*, when the divine powers are balanced, goodness goes into the world. For there is a balance between love and strict judgment. But when things are out of balance because of human evil, human evil will bring about an imbalance in the cosmic forces, and then harsh judgment overwhelms God's compassion or love or mercy, and evil results from that imbalance. So you have different theories, there's not one unified theory about it. What's most striking is that evil is seen as somehow emerging from the divine and ultimately as serving a purpose either of testing or punishment or temptation, and part of the divine economy and that sense.

MC: Another question, I know we got past the Ain Soph, but what would be the ultimate concept of godhead is that the Ayin, nothingness, and is that found in the Torah?

DM: Ain Soph, the infinite, you could say is really the ultimate level of divinity. It's very hard to distinguish between Ain Soph and what the Kabbalah calls Ayin, which is literally nothingness. Technically Ayin is the first sephirah, and Ain Soph is beyond all those sephiroth. But that first sephirah is really inseparable from Ain Soph itself. You might say that infinity manifests as a Ayin, this paradoxical nothingness. Now in Kabbalah as in Sufism and Buddhism, nothingness is not a negative term, it's just really means no thing ness. That which

is beyond material existence. So nothingness is seen as undifferentiated divine reality. It's not yet any one thing. It hasn't yet turned into the world. It's pure potential. In that sense it's no-thing-ness. So infinity and nothingness are seen as almost identical. Both of those, you could say, and the top of the ladder have to find existence. From them all the specific qualities of God emerge.

MC: So you would say that the reason we have existence at all is simply God manifesting himself. Is that why God created the world, as the kabbalists look at it?

DM: Yes, there are discussions occasionally about why did this all come about? Why, as a modern philosopher would put it, is there something rather than nothing? Nothing with a small "n", nothing as a blank. One answer is that God was lonely. God wanted someone with whom he or she or it could interact. So God created that which seems to be separate from God, but this is all part of the divine dance of eventual reunion. God yearns for the divine spark within our soul to reacquaint itself with the divine source, and that will bring about fulfilment of union and mystical oneness.

MC: Is the divine feminine in Judaism something that has evolved since the Kabbalah? Or has it always been present but only surfaced periodically and then gone back down?

DM: This is profound, because certainly if you look at the Bible it's very hard to say anything about the traditional picture of God. God seems purely masculine. It's very rare to find any feminine images. There are a few here or there, in Jeremiah or in some of the later poetic books, but in general God is the King to judge the warrior. The radical innovation in Kabbalah is that God is half male and half female. So one wonders where did this come from? Did this just emerge out of nothing? And it seems that there are roots of the divine feminine in earlier traditions. Certainly if you look at ancient Canaan itself, there were definitely goddesses, there was a widespread worship of the goddess under different names Ashirah, Maat, Astarte.

So there were goddesses worshipped in the ancient world and the Mediterranean east, and of course the prophets are always railing against this worship, seeing it as a betrayal of God to go after the goddess. But we know now from archaeological finds that there were Israelites who tried to combine the worship of of the israelite God, Yod He Vav He; they tried to combine that with the feminine. So, for example, they've dug up pieces of pottery and which you will see written this is to Yod He Vav He, to the israelite God, and his Ashirah, and his goddess. And this isn't something you find in the Bible. It's criticised, this kind of worship, of syncretism, but we know that there were Israelites who were attracted to it, and apparently it was suppressed, it was defeated, it mostly disappeared, but it must have continued to exist underground as well, as you say. It surfaces and resurfaces and what you find in Kabbalah is really a reemergence of this ancient goddess material. One scholar, Gerschem Scholem, has called this the revenge of myth. This mythic image of the feminine had been eliminated almost entirely, but it came back with a vengeance in Kabbalah. Another way to say this is that the Kabbalah now turns the goddess into something kosher. The goddess really becomes kosher in Kabbalah, and you have a feminine and masculine divinity.

MC: Aren't there are some hints in the Song of Songs and other places when they're talking about wisdom, and wisdom was there from the beginning. In Gnosticism that's considered obviously to be Sophia. How does Judaism, or the Kabbalah see it?

DM: Kabbalah would accept that. In the book of Proverbs and other wisdom literature you do have a feminine entity it seems, that apparently is God's helper and assistant. You don't find in the Bible a description of God being married to wisdom. God is creating the world through wisdom, so wisdom is a divine quality, a divine helper, a divine helpmate, so there is some feminine imagery there. But in Kabbalah it's made much more explicit, and they take all those verses, many of those verses, and apply them to the Shekhinah. So there are hints of raw material that are developed further by the Kabbalah.

MC: Yes, because another character that I've always found very interesting is the figure of the judge Deborah. For some reason I've always seen her more as a goddess than as a human being. Maybe a lot of the judges, I don't know.

DM: Well, they're historical figures, but they also become turned into divine or heavenly versions in the Kabbalah, many of them.

MC: Yeah, like in psalms, "ye are gods of the most high." Backing up just a little bit, you mentioned, and other people mention, that's there is that word in Genesis called *et*. What exactly does it mean and how to the kabbalists define it?

DM: It's a Hebrew word pronounced *ett*, it consists of two Hebrew letters, Aleph and Tav. And that is interesting because of course Aleph is the first letter of the Hebrew alphabet and Tav is the last letter. So it's a little word that contains the first letter and the last letter. As to what it means, it's very hard to pin down. In many uses, in many senses, it has no independent meaning. It's just a marker, it has to appear in a sentence in between the verb and the direct object.

MC: This was from the earliest scriptures, from the Masoretic text and so forth? It just appears there?

DM: It appears there, for syntax. For example, in Hebrew you can't say, I threw the stone. You have to say I threw *et* the stone. It precedes the direct object, it has no independent meaning. But in the *Zohar* it becomes a symbol of Shekhinah. Why? Because she is the last of the 10 sephiroth and she includes all of the others. She includes everything from the first to the last. In some ways it is similar to what Jesus says according to the new testament, "I am the alpha and the omega, I am the first and the last." Shekhinah includes in herself the entire flow of divine being. And the *Zohar* uses that very often when it wants to interpret or reinterpret a verse. But I should say that you also find that in Rabbinic Judaism. There are interpretations of the word already in Rabbinic Judaism.

MC: And, lastly, do you agree with Rabbi Ezekiel, who is in your introduction, the man you met, that in recognizing the divine feminine in all the faces is the only way to have a feeling mankind?

DM: I should say that the book you're referring to, *Zohar Annotated and Explained*, I wrote that book, meaning I translated passages from the *Zohar* and interpreted them. There's a preface written by Andrew Harvey, and it's there that you find the story about Rabbi Ezekiel, but he talks about the need to rediscover the divine feminine. I would say that it's very important to move beyond the notion of God just as a masculine power or male power or authority figure, and to celebrate the divine feminine, the intimacy of God and the presence of God in nature and the world. I think that's a very important balance.

MC: You won't find anybody who agrees with that more than I do. Could you just tell the listeners what you are working on right now?

DM: I could tell you a couple of things that other than that are available first of all. The book I can talk about most immediately is the *Zohar Annotated and Explained*. It's published by Skylights Paths, or Jewish Lights, that's a small paperback. There are a couple of other paperbacks, one is called *The Essential Kabbalah*, which is published by HarperCollins of San Francisco. And that's a selection of texts and Kabbalah translated with some written notes. There's some other material too, there's *Sefer Yetsirah*, the *Bahir*, Isaac Luria, a little bit of Hasidism. But mostly traditional kabbalistic texts organized by subject, the sephiroth, divine nothingness, Torah, how to find God in the material world, meditation, sections such as those. Then another book that I've done is called *God and the Big Bang*, which is on parallels between Kabbalah and contemporary cosmology. That was published by Jewish Lights. And my current project, which will take me many years, is a full annotated translation of the *Zohar*. The book we talked about, *Zohar Annotated and Explained*, that's a tiny percentage of the work, but I think it's a good place to start. What I'm working on now is called the *Zohar Pritzker Edition*. The Pritzkers are a family in Chicago who are enabling me to do this work. The full edition is published by Stanford University press. So far three volumes have appeared, and these three volumes cover the entire book of Genesis. I'm now working on the book of Exodus, and I imagine the entire thing will run to something like 11 volumes.

MC: Once again, thank you very much for appearing on Coffee, Cigarettes and Gnosis, Daniel, and thanks for sharing your wisdom with us.

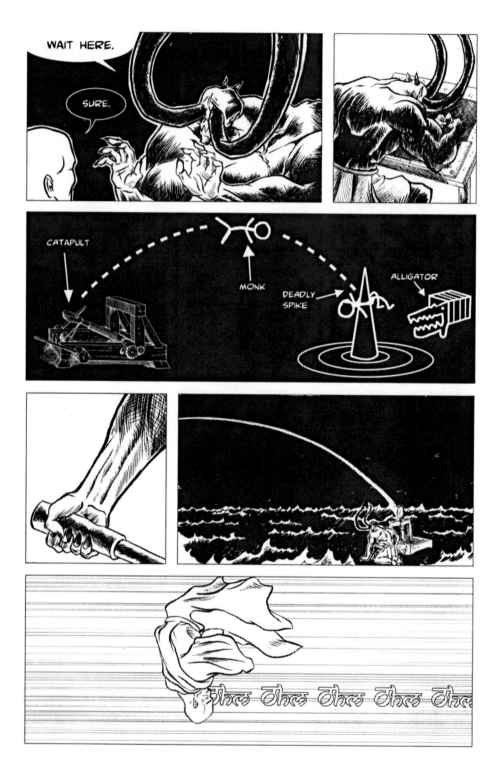

Anthony Blake

Quest for the Unreachable

The angels keep their ancient places;-
Turn but a stone, and start a wing!
'Tis ye, 'tis your estranged faces,
That miss the many-splendoured thing.
The Kingdom of God by Francis Thompson

To begin a quest for an understanding of higher intelligence, it is seemly to quote from an "expert" in the field, and none better than St. Thomas Aquinas. He presents a rational argument for the existence of angels as intellectual beings of a higher order than humanity. From Summa Theologica I, 50, 1: "Is there any entirely spiritual creature, altogether incorporeal?" by St. Thomas Aquinas (1225-1274) translated by the Fathers of the English Dominican Province.

Article 1
There must be some incorporeal creatures. For what is principally intended by God in creatures is good, and this consists in assimilation to God Himself. And the perfect assimilation of an effect to a cause is accomplished when the effect imitates the cause according to that whereby the cause produces the effect; as heat makes heat. Now, God produces the creature by His intellect and will (14, 8; 19, 4). Hence the perfection of the universe requires that there should be intellectual creatures. Now intelligence cannot be the action of a body, nor of any corporeal faculty; for every body is limited to "here" and "now."

Hence the perfection of the universe requires the existence of an incorporeal creature.

The ancients, however, not properly realising the force of intelligence, and failing to make a proper distinction between sense and intellect, thought that nothing existed in the world but what could be apprehended by sense and imagination. And because bodies alone fall under imagination, they supposed that no being existed except bodies, as the Philosopher observes (Phys. iv, text 52,57). Thence came the error of the Sadducees, who said there was no spirit (Acts 23:8).

But the very fact that intellect is above sense is a reasonable proof that there are some incorporeal things comprehensible by the intellect alone.

. . . Incorporeal substances rank between God and corporeal creatures. Now the medium compared to one extreme appears to be the other extreme, as what is tepid compared to heat seems to be cold; and thus it is said that angels, compared to God, are material and corporeal, not, however, as if anything corporeal existed in them.

. . . an angel is called an ever mobile substance, because he is ever actually intelligent, and not as if he were sometimes actually and sometimes potentially, as we are.

The idea of an "ever mobile substance" in association with intelligence helps us suspend in our thinking any naïve concept of a being or beings moving around and acting, in the manner that we as organic beings do. In essence, it corresponds with the idea of John Bennett—which we will be discussing later—of intelligence as a substance or energy. It also has some correspondence with David Bohm's concept of holomovement. Aquinas is describing a kind of "translation" between an ineffable realm of pure possibility and a more finite realm, such as ours, subject to limitations.

Any idea of intelligence "higher" or "more" than human must entail a corresponding idea of our limitations. How far can our intelligence reach? Is there any sense in saying that there could be an intelligence that reaches further than us? By "reach" here we mean to grasp and hence influence and even control. If we grasp a branch of mathematics we can do calculations based on it. If we cannot, then we are impotent in that region. So we begin with the idea that the "unreachable" is relative to us as we are in this time.

We have made considerable strides in reaching across space and time and into the depths of the construction of matter. But we seem to reach problems when we come to the limits of time, space and matter. No one can—at least yet - claim to know the initial conditions of the universe, or even if there were any. Whenever we reach a question of creation, our reasoning comes to an impasse; even though, on this side of creation, we can accomplish and understand a great deal by thought, calculation and experiment. To speak of "creation" in this rather old-fashioned way need not imply anything divine or the existence of a God, simply that there is an action in which "before and after" ceases to apply and from which all else arises. This is very close to some of our instinctual feelings of "nothingness". As the erratic mathematician Spencer Brown once put it, "Only nothingness could be sensitive to nothingness and produce something".

Questions of the origin of the universe or the deep structure of matter are fairly obvious examples of where we reach some kind of limit to what we can cope with, but there appears to be a general result of growth in exact knowledge: it enables us to more and more precisely indicate what it is that we cannot understand and/or handle. It might even be a concomitant of any increase in precise knowledge—the intangible and unreachable also increases accordingly. Once in mathematics the transfinite numbers were unreachable, now it is things we cannot decide or give a reason for. A prime example, to make a poor pun, is given by the prime numbers. We do not know how to predict them. But what could appear more evident than a prime number! It is relatively easy to find out if a given number is prime, no matter how big it is. It is quite another to be able to say what the next one will be. The image here of the landscape of prime numbers was produced by Stanislaw Ulam. It is made by plotting numbers in a square spiral and putting point for every prime. We can see that there is some pattern without being able to calculate precisely what it is.

Lack of power of prediction can make some of us feel a sense of the mysterious, or of a hidden fabric in the nature of things to which we are not yet privy. We know that we are missing something, some insight. We know this because of advances that have been made. But, for the moment, what is missing for us represents a higher mode of thinking than what we have at present. If we had that insight, we might well understand physics and mathematics quite differently and even see them as much more the same than before. There are many speculations as to what such an insight might mean but at this time, as St. Paul said, "I see as through a glass, darkly".

To say that this insight already in some way exists is to affirm the existence of higher intelligence. On many fronts, science and mathematics face into the unknown but with the confidence that much more can be discovered. We can imagine that there is a cloud of reachable insights that attenuates into the completely unreachable and it is in these regions that higher intelligence exists. But, in what form we do not know. Are new scientific and mathematical truths carried around by angels?

Or, are such truths what angels really are? Is the relatively reachable to do with higher powers, while the unreachable is what we should call "God"? What is for most only a conceptual abstraction is for others a living power of superior intelligence. For most people, the fact that at this time we cannot know the initial conditions of the universe or predict the next prime number is of no interest. However, the same consideration applies to ourselves. Where do we start from and what are we going to do next? We face the deep mystery of time.

For as long as we humans have as we say been "conscious" we have faced an immeasurable problem in understanding where our actions and impulses come from. The simple answer is just to say that, "Well my actions and impulses are what they are because I am me, I am made like that". But still we cannot see where they come from or how they arise. If I am me, how am I made? When we look at that question, we can fly off into a number of diverging paths. We now know about genetics, about the brain, about social conditioning and so on even though our knowledge is far from complete. Each of these provides or seems to provide some basis for explaining why we act as we do, though in practice we can never compute our acts in advance of them.

In our human life together, we find that at times we act very badly or very well without having any understanding of why. Of course, how we actually act is always being covered up by a process of internal explanation that continues to rationalise our behaviour and make it seem consistent. When we cannot explain how we act, this is taken as an aberration indicating mental illness. But there is much in psychoanalysis that suggests that the "inexplicable" is more common than we think.

In earlier times, it was taken for granted that a man was subject to impulses not of his own devising. The heroes of ancient Greece would be overcome with states and impulses that they regarded as coming from the "gods" or from what later become known as their "genius", the creative irrational part of their nature, which

was the source of both good and bad. The "good" and the "bad" were impulses that could not be explained, that deviated from the norm. This ancient idea became superseded in the era of modern consciousness by the supposition that something was happening "inside" us beyond awareness but still intrinsic to our own nature. The ancient idea of genius was expressed by Socrates as an encounter with his own "daimon" and it is not for nothing that the Christian church identified this with "demon" and treated it as from the devil and sinful. When Freud brought in his concept of the unconscious it was in a milieu that would regard this unconscious as the seat of irrational and perverse forces. While most people scorned the idea of an unconscious dictating what we did, the world lurched into the madness of world war!

The unconscious still carries some stigma with it, but over the last century it came to be regarded as having enormous potential for insight and wholeness, as argued in the work of Carl Jung. And it also became regarded as the source of creativity, an idea which was prominent even among scientists such as Poincare. At the same time, it became realised that what we call "consciousness" is not an opening up to what is going on in us but a closing down. We are able to be conscious because nearly all of what is happening in us is cut out of our awareness. And this is absolutely essential for us to function at all. Consider how we speak. We are totally unaware of how words come up for us to deliver. We can of course, to some degree, stop ourselves using a certain word but we cannot start the word in us, because the only way of summoning a specific word is by that word! Whatever is moving in us and interesting us, including other words and what other people say, comes out in us in what we say, but we do not know how this happens. We might as well admit that one word speaks to another in us rather than we make speaking happen the way it does.

If we know something is coming up in us it is possible for us to stop it. But this only applies when something is already on its way. I am sitting here at the keyboard, paying attention to some questions, often waiting for something to form in me. Some of the sentences I write down are later deleted, something I can do while writing but is hardly possible when I am speaking. When I am about to speak I can inhibit myself but once I have spoken it is irretrievable: "The words just came out of my mouth, I didn't mean it" we will say. This has led some to conclude that we do not have any real identity at all. The one who blurts something out is not the one who then regrets what they have said.

The Russian mystic Ouspensky wrote a novel *The Strange Life of Ivan Osokin* to express the idea that even if we knew the future we would not be able to change what we did. When in life we do not do what we set out to do, then we explain this in terms of a reason that avoids

do with accessing what can be called "will". I say that I want to do X but I end up doing Y. We sometimes admit to ourselves that we do not really know what we want. So, even if we knew what we will do next we do not know what "we" this entails or whether it is really us at all. When we come to the next moment, will we properly remember this one? In a pragmatic sense, yes, because we function according to a continuity of self. In any deeper sense, No. What is really going on remains in the unconscious, which we have to infer by noticing lapses of memory, inconsistencies of behaviour, and surprising impulses.

The unconscious is unreachable. If it were reachable, "we" would cease to exist at all. If we seek to extend our consciousness into the

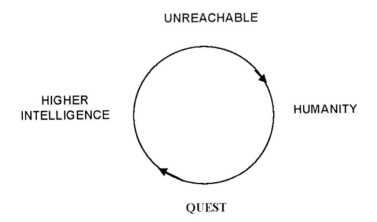

UNREACHABLE

HIGHER INTELLIGENCE   HUMANITY

QUEST

recognising that we are not able to do.

Not only are we not aware of where things start in us but we are also not aware of what will happen next. The simplistic argument is that if I know what I will do next I could always not do it. This is simplistic because it does not take into account the fact that we can be aware but incapable in fact of changing what is happening or going to happen. It is one of the "horrors" of consciousness that we can "see" ourselves doing things that we judge as being "bad" or "stupid" without being able to stop ourselves. This is a third kind of unreachable that has to

unconscious we become unconscious! This is not to be taken in an absolute sense. There is a "fuzziness" between conscious and unconscious.

The principle of unreachability is reflected in the physical universe, according to the principle that no computer could be built in the universe capable of computing the state of the universe. We are not able to demonstrate or even argue this here and we ask you just to imagine that such a computer would have to built out of something and have storage capacity and operating systems and so on, analogously with your own PC, but would have to compute the beginning and end of all things! It would be an "apocalypse" machine in the true sense of the word - "lifting the veil". Such a prospect has been wonderfully satirised in Douglas Adams' masterpiece *The Hitch Hiker's Guide to the Galaxy*, where the Earth is really a supercomputer run by white mice to answer the question of life, the universe and everything only to require an even greater computer able to compute what the question is! He could well have gone on to suppose a greater computer still to work out the meaning of the question, and even greater still to calculate why the question was asked in the first place! Of course, the suggestion here is that intelligent life (such as us?) is the equivalent of Adams' white mice computer programmers and we have in principle the whole physical universe to build from. As far as we know, no one has yet proved that no physical system can fully compute itself. It reflects on the apparently inevitable sense we have that self-knowledge is limited by some kind of barrier perhaps defined by the physical nature of thought. Such a limitation might be expressed in terms of a velocity, or in terms of a "size" of content, or in terms of complexity, though there has been insufficient measurement of thought. A physical system that devotes some of its energy to computing itself can be called "conscious". Consciousness then appears as energy transformed into self-information. Such information is inherently incomplete, which then implies what is beyond any consciousness, or *will*. Will *cannot* be within consciousness.

The quest for the unreachable points towards beginnings and endings, towards will and self-knowledge, towards the realm of creativity and madness.

Countless humans believe that higher powers intervene in their lives. In a more sophisticated way, some believe that our very aims and purposes have been stimulated in us by a superior order of intelligence. This was given the most sublime expression by Jalalludin Rumi, the Sufi poet of the 13th century, in his Mathnawi. In this book of many stories there is one about a man praying who is tempted to question whether his prayers are being answered. The hidden teacher Khidr appears, representing God, and chides the man for his lack of understanding—that, in fact, he would not be able to pray to Allah unless Allah had "answered" him by giving him the impulse to pray in the first place.

Simone Weil made a point of insisting that in the Gospels we can find no reference to man seeking God, only to God seeking man.

If we could see from where our initiative starts, then we could change it and it would no longer be the origin. This is tantamount to changing the past. As it is, it is just because the origin is unreachable that we can act at all. This may not be apparent at first. After all, our common language is full of absurdities which are used everyday. Prime amongst them is the phrase "use my will". This is absurd. Will is that which acts and originates. The phrase is tantamount to saying "I will my will" or even "will wills my will".

Religious people believe in a "higher will" and the possibility of a relationship between their own will and this higher form. An action such as prayer is supposed to exemplify this relation. But in the example of the story from the Mathnawi the relation does not originate in us but in the divine. It is even felt that when we pray or act in some way to reflect the relationship, that this has already been done in the divine sense and we are merely carrying out what is already accomplished. In traditional religion there is never any sense that we can reach God. In fact such a proposition is consistently treated as heresy, and for a good reason. The consistent teaching is that although we cannot reach God, God can reach us, as in the Islamic saying, "Man takes one step towards God and God takes ninety-nine steps towards man."

The quest for the unreachable is, of course, the quest for God. The hint from religion we get is that the unreachable is capable of reaching us! In the little diagram above, ourselves and our search appear in only part of the whole. This is an unusual portrayal because it suggests that we and our intelligence simply play a part in a whole that is vastly greater than us. We could play around with such imagery, for example to suggest that we humans operate within a certain bandwidth of intelligence. For such ideas we have no proof, only an extrapolation from our experience of other life forms on this planet. Incidentally, "quest" represents us at our best, giving it our best shot, not the statistical average.

The image of a circular action can be replaced by a fractal one. To make the concept familiar, we can think of the coastline of the British Isles. As we look at this coastline in more and more detail, its effective length gets larger and larger and approaches infinity in the limit while the area of the land remains the same. It is another image of the unreachable in an almost literal

states to exist even though they are of low probability. We cannot exist "too far"—and this is a kind of "distance"—from such regions. Our sense of time is said to derive from the entropy gradient between lower and higher regions of entropy. One consequence of this view is that we will always tend to think in terms of a "creative origin" of the universe—such as a Big Bang—and this is not so different from thinking in terms of a "creator god". The highest state of lowest entropy would also correspond to our intuitions of "heaven" or the "angelic realm". It is a feature of the lore of angels that they are not subject to decay! Religion then appears as founded on a real sense of *qualities of order*.

We are of course acting in a cavalier way with

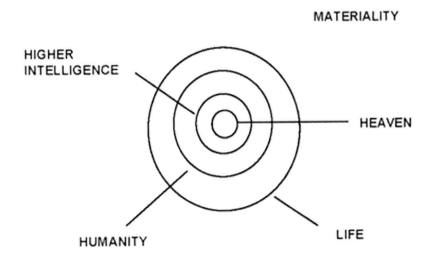

form. There is a saying that "God is in the details".

The issue of complexity is prevalent. As we said, our consciousness is founded on a massive filtering of information, so that we deal with the merest outline of what is going on. An interesting concept is that we, as complex and highly organised entities, must exist somewhere near regions of very low entropy. According to physical law, it is possible for highly ordered

all kinds of concepts from many sources. We are now asking you to consider an understanding of higher intelligence in terms of diminution or relative absence of entropy. One of the tricks of higher intelligence is to get from a state of greater entropy to one of lesser entropy. In traditional spiritual paths, we come across an extreme version of this such as "liberation" and "immortality". But, if we try to imagine what it would like "in heaven" we find it hard. We have some hope in terms of how "this life" might look from the standpoint of heaven. Perhaps we can have actual tastes of higher intelligence. Our "position" whatever that is in the scheme of things may not be single-valued.

This is a liberating concept. It means that heaven is here and now, though in a very "fractional" way. It means that we ourselves actually do participate in higher intelligence, although this might be quite "unconsciously". We could easily come to ascribe this to our "unconscious" if we are modern people, or our "daimon" if we would be Socrates. Speaking of that, our broad notion of higher intelligence includes such a possibility. From the standpoint of heaven every one of us might be, in some slight sense, Socrates.

When Dante in his *Divine Comedy* finally enters Paradise, he doubts where he is. The higher powers then command him to speak of heaven. The fact that he is able to do so "proves" that he is in heaven. It is interesting that he is guided to the gates of heaven by Virgil, the higher intelligence, but taken in by Beatrice who is more than that.

".......the end point of the universe comes when the maximum information storage is reached"

In their book *Anthropic Cosmological Principle* Barrow and Tipler refer to the question of whether the universe is "open" or "closed". They state, "it seems on anthropic grounds that the universe is more likely to be closed than open, but this is only a weak prediction". Their scenario for the end of the universe is thus based on this assumption of a closed universe. In that scenario, life eventually engulfs the entire universe; and the end point of the universe comes when the maximum information storage is reached. At that Omega Point, no further activity is possible. In a note, the last words of text in the book, they add, "A modern-day theologian might wish to say that the totality of life at the Omega Point is omnipotent, omnipresent, and omniscient!"

Donivan Bessinger, *The Psychology of God*

The idea of regions of low entropy or "heaven" does not easily let us consider a most important feature of higher intelligence, which is perception of reality. In our human experience, we have to "make do" with inference to arrive at knowledge of phenomena hidden to our senses. It seems that we do not directly perceive quarks, nor motions near the speed of light, nor the fields that surround us. It is not obvious that

a region of low entropy must include a different order of direct perception to the one we have. Some have speculated that we call "mind" corresponds to a mode of perception that has not yet become part of our organic nature. It is not for nothing that this mind finds expression in artefacts and relationships outside of our bodies. Of course, the standard view is that this mind is not to do with perception at all but is a kind of inner processing that takes place in the dark cave of the brain! So, for some thought is what we "do" or "make up" while for others, a minority, it is something akin to a perception of "what is there".

It is a feature of our present human life that we set thought and perception apart, as if they were two different kinds of thing. This has immense influence on how we regard ourselves and our relation to reality. This is because, in such a separation, we have to take thought as private, subjective, artificial in contrast with perception that is of the "world", objective and natural. But in higher intelligence these are not at all separate. There is the intuition or belief that higher intelligence can see what is *really going on*. This idea is not confined to religious systems. Science sometimes makes use of the idea of a "cosmic intelligence" able to see the real structure of the universe, even though of course, this does not mean that scientists actually believe in the existence of such an observer. However, the concept is used to argue a view of the universe that is contrary to our "normal" experience. Just as we came to realise the earth was round, rotating and in orbit by a long chain of inference, long before we could actually see this from space by going there, so we anticipate what we might see from a much greater perspective than we can have at this time as organic beings. This includes the greater perspective of long periods of time. It is totally extraordinary that we can contemplate processes over billions of years, something that has only been possible for just over 100 years.

We are now much used to scientists telling us about all kinds of strange and "invisible" things, but it is surprising to what extent this is accepted. For example, the vast majority of people rapidly accepted the discovery of a hole in the ozone layer, even though this was entirely outside any possible human experience through the senses. However, when it comes to things such as depicted in relativity and quantum mechanics, they are so radically different from what we expect that we find them difficult to take on board. The reason is that they demand of us a change in the very way we see how things happen. In the end, we only go along with such theories because of such things as the atomic bomb dropped on Hiroshima.

It is interesting and not trivial to draw a parallel between our relation to relativity and our relation to religion. At least in the past, we looked to miracles as evidence of our faith in what we could not actually see as real for ourselves. So we look for spectacular manifestations of the scientific "theories" - that are dealt with in ways we cannot possibly grasp - to convince us that they are "real perceptions". Such manifestations amount to creating events in laboratories on Earth that could not otherwise take place here. They are practical and repro-ducible "miracles".

It is both in the domain of the very small and in the domain of the very large that we are most lacking in terms of direct perception. We should add to this short list the domain of the very complex, because we do not see what is "really going on" in natural processes but have to compute them in indirect ways. In the domain of the very small we have the underlying structure of matter and, in the domain of the very large, the nature of the fabric of the universe, the very structure of space, time and energy. The scientist does imagine himself in the role of cosmic intelligence, however modest he may be.

An important point to add here is that there is very little evidence for any mystic or religious prophet giving us any substantial information about the universe other than that available in the time they lived. This is an awkward point for spiritual people to answer: if you claim to develop different orders of perception where is the evidence? Of course, there is a plethora of fringe acitvities purporting to do just that but none have stood up to any strong testing. Science has now commandeered the domain of the "unseen" as its province. And what is coming out of science is challenging just about every "common sense" view of things.

The most commonly cited example of this is the cheery claim that "matter is mostly empty space", a saying that came out of research into atomic structure. We think this table is solid whereas "in fact" it is made of atoms separated from each other which are also composed of particles whirling around each other at relatively immense distances. This persuades us to think in terms of our actual perception being defective. So also with regard to recent ideas about the nature of the universe. It is becoming a more and more common contention that our experience of time is an illusion. Now, this really strikes a blow against our common sense! What is strange is that assimilating this idea can change how we interpret our experience so that time actually feels differently to us.

Whatever one's attitude to the "truths" of science, it remains the case that what is suggested to us is that the way we see things is as best partial and that a totally different view could be much nearer to how things are (some scientists like to play at God, while others seriously believe that the universe is governed by a higher intelligence). While we are organic beings, dependent on structures that have evolved on this planet through natural selection, it is not possible for us to directly perceive or in some sense "see" how things are. We cannot see the structure of matter and we cannot see the structure of the universe. These things are unreachable as perceptions. We can only "think" about them, or just "imagine" how they might be. It is not for nothing that Einstein relied heavily on what are called *gedanken* or "thought" experiments, as well as on calculation and observation.

Now, what if "mind" were a rudimentary organism of emergent character? Would not such an organism have its own corresponding perceptions? And then, would not these perceptions be similar to what has been proposed for higher intelligence? We might even here appeal to a very unscientific person in the form of William Blake, for whom the human imagination was the divine itself!

Because of the split in science between the way that "visions" or, more austerely, "hypotheses" are generated and the way in which we test them against measurement and observation, the reliance of scientists on such things as "physical intuition" is minimalised. The human power of imagination is gener-ally supposed to operate without any reference to how things really are, being considered something that arises in the brain or private mind. Because the results of imagination are often found to be "unreal" and not correspond with the facts, it gets dismissed out of hand. In practice, scientists—such as Einstein—draw upon this power to do their work. Scientists at the beginning of the twentieth century were conscious of attempting to "project" themselves into atomic structures to understand what they were like. This was even given a special name—*projicience.*

The general argument here is that our minds have fuzzy boundaries in which we exercise powers similar to those supposed to be the property of higher intelligence. However, we also take into account that these powers operate in us in a sporadic and uncertain manner. We can say that every act of imagination is valid but that we often do not know in what way it is valid. Hence strong convictions can arise about the nature of things that have some substance but are misconstrued. This leads to the idea that what is "broken" in us is "whole" in higher intelligence. The brokenness of our condition represents a higher entropy than that of higher intelligence.

There are hints of a perception of reality breaking through the veils of disorder, as it were. But, for us to access these in more than a fleeting way, we need to build up corresponding energies to support them. This is a rationale for science, in which great amounts of work go into providing a suitable vehicle for imaginative insights. In quite another way, some yogis and mystics claim that they can do inner work that provides them with the power and an apparatus to see a deeper reality. An unprepared mind lacking instruments is unable to register higher events.

If we imagine that human beings are in fact operating simultaneously in different worlds of perception, then we need to suppose that our "presence" in some of them is very small indeed but that, still, our multiple presence leads to these various perceptions interfering with each other. When we try to "reach" a region of higher intelligence, or very low entropy, the way we do this makes it impossible to achieve. Our "trying" sends us further downhill along the entropy gradient. To get round this, we have turned to the means of using artefacts such as mathematics which themselves have very low entropy. A similar but more subtle example is that of works of art. This leads us to consider the unreachable in aesthetic terms as well as scientific ones.

One of the great appeals of a genius such as Mozart is the apparent ease with which he could produce masterpieces, as if they just flew out of him complete, as Athena broke forth from the head of Zeus. Although these days much is made of the sweat and tears that go into most works of genius, there remains the feeling—and we believe it to have validity—that the real art comes of itself without effort. At this point, we do not want to dwell on the contradiction here. We want to focus on the possibility that real works of art, which have their own "truth" and being, come of themselves into human life. An im-portant idea is that our sweat and tears do not concern the making of the art but enabling us to bear its manifestation in us.

Intimations of this conception of higher intelligence are to be found in Rilke, the German poet, especially in his masterpiece *The Duino Elegies.*

> Who, if I cried, would hear me among the
>   angelic orders?
> And if one of them suddenly
>   pressed me against his heart,
> I should fade in the strength of
>   his stronger existence.
> For Beauty's nothing but beginning
>   of Terror we're still able to bear
> and why we adore it so is because it
>   serenely disdains to destroy us.
> Every angel is terrible.

And this then leads us to suppose that in higher intelligence we have something like a beauty machine: a way of producing beauty that is akin to just "turning a handle". At the same time, we have in this realm a perception of beauty that is infallible. Of course, such suggestions are unproven and almost certainly unproveable: to be able to prove them would be to contradict them; but there are such things in mathematics also. We have to realise that Beauty is more than something that pleases us, as the poet Rilke declares. In fact, we have to say that we do not see beauty as it really is. In saying this, we very much go against contemporary culture, in which all things of value are considered subjective and unrelated to the nature of things. We say that just as it is difficult to see what the facts are, so it is to see what the values are. Beauty, truth, goodness and so on may be far more than the sensations and emotions that we have can support. What we see of them is the mere outline of what they are.

Values figure predominantly in any traditional spiritual view of things. It is fairly common to regard the realm of higher intelligence to be *composed of qualities.* Further, that it is only in this realm that they can be seen for what they are. In our realm of experience, they tend to manifest through what is most frail and fleeting. Their embodiment in works of art is only a partial realisation and, even then, as we indicated, the circumstances of their making are often fraught with difficulties, as the life of Mozart exemplifies. In his book *Hazard,* J. G. Bennett argues that such things as virtue have to manifest under extremes of uncertainty. His realism here is striking, since the general tendency is to regard virtue as some kind of personal possession, an attitude that lends itself to self-deception.

Let us stay with the conception of the realm of low-entropy higher intelligence as one in which the truth of how the universe is seen in a way that puts both fact and value on the same footing. For us they are of separate natures. For the higher intelligence, they are not. Some people have intimations of this. They insist that "understanding" the universe must include a direct perception of beauty, goodness and truth; that these values are not some "gloss" on things that arises from superfluous aspects of our experience. The essence is in the possibility of seeing fact and value as not-different. The world is as it is because it is beautiful. We can also remember the words of *Genesis* in which God "sees that it is good", an understanding that was first given religious expression in Zoroastrianism.

Naturally enough, in spite of the fact that many scientists are not immune to a sense of beauty and goodness, they would never consider these are criteria of scientific truth. In spite of which, we can still come across scientists and mathematicians who appeal to a sense of beauty to justify their work. The gen-eral scepticism has one great virtue: that it does not allow us *to impose our sense of beauty on reality.* Nevertheless, without some contact with beauty, goodness and truth, we might well be lost, even when engaged in research into what appear to be matters of fact. Poincaré said:

> The scientist does not study Nature because it is useful; he studies it because he delights in it, and he delights in it

because it is beautiful. If Nature were not beautiful, it would not be worth knowing, and if Nature were not worth knowing, life would not be worth living.

Beauty, goodness and truth are an important aspect of what is (relatively) unreachable for us. Some of us have the experience of something beautiful as if it were torture! We say, even of something fairly common such as the sight of a beautiful sunset, that "it hurts, it is so beautiful". This has to do with what we can bear. We have dallied with this aspect and it is time to state it more directly: we cannot dwell in the realm of higher intelligence because we could not bear it. The realm of values is unreachable, or "relatively unreachable" because it renders us unconscious because it is unbearable! So we come full circle. What we cannot reach is in our "unconscious"— though whether this "unconscious" is the same as the psychoanalytic one is questionable and any attempts to reach it renders us "unconscious". This may be just a matter of getting used to *another kind of consciousness*. One value of the psychoanalytic view is that it suggests that we are "sort-of" conscious of a great deal that we do not allow ourselves to access in a regular way, but have to come to through such indirect means as dreaming and imaginative art, or through some "shock" that awakens us to what we have suppressed, in what is unique and fleeting

People ask why, if there is a higher intelligence, does it not come forth and speak to us and help us? The reason offered here is that it might render us inoperative.

We have talked about the unreachable in terms of the far reaches of space and time, in terms of the basic structure of matter, in terms of complexity, in terms of our own nature and in terms of qualities and values. What remains?

We mentioned in passing that we enable ourselves to deal with higher intelligence by creating artefacts, which can "carry" the higher information safely. These are such things as mathematics and art—and, as we shall explore later, language. This is most important. What it implies is that *we are simulations of higher intelligence*, where the term "we" includes the meaningful adjuncts to ourselves that enable us to see beyond what we are able to see unaided in separate organic bodies. In this sense, our science, art and technology really are manifestations of higher intelligence and it is possible to look at human history as a hazardous attempt to bring us into closer communication with higher intelligence. The fact that recent advances appear to have made belief in higher intelligence recede is par for the course. What may be under way is a communication with higher intelligence that is far more "realistic" then ever before. We can adopt the view that higher intelligence is trying to get through to us and that it is our very own nature that is making this difficult.

So, we turn our quest in its head: we are unreachable as far as higher intelligence is concerned. One of Gurdjieff's many pithy sayings was, "If a man can make shoes one can talk to him". Contrary to contemporary assumptions it is only possible to communicate to someone significant "know-how" if they already are able to do something for themselves! The historical equivalent of "making shoes" is our science and technology. Of course, if someone is identified with making shoes, we have a problem!

Spiritual lore has it, of course, that some of us are able to detect influences coming from the realm of higher intelligence and that it is not unreachable. Still, the link is portrayed as tenuous in the extreme, as if through faint shining threads. From our side, following back the "luminescent threads" (see below) to their origin is an act of decision and faith. It can have no justification from "our side" of the relationship. It requires an act of "as if"—in this case to act as if we were ourselves the higher intelligence. The apparent "barrier" to communication is created by our own nature. We are that barrier. So being told about a communication is of little use to us, because the operations involved cannot be explained.

It will be useful to give an example of a very important way in which a "communication-gap" between ourselves and higher intelligence must arise. If we can associate higher intelligence with a "greater vision" than we have as organic beings this vision will have a very significant property: as our span of attention is to be measured in seconds, minutes, hours, days at best that of a higher intelligence may well be measured in years, centuries and millennia. Imagine an intelligence for which one action or meaning embraces many of our centuries. How would it be possible for such a vision to be transmitted to us?

> According to the 13th century Andalusian Sufi Ibn Arabi there exist "delicate tenuities" that stretch between heaven and earth like Jacobs-ladders - and the "meanings" which descend along these tenuities are like angels . . . if the meaning that appears in the tenuity is real, it can be traced back to its source which is real - or real enough for our present purposes - and this tracing-back is called (by the Ismaili gnostics) ta'wil, or 'Interpretation.'"

Hakim Bey, *For and Against Interpretation*

We are well aware of the tendency towards short-term thinking that prevails in just about every human activity. Attempts to artificially claim a vision beyond that of a year or so seem to enjoin us in disaster—as in the five-year plans of the Soviets and the dreadful nightmare of the Third Reich. In contrast, a real perception that would embrace a thousand of years seems so unlikely as to be dismissed out of hand. Yet we do have experience of a narrowing and broadening of the scale of our own subjective present moment. With this, we also have the experience that when we are in a "longer" state, that it is next to impossible to communicate to ourselves when we are in a "shorter" state. We then lose contact with our own vision! In times of great meaning for us, we can even experience the poignant pain of being unable to ensure that we will not forget what we have seen. Even if we write for ourselves a "message" we will find ourselves unable to decipher its true meaning when the moment has passed. It is one of the greatest arts to be able to communicate with oneself in a future state of relative oblivion.

So could it be for a higher intelligence that sees what we cannot see. There is just not enough "room" in us for this kind of information. This does not mean that it never happens but that it must happen in unexpected ways. The evidence is that we have made little or no progress in managing our side of the communication. But the best things are not easy—on either side. To be sure, the result of any communication between ourselves and higher intelligence should increase meaning in the whole. The hardest thing to grasp, we feel, is that even though there may be a higher intelligence, superior to our own, still it must lack something that only we can provide.

> . . . man has not yet learned how to communicate with an ant. When he does, will the questions put to the world around by the ant, and the answers that he elicits contribute their share, too, to the establishment of meaning?"

John A. Wheeler in "Information, Physics, Quantum: The Search for Links" from *Complexity, Entropy and the Physics of Information.*

This idea can be turned on its head to regard us as the "ant" relative to higher intelligence.

One of the aspects of a view of higher intelligence that includes in it the power to perceive across hundreds of years in a single act of attention is that it entails that history is meaningful. By this we mean that events stretching over hundreds and thousands of years, perhaps longer, have a wholeness that we cannot easily see. If we do not see it, it might be argued, then why bother to consider such a possibility? One argument is to extend the ideas that surround the issues of quantum mechanics, some of which focus on the act of measurement or observation as a crucial and integral part of the reality that is taking place. If we accept that we do not see the pattern in the greater whole, we may still be able to accept that something does. That there is a seeing that embraces our history—holds it in trust as it were—and that without this seeing our history would indeed be a record of madness, as some of us feel.

One of the most extraordinary features of some experiences of expanding consciousness has been the sense that it is not our consciousness that is becoming greater but that we come into some rudimentary awareness of a consciousness that is aware of us. It is something like this that informs the sense that some have of being watched over and even cared for. It is perfectly logical, of course, still to ascribe this to ourselves, as an aspect of a multiplicity of consciousness in us. However, if for the moment we accept this as a genuine insight—that is, if we choose to do so knowing full well that we can never demonstrate this to another person—then we can come to understand that it is in being seen that we are enabled to see anything for ourselves.

We are not used to thinking that "mere" seeing can have a real effect on what is. We tend to treat "seeing" as if it were either a passive response or an active fabrication. What if it is neither? This is the kind of view we can now find in regard to quantum phenomena. What if it can be applied to ourselves? We ask only that you visualise this prospect and simply imagine a consciousness able to be aware of you, a consciousness that "knows" you from childhood to death, your ancestors and descendants, your place in history. This may be what is sometimes labelled "destiny".

Would a higher intelligence be concerned with you or us? In the Bible it is written, "Not a sparrow falls but that the Lord they God knows it." But this is the highest god and maybe the higher intelligence is not capable of such a feat of attention but can only have it partially. This is a question we will follow through as best we can.

Awareness of complexity over a myriad of years may even extend deeply into the cosmos. We can imagine that throughout the fabric of the universe, but not in a guise we can readily grasp in terms of our own time-experience, the seeing of wholeness is carried by vast intelligences capable even of perceiving the destiny of a galaxy. This does not determine what will happen—nor even what has happened! - because any act of communication on whatever scale produces new meaning. If a higher intelligence sees what is possible, we on our part have to make what it is actual. Just as a provisional analogy, imagine that there is a theatrical director/writer who has a script in mind but must allow us to play our parts as we see fit. A skilled director will allow this to happen and not impose his own set ideas; and, by doing so, the drama is enriched. It may well be that, by playing our seemingly humble part, the unreachable reaches us.

Our own time-experience reflects the kind of present moment we have. Our thinking about time is a projection based on what we regard as "now". As is acknowledged in physics, the current view of physical reality in science does not admit to any sense of now in the special sense it means for us. A few scientists are beginning to question this and make the sense of "now" as a fundamental aspect of the universe and the concept we have of linear time as a very partial and distorted reading of what "now" means.

Julian Barbour in his *The End of Time* argues a model of the universe he calls "Platonia", in which "instants" or "time-capsules" are nested in each other to embrace the whole. Then there is no such thing as a "movement" from one instant to another. This was in fact anticipated by Descartes who said that each instant is connected to others only by God. If we accept a kind of perception and attention that can embrace the phenomena of a thousand of our years, then this cannot be located in our standard concept of linear time. It leads to the contradiction of something knowing our future while we yet remain free to act otherwise. It is necessary to look for an understanding of time that does not rely on there being any one single track of time along which all phenomena can be "located". A similar sort of requirement is in front of anyone who wishes to believe in reincarnation, or many lives. These are usually presented in terms of an assumed line of time so that one life follows after another along a single track. We learned from relativity that "simultaneity" is questionable—the idea that something happening here is "at the same time" as something happening for that moving object over there - and it is a truly revolutionary insight. In spite of that, even physicists cling to the idea that there is some universal time line that embraces the whole universe. Once we give up on the idea of Newtonian absolute time, we can begin to accept a multiplicity in time values. It may well be that such a multiplicity is the basis for impressions of many lives.

A higher intelligence will not see time as we do (we should remember our contention that perception and thinking will not be divided as in us). By trying to place higher intelligence in our usual concept of time we get it wrong and, consequently, cannot understand anything about the influence of higher powers on our lives. It is to be regretted that, as far as we know, nothing has been realised of this in the plethora of documents purporting to be derived from contact with "angels" in which conversations are reported in terms of human time.

The linear time concept brought us factories and western scientific-technological expansion. It still governs our thinking in all regions of human activity. Some writers have harked back to what they see as a more archaic view of time in terms of "circularity", as in Mercia Eliade's *Myth of the Eternal Return* as the only alternative. It is not so. There is a third concept that is just emerging, allowing for time to be multiple and in which both linearity and circularity can be seen as partial aspects. The third concept can be seen as "descending" into human consciousness from the supra-mental, the name given by the Indian Yogi Sri Aurobindo to higher intelligence. We can go along with this term since it basically means what is in our own present moment beyond our minds.

The unreachable of one moment may not be unreachable in another. Nevertheless, we may always find that we have to return again into our own basic present moment to do what only we can do. This is, of course, just the same as we can find in a methodology such as Buddhism: the *mahayana* or "greater path" is to return into life again after liberation to help the liberation of others. This return is echoed in Christianity by the megamyth of Christ as the Son of God, coming into human existence to bring salvation. John Lilly, famous for his work with dolphins, underwent an intense series of experiments involving drugs and isolation tanks to enable him to enter into higher (or at least different) world views. In doing so, he reports encountering higher intelligences who instructed him to return to ordinary life and learn how to be a human being!

From time to time we have touched upon religious questions and have intimated that God is beyond higher intelligence. Even higher intelligence cannot reach God. God is the supreme unreachable that we cannot get to but, yet, can get to us. And, in the sight of God, higher intelligence, human beings, other life forms, etc. are all equal. This kind of equality is unthinkable for us. This is largely because it demands of us that we abandon all concepts. The reason for this is that concepts remove uniqueness. We cannot imagine a reality in which everything is regarded in its pristine uniqueness. This would conjure up an image of such overwhelming complexity that we could not bear it.

Many traditions make it clear that higher intelligence is not to be identified with God. Even the Thomist view of angels as intellectual creatures between us and God is not enough. There is nothing between us and God, even though we cannot reach the perfection of God. Our exploration has considered the universe to be like an unfinished symphony. The direction of perfection is located in every moment and is not the same as conveyed by shallow views of evolution, which presume there is a single line of time. When we appeal to the idea of higher intelligence, this is just a beginning and not an explanation that can let us rest. The ultimate unreachable is *who we are*.

Andrew Phillip Smith

Robert Graves, the Bull God and the Angry Shepherd

Though he thought of himself primarily as a poet, Robert Graves is best known for his two Claudius novels, *I Claudius* and *Claudius the God*, and two works of nonfiction, his encyclopaedic though eccentric the *Greek Myths* and his brilliant, and also eccentric, *The White Goddess*. This last work is a complex creation that draws on an associative network of myth, ritual and sacred calendar to emphasize the central importance of the goddess. This white goddess, who has a threefold nature, is the fount of true poetry. Each woman is potentially an avatar of the goddess. The role of the male should be subservient to the goddess. Man is the poet, inspired by the Muse; the son of the mother, the lover of the queen, and finally the corpse lain out by the ancient hag. Like the kings of ancient societies he is sacrificed to the queen and replaced by his deputy. Graves' argument takes in tree alphabets distilled from the obscure medieval Welsh poetry, the symbolism of the solar year and quirky interpretation of the ancient myth and folklore. *The White Goddess* owes its genesis to a moment of intuition in which Graves felt that he could solve the riddle of the medieval Welsh poem *Cad Godeu*, the *Battle of the Trees*, found in the *Book of Taliesin*. His thesis, partly influenced by his sometime partner the American poet Laura Riding, continued to influence his poetry and thought until the very end of his life. His dedication to the female deity led him to consider masculine religion, in which a male god was central, as an abomination. Father gods were usurpers, forcing out the natural position of the Goddess.

What better example of a patriarchal male god is there than Jehovah? Graves treated the God of the Old Testament as a mere tribal deity of the Hebrews and usurper of the goddess. His novel *King Jesus* contains a succinct account of Graves' view of Jehovah: "Jehovah, it seems clear, was once regarded as a devoted son the Great Goddess, who obeyed her in all things and by her favor swallowed up a number of variously named rival gods and godlings—the Terebinth-god, the Thunder-god, the Pomegranate-god, the Bull-god, the Goat-god, the Antelope-god, the Calf-god, the Porpoise-god, the Ram-god, the Ass-god, the Barley-god, the god of Healing, the Moon-god, the god of the Dog-star, the Sun-god. Later (if it is permitted to write in this style) he did exactly what his Roman counterpart, Capitoline Jove, has done: he formed a supernal Trinity in conjunction with two of the Goddess's three persons, namely, Anatha of the Lions and Ashima of the Doves, the counterparts of Juno and Minerva; the remaining person, a sort of Hecate named Sheol, retiring to rule the infernal regions. "[1]

Though there is only the slightest of parallels between Graves downgrading of Jehovah and the Gnostic interpretation of Jehovah as the demiurge Yaldabaoth, Graves' eccentric ideas on religion are worth exploring.

Graves was from an upper-middle-class English family, with Irish and Anglo-Irish connections on his father's side (his grandfather was an amateur Celtic scholar). His difficult relationship with his German mother was at odds with (or perhaps at the root of) his worship of the feminine. His family life was strong on German tradition, but he identified more with the Irish side of the family, particularly as he encountered hostility to Germany in school and public life. His typically severe boarding school experiences at Charterhouse and his life in the trenches as a Captain in World War I are chronicled in his early memoir *Goodbye to All That*. He comments that,

I was brought up with a horror of Catholicism and this remained with me for a very long time. It was not a case of once a Protestant always a Protestant, but rather that when I ceased to be a Protestant I was further off than ever from being a Catholic. I discarded Protestantism in horror of its Catholic element. My religious training developed in me a great capacity for fear (I was perpetually tortured by a fear of Hell), a superstitious conscience, and a sexual embarrassment.... The last thing that is discarded by Protestants when they reject religion altogether is a vision of Christ as the perfect man. " [2]

He disliked Catholic imagery, apart from the virgin Mary, and when on holiday in his mother's native Bavaria as a child detested "the wayside crucifixes with the realistic blood and wounds, and the *ex-voto* pictures, like sign-boards, of naked souls in Purgatory, grinning with anguish in the middle of high red and yellow flames. We had been taught to believe in Hell, but we did not like to be reminded of it." [3]

Along with many other young men he was hospitalised and treated for shell shock but, despite his never lost his respect for soldiering.

His first marriage to Nancy Nicholson disintegrated quickly (though the divorce took years to go through as she, supported by Robert, refused to file for divorce under her married name as was legally required) and he fell under the spell of the American poet Laura Riding, with whom he had an intense and devoted relationship: when she threw herself from a fourth-floor window in a failed suicide attempt in 1929 Graves rushed down a floor and threw himself after her out of the third-floor window. For Graves, Riding was the most important poet of her time and the living embodiment of the cruel muse. After they split up he slowly emerged from her influence, taking his second wife Beryl back to Deyá in Majorca, where he had previously co-habited with Riding. He remained married to Beryl to the end of his life, though he took on a succession of young "muses" as mistresses from his late middle age.

His poetry was extensive, encompassing prosy mythography, occasional verse and heartfelt, crystalline lyrics. He wrote many novels, mostly with well-researched historical backgrounds, ranging from the popular Claudius books to the Byzantine Count Belisarius, Homer, Milton and the eighteenth century America of Sergeant Lamb. His articles, essays and lectures, chiefly on the subjects of poetry, myth and ancient religion, were always opinionated and erudite, drawing unorthodox conclusions based on a close reading of the primary sources and blithely ignoring mainstream scholarship.

Throughout his life, Graves grappled with Christianity, and tried to interpret and rehabilitate the figure of Jesus. Unable to disregard it, he reinvented it in the image of his mythic theories, and even rewrote the gospels. His 1914 poem "In the Wilderness," sympathetically depicts "Christ of His gentleness/Thirsting and hungering,/Walked in the wilderness." During his isolated fast of forty days and nights he meets the scapegoat. Graves later described the poem as silly and quaint, but it was one of the few early poems to be retained in successive editions of his collected poems. In *Goodbye to All That* he prints a long begging letter from a devoted reader who hopes that the

Christ-like Graves might donate a few quid to her.

He was heavily influenced by the *Golden Bough*, that compendious and influential work of folklore, ritual and naive anthropology by James Fraser who, Graves commented, was only able to keep his place in academia by "methodically sailing all round his dangerous subject, as if charting the coastline of a forbidden island without actually committing himself to a declaration that it existed. What he was saying-not-saying was that Christian legend, dogma and ritual are the refinement of a great body of primitive and even barbarous beliefs, and that almost the only original element in Christianity is the personality of Jesus."[4]

While no one could claim that Graves understood Gnosticism correctly, in each case in *The White Goddess* he shows admiration for the Gnostics. (On page 150, he writes, rather extravagantly, that a particular alphabet was brought to Ireland "in early Christian times, by Alexandrian Gnostics who were the spiritual heirs of the Essenes after Hadrian suppressed the order in 132 AD.") Elsewhere he associates the Gnostics with paganism and with what he sees as Paul's perversion of Christianity. In *King Jesus* the narrator Agabus considers that the Gentile Christians present Jesus "as a Jew of doubtful parentage, a renegade who abrogated the Mosaic Law and, throwing in his lot with the Greek Gnostics, pretended to a sort of Apollonian divinity... [whereas] Jesus was in fact not only royally born but as scrupulous in his observance of the Mosaic Law as any Jew who ever lived..."[5]

An incomplete and fairly early work, the *Autobiography of Baal*, is an unsuccessful satire, an interesting philosophical idea that is overworked. The speaker is God ("I am using, as a matter of literary good manners, not my principal name, which would look a trifle overwhelming on the dust-cover of an octavo volume but a subsidiary and even somewhat invidious one that I have not used for a number of centuries." *But It Still Goes On*, p. 171) He is the author of the Pentateuch and the Koran and the Book of Mormon and Mary Baker Eddy's *Science and Health: With the Key to the Scriptures*. The gist of it is this: though God is the narrator, the concept of God actually originated in the human question "why?" This in turn becomes "how" as formal religion takes over and the why is forgotten. God starts off as a sincere question and ends up as a series of formalised ritual answers. The message is clear: God is a human construct.

His novel *King Jesus* began life as the *Angry Shepherd,* and was for a while known, obliquely, as *The Power of the Dog.* Though a work of fiction, Graves seems to have been convinced (at least at the time) of the veracity of his unconventional ideas about Jesus. Jesus was a genuine claimant to the royal line, the bastard son of Herod Antipater and Miriam/Mary who, in line with the *Protoevangelium of James*, was a temple virgin; not only that but she was an heiress of Michal, the wife of David, and "one of a line of priestesses in whom a divinity is held to be incarnate."

It is certainly not one of Grave' better novels, at least in terms of reader interest, character, dialogue and prose style, and can be tedious. Characters have barely met each other before they launch into convoluted discussions of ancient genealogies and mythography, which are prime examples of the mythic reasoning that makes the White Goddess so fascinating. It is framed as a discursive history written by an Alexandrian pagan Agabus, who approaches the story from a point of view of educated disinterest.

Herod Antipater needs to get a child on Miriam to ensure his legitimacy in the matrilinear line. Jesus, the resulting heir, grows up feeling that he should claim his right to the throne of Israel. He sees himself as a prophet of Jehovah and in his enthusiasm for the masculine God comes to reject the feminine, even though his bloodline depends principally on the female transmission. In turn he also rejects marriage with Mary Cleopas, thereby hoping to defeat death and hopes to see the end of days and establish the kingdom. This anti-female Jesus is drawn from sayings preserved by Clement of Alexandria from the apocryphal *Gospel of the Egyptians*, "When Salome enquired, 'For how long will death have power?' the Lord said, 'As long as you women bear children.'"; and "I have come to destroy the works of the female."

This rejection of the female is his undoing. His crucifixion is the ritual death of a king, attended by the triple goddess in the form of the three Marys: his mother, lover (Mary Cleopas) and layer out (Mary Magdalene or Mary the Hairdresser, the representative of the ancient goddess religion.)

The book draws on Graves' extensive knowledge of the classical world and his research into the apocrypha and polemical Jewish traditions of Jesus such as the *Toledot Yeshu*. Pre-publication, Graves claimed that, "No one who has read it has felt that it is anyway derogatory to the dignity of Jesus."[6] Once published the book had a fairly rough reception, particularly in the USA, and never sold all that well, though it is still in print.

In 1943, when Graves and his family were living in England, having vacated the house in Deya due to WWII, he met Joshua Podro, a Jewish businessman who invented the newspaper clipping agency who was also an amateur Talmudic scholar and historian.

Graves' association with Podro had already led to a more positive portrayal of the Pharisees in *King Jesus* and eventually to an abandonment of the goddess-hating theme. However, their collaborative work, The *Nazerene Gospel Restored* would prove to be just as controversial. Graves would again be gung-ho about the historical reality and reliability of his claims and sales would be even worse than King Jesus.[7] Hyam Maccoby, author of *Paul the Mythmaker* and a controversial scholar himself, felt that the *Nazerene Gospel Restored* was a "mine of insights" that deserved serious though critical attention from mainstream scholars.

The goddess is no longer the hermaneutic key to the story of Jesus. Replacing her is the central importance of rabbinic Judaism and a revival of the Tuebingen theory of F.C. Baur, in which the Jewish religion of Jesus, James and Peter has been hijacked by Paul's new gentile mystery religion. Jesus is still King Jesus, but now of a more conventional first-century messianic apocalyptic type.

Like many modern researchers, Graves wished to separate "the idea of Jesus from the idea of the Man-god-ethics in fact, from myth." adding that there was "a place for both in this world, but not confused together as in the gospels."[8] The Christianity of Paul and the canonical gospels is seen as spiritualised and depoliticised. The gospels have been heavily edited by Syro-Greek gentiles, and Graves and Podro intend to restore the original Nazerene Gospel, so gospel pericopes are modified to be in line with presumed first century rabbinical practice

Graves was a considerable scholar of Greek and Latin and had a voluminous knowledge of ancient literature in the original languages. But he lacked a conventional critical sense. Though he has a sure sense of direction, his method is all throttle and no brake. Graves used "analeptic" thought and creative imaginative inspiration to work the clay of scholarship. His aim was "to stop Jesus writhing endlessly on that cross; to give his spirit rest."

The *Nazerene Gospel Restored* is a weighty volume of over 1000 pages. Like Graves' other work, it is learned yet does not adopt the academic critical method or, some might argue, the self-critical method too. The first section of the book lays out Graves' and Podro's premises, method and view of early Christianity. Part two follows the gospel story in chronological order, giving all of the parallels for each gospel pericope—all four canonical gospels plus a selection of apocryphal gospels such as the *Protoevangelium of James* for the infancy stories, or the Jewish-Christian the *Gospel of the Nazarenes*, the *Gospel of the Ebionites* as and when they are relevant. The parallels are given, then they are discussed, then the supposedly true and original gospel account of the particular episode is reconstructed. Graves' rewriting extended to inventing new dialogue for Jesus, his family and disciples. The third section, which was issued separately as a limited edition, reiterates the complete reconstructed Nazerene Gospel from beginning to end uninterrupted.

According to the authors, "Christianity became a strange compound of laughter-loving Mediterrannean Goddess worship, Gothic sword-worship, Greek speculative philosophy and ascetic Jewish monotheism.[9] Among the odd statements are that Pauline Christianity made an "identification of Jesus with the second person of the Gnostic trinity..."

The original title of the *Nazerene Gospel Restored*, which survived as a chapter title, was "The Hand of Simon Magus," as Graves initially believed that a Samaritan editor had been the principle corruptor of the original gospel. Graves gives us an inventive history of Simon Magus. He sees a bias towards Samaria in the gospels--the Good Samaritan, the Samaritan woman who is an adulterer and the Samaritan leper in Luke xvii:"The early fathers' intense preoccupation with Simon Magus suggests that, before his megalomaniac derangement, he had assisted greatly in the formation of Church doctrine... At first, Simon Magus had been a Samaritan mystic connected with the local cult of the Dove-goddess Astarte... next he became a convert of the Nazerene faith; and then a Pauline, with Gnostic leanings." Thus the spoiling editor of the extant gospels was a Samaritan, and most likely Simon Magus.[10]

Despite his eccentricity, Graves is a rationalist in his interpretation, aiming to make "good historical sense" out it. Graves demanded that the gospels should be sifted and remoulded to make good historical sense. He treats them as problems to be solved intact, as he does with myth in general, and ignores such difficulties as source criticism or academic method.

Graves rejects allegory in the gospels, allows for midrashic reference to the Hebrew Bible, yet sees the miracles as either straightforward faith healings or misunderstood ritual symbolism. After the Annunciation section, comes the Coronation. This is Graves' interpretation of the baptism, John the Baptist reviving Jewish monarchy. "There need be no doubt that Jesus was anointed and crowned king of Israel; but the Gospel editors have done their best to conceal this, for political reasons, even while referring to him as Christ."[11] "At the coronation "Mary of Cleopas will have spread her skirt over Jesus and thus borne him; with Salome a kinswoman, acting as midwife and testifying to her virginity."[12] The famous "Son behold thy mother" is rejected as this would have been an insult to the brothers of Jesus, whose duty it was to provide for their mother. The Feeding of the 5000 was an actual non-miraculous demonstration by Jesus of calendar symbolism. His interpretation of the transformation of water into wine at the marriage in Cana is banal in its simplicity. They ran out of wine and started to drink water pretending it was wine in deference to Jesus who as the messiah was forbidden to taste wine (Prov xxxi,3-5).

Judas realised that Jesus was leading them astray and had Jesus arrested in order to put him into protective custody, but Jesus welcomed this as the preparation for his ritual death in fulfillment of prophecies in Zechariah. In this reconstruction, "Satan entered his soul for he loathed the task that was laid upon him."[13]

Jesus didn't die during the crucifixion, but went into a trance. The angel in the tomb is John the disciple; Jesus is rescued and lives out his life. A separately published epilogue, *Jesus in Rome*, which I have not been able to consult, covered Jesus' post-resurrection life in the Roman capitol.

Graves had no time for metaphysics and blamed Paul for spiritualising Christianity. Graves shows so little interest in a transcendent God or a theistic God or in the search for ultimate meaning that he might almost be counted as an atheist. It is not clear that his much-vaunted goddess is anything more than a personification of the female role in human relations. Or perhaps Graves is a true pagan, seeing true significance only in the natural world and the archetypal relationship of the sexes.[14]

His useful and thorough, and, once again, eccentric classic *The Greek Myths* was followed up by a volume on *The Hebrew Myths*, produced in cooperation with another Jewish scholar Raphael Patai. They plundered the Talmud, midrash, targum, apocrypha and Near-Eastern parallels to bolster the stories of Genesis. Variants from the post-Biblical centuries are used achronically to build up a picture of a genuine Jewish mythology. Patai was a more sober scholar than Graves, but the commentary is, like that of *The Greek Myths*, full of cavalier insight. As with *The Greek myths*, Graves saw a running theme of "the gradual reduction of women from sacred beings to chattels." (*The Hebrew Myths* p.4) Half a dozen references to Gnostic ideas are scattered throughout the commentary, but there is no attempt to include the gnostic variations on the creation myth.

Graves states his admiration for the virgin Mary in "Goddesses and Obosoms," an article also in *Difficult Questions, Easy Answers*. Graves sees the virgin Mary (and also the Queen of England) as an obosom, a word used by West African tribes to designate a woman who has received in part the powers of the goddess. Her emphasises the role of a female figure in providing spiritual comfort,

> ...men and women in real trouble naturally prefer the support of a calm mother to that of a miserably suffering older brother. Women, indeed, have a natural aversion to spectacles of extreme misery caused by man's injustice to man. Few young women in love, especially if they are carrying or nursing a baby, or tending the sick, wish to expose themselves to this commemorative record of male torture, and therefore to a symbolic denial of their own powerlessness in face of male perversity."[15]

Typically, Graves takes his argument too far, "If a sensitive woman ponders too painfully on the seven stations of the Cross she risks souring

her milk, aborting her child and turning her own wits...." It is Graves' stubborn certainty in his insight about these matters that makes his work simultaneously compelling and irritating. He held forth on his views in interviews and lectures. A 1970 interview gives an interesting summary of his view of the shift away from the goddess.

> ... the "White Goddess" is a historical character: the goddess of love and battle, the goddess of life and death, who ruled Europe long before any male gods appeared there. She was a harsh taskmistress and kept her male subjects in very good order, until eventually they broke allegiance after the arrival of our Indo-European ancestors from Central Asia, who were cattle people. Cattle people have gods, not goddesses, for the simple reason that the bull rules a herd, and that the cows count on him for protection. Any challenger for the headship has to meet the horns of the king bull; so also with cattle kings and their challengers. Those cattle people did no planting, but simply drifted from one pasture to the other. The whole fertility mystique in Europe and other parts of the world where nomadic patriarchal herdsmen are not found, is dependent on agriculture. The woman's job is to plant, sow and harvest. She alone has the right touch, is at one with nature and knows exactly what to do. So, when these two opposed cultures mix, there's great confusion at first.
>
> The White Goddess had to keep firm control of men; otherwise they would soon have got out of hand. And she did so for a long time. Few people realise that this same Goddess, under the name of Ashera, was in charge of Jerusalem until long after the earlier books of the Bible had been written; and that she had a temple on the Temple Hill about five times the size of

Jehovah's. And that she took all political decisions herself until she found at last that she could no longer trust men, and decided, 'Very well, let them see how they can manage by themselves.' And so she retreated. She is still always there privately for those who need her, in the person of the Virgin Mary or of the woman whom one adores; but politically she has stepped aside and let men make a mess of things."[16]

In later life Graves was interested in mushroom cults, arguing that the phenomenon of cultural mycophobia (fear or dislike of mushrooms) is a taboo that has its origins in the sacred use of hallucinogen fungi. Like Dead Sea Scrolls scholar John Allegro, he saw the consumption of psychoactive mushrooms as fundamental to the visionary experiences of mystery cults, even attributing the conception of ancient religious paradises with their attendant serpents to the snakelike properties of visual hallucinations. In 1960 he ingested mushrooms and experienced the archetypal paradise for himself. He was less impressed with the more chemical experience of an LSD trip taken in a New York apartment. Until he succumbed to Alzheimer's and became bed-ridden his house in Deya was a magnet for writers, well-wishers and the curious. When my friend the poet and alternative culture figure John Esam, recommended to Deya by the musician Robert Wyatt, first met Graves the older man challenged him to a fistfight. He felt it was a standard ploy.

The roguish Anglo-Afghan sufis Idries Shah and Omar Ali Shah persuaded him to versify a new translation of Omar Khayyam, supposedly from a previously unknown manuscript which, when challenged by scholars, the Shahs were unable to produce. Before his association with Idries Shah he was largely indifferent to Islam, but he became convinced him that a different relationship to woman maybe be possible through the Black Goddess of Sufism.

Graves' ideas on religion are an intriguing

hodgepodge of woman-worship, poetic myth and erudite though erratic scholarship. Jehovah remained a brutish usurper, pushing out the female goddesses who should have been his mother, lover and layer-out. Graves' Jesus began as meek, in *King Jesus* became a woman-hating prophet of the male God, and in the *Nazerene Gospel Restored* reverted to a more straightforward failed political messiah. References to Gnosticism are scattered among Graves' reassessment of Christianity, but he was not well-informed about Gnosticism, somewhat admiring it but seeing it mostly as a religion of pagan origin used to distort the life and message of the historical Jesus. If only Graves had addressed the myth of Sophia, a figure well-suited to his love of the divine feminine. He never did. Sophia as mother of Jehovah-Yaldabaoth; the fall and redemption of the female soul; Barbelo as divine mother; the Gnostic Mary Magdalene, all these would have been grist to the mill for Graves. The lack of what would surely have been a contentious, idiosyncratic, infuriating and thought-provoking examination of these central Gnostic figures is our loss.

NOTES

1 *King Jesus* (Farrer Straus Giroux, 1946), p. 5.
2 *Good-bye to All That: An Autobiography* (Berghan books, 1995) p.19 3 Ibid., p.32
4 *The White Goddess* p.
5 *King Jesus* p. 284.
6 *Robert Graves and the White Goddess* p.97
7 *The Nazerene* [sic] *Gospel Restored* has been out of print since the first and only edition sold out. Caracanet plan to finally reprint it this year in their uniform edition of Graves' works.
8 *Robert Graves and the White Goddess* p.161
9 Ibid. p.xii 10 Ibid. p.31 11 Ibid. p.106
12 Ibid. p.111 13 Ibid. p.970
14 Graves' conclusions (or premises) for the *Nazerene Gospel Restored* are summed up in an essay on the early history of Christianity, "The Bible in Europe," included in *Difficult Questions, Easy Answers*, (Doubleday, 1973).
15 *Difficult Questions, Easy Answers* p.73
16 *Conversations with Robert Graves* (Univ Press of Mississippi, 1989), p.110-111

Excerpts from Theodotus

EXTRACTS FROM THE WORKS OF THEODOTUS AND THE SO-CALLED ORIENTAL TEACHING AT THE TIME OF VALENTINUS

1 "Father," he says, "I deposit into thy hands my spirit." Wisdom, he says, put forth a receptacle of flesh for the Logos, the spiritual seed; clad in it the Saviour descended. Wherefore, at the Passion, it is Wisdom which he deposits with the Father, in order that he may receive her from the Father and not be held back here by those who have the power to deprive him. Thus, by the word already spoken of, he deposits the whole spiritual seed, that is, the elect.

We admit that the elect seed is both a spark kindled by the Logos and a pupil of the eye and a grain of mustard seed and leaven which unites in faith the genera which appear to be divided.

2 But the followers of Valentinus maintain that when the animal body was fashioned a male seed was implanted by the Logos in the elect soul while it was asleep and that this is an effluence of the angelic <seed>, in order that there may be no gap. And this worked as leaven, uniting what seemed to have been divided, soul and flesh, which had also been put forth separately by Wisdom. And Adam's sleep was the soul's forgetting, which restrained from dissolution, . . . just as the spiritual thing which the Saviour inserted into the soul.. The seed was an effluence of the male and angelic <element>. Therefore the Saviour says, "Be saved, thou and thy souL"

3 Therefore when the Saviour came, he awakened the soul and kindled the spark. For the words of the Lord are power. Therefore he said, "Let your light shine before men." And after the Resurrection, by breathing the Spirit on the apostles, he was blowing off and removing dust like ashes, but kindling and giving life to the spark.

4 By reason of great humility the Lord did not appear as an angel but as a man, and when he appeared in glory to the apostles on the Mount he did not do it for his own sake when he showed himself, but for the sake of the Church which is "the elect race," that it might learn his advancement after his departure from the flesh. For on high, too, he was Light and that which was manifest in the flesh and appeared here is not later than that above nor was it curtailed, in that it was translated hither from on high, changing from one place to another, so that this was gain here and loss there. But he was the Omnipresent, and is with the Father, even when here, for he was the Father's Power. And besides, it was necessary that that word also which the Saviour spoke should be fulfilled, "There are some of those standing here who will not taste death until they see the Son of Man in glory." Therefore, Peter and James and John saw and fell asleep.

5 How was it that they were not frightened when they saw the vision of light but fell on the earth when they heard the voice? Because the ears are more sceptical than the eyes and an unexpected voice is more terrifying. But John the Baptist, when he heard the voice, was not afraid, as if

he heard in the spirit, which was accustomed to such a voice. But it was just as any ordinary man on merely hearing would have been frightened; therefore the Saviour said to thern, "Tell no one what you saw." Yet they had not even with eyes of the flesh seen the light (for there is no bond of kinship and relation between that light and the present flesh) but as the power and will of the Saviour enabled the flesh to have vision. Moreover, that which the soul saw it shared with the flesh that companied with it. . .. And "tell no one" was spoken lest any, when they knew what the Lord is, should refrain from laying hands on the Lord and the plan of God be made incomplete and death refrain from the Lord as from a vain attempt on the unapproachable. And, moreover, the voice on the mountain came to the elect who already understood, so that they were also amazed when testimony was given to that which they believed; but the voice at the river was for those who were going to believe. Therefore, too, the voice was disregarded by them, held down as they were to the discipline of the Scribes.

6 The verse, "In the beginning was the Logos and the Logos was with God and the Logos was God" the Valentinians understand thus, for they say that the "beginning" is the "Only Begotten" and that he is also called God, as also in the verses which immediately follow it explains that he is God, for it says, "The Only-Begotten God who is in the bosom of the Father, he has declared him." Now they say that the Logos in the beginning, that is to say in the Only-Begotten, in the Mind and the Truth, indicates the Christ, the Logos and the Life. Wherefore he also appropriately calls God him who is in God, the Mind. "That which came into being in him," the Logos, "was Life," the Companion. Therefore the Lord also says, "I am the Life. "

7 Therefore, the Father, being unknown, wished to be known to the Aeons, and through his own thought, as if he had known himself, he put forth the Only-Begotten, the spirit of Knowledge which is in Knowledge. So he too who came forth from Knowledge, that is, from the Father's Thought, became Knowledge, that is, the Son, because "through' the Son the Father was known." But the Spirit of Love has been mingled with the Spirit of Knowledge, as the Father with the Son, and Thought with Truth, having proceeded from Truth as Knowledge from Thought. And he who remained "Only-Begotten Son in the bosom of the Father" explains Thought to the Aeons through Knowledge, just as if he had also been put forth from his bosom; but him who appeared here, the Apostle no longer calls "Only Begotten," but "as Only-Begotten," "Glory as of an Only-Begotten." This is because being one and the same, Jesus is the "First-Born" in creation, but in the Pleroma is "Only-Begotten." But he is the same, being to each place such as can be contained <in it>. And he who descended is never divided from him who remained. For the Apostle says, "For he who ascended is the same as he who descended." And they call the Creator, the image of the Only-Begotten. Therefore even the works of the image are the same and therefore the Lord, having made the dead whom he raised an image of the spiritual resurrection, raised them not so that their flesh was incorruptible but as if they were going to die again.

8 But we maintain that the essential Logos is God in God, who is also said to be "in the bosom of the Father," continuous, undivided, one God.

"All things were made by him"; things both of the spirit, and of the mind, and of the senses, in accordance with the activity proper to the essential Logos. "This one explained the bosom of the Father," the Saviour and [Isaiah said, "And I will pay back their deeds into their bosom," that is, into their thought, which is in the soul, from which it is first activated] "First-Born of all creation." But the essential Only-Begotten, in accordance with whose continuous power the Saviour acts, is the Light of the Church, which previously was in darkness and ignorance.

"And darkness comprehended him not": the apostates and the rest of men did not know him and death did not detain him.

9 Faith is not single but various. Indeed the Saviour says, "Let it be according to thy faith." Wherefore it is said that some of those of the Calling will be deceived at the coming of the Antichrist. But this would be impossible for the elect. Therefore he says, "And if it were possible, my elect"; again when he says, "Get ye out from my Father's house," he is speaking to those who are called. Again he utters the call to the one who came back from a journey and had consumed his goods, for whom he killed the fatted calf; and where the King called those who were on the highways to the wedding feast. All, therefore, have been called equally, "for he sendeth rain upon the just and on the unjust and maketh the sun to shine upon all," but the elect are those who have superior faith, for he says to them, "No man hath seen my Father except the Son," and "Ye are the light of the world" and "Holy Father, sanctify them in thy name."

10 But not even the world of spirit and of intellect, nor the archangels and the First-Created, no, nor even he himself is shapeless and formless and without figure, and incorporeal; but he also has his own shape and body corresponding to his preeminence over all spiritual beings, as also those who were first created have bodies corresponding to their preeminence over the beings subordinate to them. For, in general, that which has come into being is not unsubstantial, but they have form and body, though unlike the bodies in this world. Those which are here are male and female and differ from each other, but there he who is the Only-Begotten and inherently intellectual has been provided with his own form and with his own nature which is exceedingly pure and sovereign and directly enjoys the power of the Father; and the First-Created even though numerically distinct and susceptible of separate distinction and definition, nevertheless, are shown by the similarity of their state to have unity, equality and similarity. For among the Seven there is neither inferiority nor superiority and no advance is left for them, since they have received perfection from the beginning, at the time of the first creation from God through the Son. And he is said to be "inapproachable Light" as" Only-Begotten," and "First-Born," "the things which eye hath not seen, nor ear heard, and which have not entered into the heart of man,"—and such a one shall not be found either among the First-Created or among men,—but they "always behold the face of the Father" and the face of the Father is the Son, through whom the Father is known. Yet that which sees and is seen cannot be formless or incorporeal. But they see not with an eye of sense, but with the eye of mind, such as the Father provided.

11 When, therefore, the Lord said, "Despise not one of these little ones. Verily, I say .unto you, their angels do always behold the face of the Father," [as is the pattern, such will be the elect,] when they have received the perfect advance." But "blessed are the pure in heart for they shall see God." And how could there be a face of a shapeless being? Indeed the Apostle knows heavenly, beautiful and intellectual bodies. How could different names be given to them, if they were not determined by their shapes, form, and body? "There is one glory of the heavenly, another of the earthly, another of angels, another of archangels, because in comparison with bodies here, like the stars, they are incorporeal and formless, as in comparison with the Son, they are dimensional and sensible bodies; so also is the Son, if compared with the Father, and each one of the spiritual beings has its own power and its own sphere of action just as those who were first created both came into being together, and received completion, their common and undivided service.

12 Therefore the First-Created behold both the Son and each other and the inferior orders of being, as also the archangels behold the First-

Created. But the Son is the beginning of the vision of the Father, being called the "face" of the Father. And the angels, who are intellectual fire and intellectual spirits, have purified natures, but the greatest advance from intellectual fire, completely purified, is intellectual light, "into which things the angels desire to look," as Peter says. Now 'the Son is still purer than this: "light unapproachable" and "a power of God" and, according to the Apostle, "we were redeemed by precious and blameless and spotless blood." And his "garments gleamed as the light, and his face as the sun," which it is not easy even to look at.

13 He is "heavenly bread" and "spiritual food" furnishing life by food and knowledge, "the light of men," that is, of the Church. Therefore those who ate the heavenly bread died, but he who eats the true bread of the Spirit shall not die. The Son is the living bread which was given by the Father to those who wish to eat. "And my flesh is the bread which I will give," he says, that is, to him whose flesh is nourished by the Eucharist; or better still, the flesh is his body, "which is the Church," "heavenly bread," a blessed Assembly. And perhaps just as the elect are essentially derived from the same substance, and as they will also attain the same end. . .

14 The demons are said to be incorporeal, not because they have no bodies (for they have even shape and are, therefore, capable of feeling punishment), but they are said to be incorporeal because, in comparison with the spiritual bodies which are saved, they are a shade. And the angels are bodies; at any rate they are seen. Why even the soul is a body, for the Apostle says, "It is sown a body of soul, it is raised a body of spirit." And how can the souls which are being punished be sensible of it, if they are not bodies? Certainly he says, "Fear him who, after death, is able to cast soul and body into hell." Now that which is visible is not purged by fire, but is dissolved into dust. But, from the story of Lazarus and Dives, the soul is directly shown by its possession of bodily limbs to be a body.

15 "And as we have borne the image of the earthly, we shall bear also the image of the heavenly," that is of the spiritual, as we advance towards perfection. Again he says "image" in the sense of spiritual bodies. And again, "For now we see in a mirror, confusedly, but then face to face"; for immediately we begin to have knowledge. . . there is not even "face"—form and shape and body. Now shape is perceived by shape, and face by face and recognition is made effectual by shapes and substances.

16 Now the Dove also appeared as a body when it made its descent upon the flesh of the Logos —the Dove, which some call the Holy Spirit, but the followers of Basilides call the Servant, while the followers of Valentinus call it the Spirit of the Father's thought.

17 According to the Valentinians, Jesus and the Church and Wisdom are a powerful and complete mixture of bodies. To be sure, human commingling in marriage produces the birth of one child from two commingled seeds and. the body, dissolved into earth, mingles with the earth, and water mingles with wine. And the greater and more excellent bodies are capable of being easily mixed, for example, wind mingles with wind. But to me it seems that this happens by conjunction and not by admixture. Therefore, does not the divine power, immanent in the soul, sanctify it in the final stage of advance? For "God is spirit" and "inspires where he will." For the immanence of the divine power does not affect substance, but power and force; and spirit is conjoined with spirit, as spirit is conjoined with soul.

18 When the Saviour descended, he was seen by the angels and so they proclaimed him. But he was also seen by Abraham and the other righteous men who are in Paradise on his right hand. For he says, "He rejoiced to see my day," that is the advent in the flesh. Wherefore, the risen Lord preached the good tidings to the righteous who are in Paradise, and moved

them and translated them and they shall all "live under his shadow." For the advent here is a shadow of the Saviour's glory which is with the Father, and a shadow of light is not darkness but illumination.

19 "And the Logos became flesh" not only by becoming man at his Advent <on earth>, but also "at the beginning" the essential Logos became a son by circumscription and not in essence. And again he became flesh when he acted through the prophets. And the Saviour is called an offspring of the essential Logos; therefore, "in the beginning was the Logos and the Logos was with God" and "that which came into existence in him was life" and life is the Lord. And when Paul says, "Put on the new man created according to God" it is as if he said, Believe on him who was "created" by God, "according to God," that is, the Logos in God. And "created according to God" can refer to the end of advance which man will reach, as does. . . he rejected the end for which he was created. And in other passages he speaks still more plainly and distinctly: "Who is an image of the invisible God"; then he goes on, "First-Born of all creation." For he calls the Logos of the essential Logos "an image of the invisible God," but "First-Born of all creation." Having been begotten without passion he became the creator and progenitor of all creation and substance, for by him the Father made all things. Wherefore it is also said that he "received the form of a servant," which refers not only to his flesh at the advent, but also to his substance, which he derived from its underlying reality, for substance is a slave, inasmuch as it is passive and subordinate to the active and dominating cause.

20 For we thus understand "I begot thee before the morning star" with reference to the first-created Logos of God and similarly "thy name is before sun" and moon and before all creation.

21 The Valentinians say that the finest emanation of Wisdom is spoken of in "He created them in the image of God, male and female created he them." Now the males from this emanation are the "election," but the females are the "calling" and they call the male beings angelic, and the females themselves, the superior seed. So also, in the case of Adam, the male remained in him but all the female seed was taken from him and became Eve, from whom the females are derived, as the males are from him. Therefore the males are drawn together with the Logos, but the females, becoming men, are united to the angels and pass into the Pleroma. Therefore the woman is said to be changed into a man, and the church hereon earth into angels.

22 And when the Apostle said, "Else what shall they do who are baptised for the dead?" . . . For, he says, the angels of whom we are portions were baptised for us. But we are dead, who are deadened by this existence, but the males are alive who did not participate in this existence.

"If the dead rise not why, then, are we baptised?" Therefore we are raised up "equal to angels," and restored to unity with the males, member for member. 'Now they say "those who are baptised for us, the dead," are the angels who are baptised for us, in order that when we, too, have the Name, we may not be hindered and kept back by the Limit and the Cross from entering the Pleroma. Wherefore, at the laying on of hands they say at the end, "for the angelic redemption" that is, for the one which the angels also have, in order that the person who has received the redemption may, be baptised in the same Name in which his angel had been baptised before him. Now the angels were baptised in the beginning, in the redemption of the Name which descended upon Jesus in the dove and redeemed him. And redemption was necessary even for Jesus, in order that, approaching through Wisdom, he might not be detained by the Notion of the Deficiency in which he was inserted, as Theodotus says.

23 The followers of Valentinus say that Jesus is the Paraclete, because he has come full of the

Aeons, having come forth from the whole. For Christ left behind Sophia, who had put him forth, and going into the Pleroma, asked for help for Sophia, who was left outside; and Jesus was put forth by the good will of the Aeons as a Paraclete for the Aeon which had passed. In the type of the Paraclete, Paul became the Apostle of the Resurrection. Immediately after the Lord's Passion he also was sent to preach. Therefore he preached the Saviour from both points of view: as begotten and passible for the sake of those on the left, because, being able to know him, they are afraid of him in this position, and in spiritual wise from the Holy Spirit and a virgin, as the angels on the right know him. For each one knows the Lord after his own fashion, and not all in the same way. "The Angels of the little ones" that is, of the elect who will be in the same inheritance and perfection, "behold the face of the Father."And perhaps the Face is now the Son, and now as much of that comprehension of the Father as they perceive who have been instructed by the Son. But the rest of the Father is unknown.

24 The Valentinians say that the Spirit which each one of the prophets had adapted to service was poured out upon all those of the Church. Therefore too the signs of the Spirit, healings and prophecies, are fulfilled through the Church. But they do not know that the Paraclete, who now works continuously in the Church, is of the same substance and power as he who worked continuously according to the Old Testament.

25 The followers of Valentinus defined the Angel as a Logos having a message from Him who is. And, using the same terminology, they call the Aeons Logoi.

He says the Apostles were substituted for the twelve signs of the Zodiac, for, as birth is directed by them, so is rebirth by the Apostles.

26 The visible part of Jesus was Wisdom and the Church of the superior seeds and he put it on through the flesh, as Theodotus says; but the invisible part is the Name, which is the Only-Begotten Son. Thus when he says "I am the door," he means that you, who are of the superior seed, shall come up to the boundary where I am. And when he enters in, the seed also enters with him into the Pleroma, brought together and brought in through the door.

27 The priest on entering within the second veil removed the plate at the altar of incense, and entered himself in silence with the Name engraved upon his heart, indicating the laying aside of the body which has become pure like the golden plate and bright through purification. . . the putting away as it were of the soul's body on which was stamped the lustre of piety, by which he was recognized by the Principalities and Powers as, having put on the Name. Now he discards this body, the plate which had become light, within the second veil, that is, in the rational sphere the second complete veil of the universe, at the altar of incense, that is, with the angels who are the ministers of prayers carried aloft. Now the soul, stripped by the power of him who has knowledge, as if it had become a body of the power, passes into the spiritual realm and becomes now truly rational and high priestly, so that it might now be animated, so to speak, directly by the Logos, just as the archangels became the high-priests of the angels, and the First-Created the high-priests of the archangels. But where is there a right judgment of Scripture and doctrine for that soul which has become pure, and where is it granted to see God "face to face"? Thus, having transcended the angelic teaching and the Name taught in Scripture, it comes to the knowledge and comprehension of the facts. It is no longer a bride but has become a Logos and rests with the bridegroom together with the First-Called and First-Created, who are friends by love, sons by instruction and obedience, and brothers by community of origin. So that it belonged to the dispensation to wear the plate and to continue the pursuit of knowledge, but the work of power was that man becomes the bearer of God, being controlled directly by

the Lord and becoming, as it were, his body.

the loss of the Name.

28 The followers of Basilides refer "God visiting the disobedient unto the third and fourth generation" to reincarnations, but the followers of Valentinus maintain that the three places mean those on the left, while the "fourth generation" is their own seed, and "showing mercy unto thousands," refers to those on the right.

29 They say that Silence, who is the mother of all who were put forth by Depth, with regard to what she had nothing to say kept silence about the inexpressible and with regard to what she did not understand she called it incomprehensible.

30 Then forgetting the glory of God,. they impiously say he suffered. For inasmuch as the Father shared in suffering, though he is, says Theodotus, rigid and unyielding in nature, by showing himself yielding, in order that Silence might understand this, it was suffering. For sympathy is the suffering of one for the sake of another's suffering. Moreover when the Passion took place, the whole shared in the same suffering for the recovery of the sufferer.

31 Moreover, if he also who came down was the "good will" of the whole, "for in him was the whole Pleroma bodily," and the Passion was his, it is clear that the seed in him shared also in the Passion, and that through them the "whole" and the "all" are found to be suffering. Moreover through the persuasion of the twelfth Aeon the whole was instructed, as they say, and shared in his Passion.. For then they knew that they are what they are by the grace of the Father, a nameless name, form and knowledge. But the Aeon which wished to grasp that which is beyond knowledge fell into ignorance and formlessness. Whence it effected an abstraction of knowledge which is a shadow of the Name, that is the Son, the form of the Aeons. Thus the distribution of the Name among the Aeons is

32 Therefore though there is unity in the Pleroma, each of the Aeons has its own complement, the syzygia. Therefore, whatever come out of a syzygia are complete in themselves (pleromas) and whatever come out of one are images. So Theodotus called the Christ who oame out of the thought of Wisdom, an "image of the Pleroma." Now he abandoned his mother and asoending into the Pleroma was mixed as if with the whole and thus also with the Paraclete.

33 Indeed Christ became an adopted son as he became "elect" among the completed beings and "First-Born" of things there.

Now this doctrine is a misunderstanding of ours which holds that the Saviour is the first-born from the "underlying reality" and he is, as it were, our root and head, and the Church is his fruits.

They say that when Christ fled that which was foreign to him and was drawn into the Pleroma, after he had been begotten from his mother's thought, the Mother again produced the ruler of the dispensation as a type of him who had deserted her, according to her desire for him, in that he was better, for he was a type of the Father of the universe. Therefore, he was made less, as if he was created from the passion of desire. Indeed in view of his harshness, she was disgusted, as they say.

34 But also the powers on the left hand, which were the first to be put forth by her from those on the right, received no form by the advent of the Light, but those on the left hand remained behind to be formed by Space. So after the entry of the Mother with. the Son and the seeds into the Pleroma, then Space will receive the power of the Mother and the position that the Mother now has.

35 "Jesus our light" "having emptied himself," as

the Apostle says, that is, according to Theodotus; having passed beyond the Boundary, since he was an angel of the Pleroma, led out the angels of the superior seed with him. And he himself had the redemption inasmuch as he had proceeded from the Pleroma, but he led the angels for the correction of the seed. For, inasmuch as they are bound for the sake of the parts, and plead and, being restrained for our sakes in their zeal to enter, they beg remission for us, that we may enter with them. For, since they may almost be said to need us in order to enter, for without us they are not permitted (therefore not even the Mother has entered with them without us, they say), they are obviously bound for our sake.

36 Now they say that our Angels were put forth in unity, and are one, in that they came out from One. Now since we existed in separation, Jesus was baptised that the undivided should be divided until he should unite us with them in the Pleroma that we "the many" having become "one," might all be mingled in in the One which was divided for our sakes.

37 According to the Valentinians, of those who proceeded from Adam, the righteous, making their way through created things, were held in Space, but the others are held among those who are on the left, in the place created for darkness, and feel the fire.

38 A river goes from under the throne of Space and flows into the void of the creation, which is Gehenna, and it is never filled, though the fire flows from the beginning of creation. And Space itself is fiery. Therefore, he says, it has a veil in order that the things may not be destroyed by the sight of it. And only the archangel enters it, and to typify this the high priest every year enters the holy of holies. From thence Jesus was called and sat down with Space, that the spirits might remain and not rise before him, and that he might subdue Space and provide the seed with a passage into the Pleroma.

39 The Mother who brought forth Christ complete, and was abandoned by him, in future no longer brought forth anything complete, but supplied what was possible by herself, so that even of Space. . . . Therefore having produced the angelic elements of the "called" she keeps them by herself, for the angelic elements of the elect had been put forth still earlier by the Male.

40 Now those on the right were put forth by the Mother before the demand for the Light but the seeds of the Church after the demand for the Light, when the angelic elements of the seed had been put forth by the Male.

41 The superior seeds, he says, came forth neither as passions, the seeds of which would have perished when they perished, nor as a creation, but as offspring; since otherwise, when creation was being put together, the seeds would have been put together with it. Therefore, also it has an affinity with the Light, that is Jesus, whom the Christ, who besought the Aeons, first put forth.

And in him the seeds were refined, as far as possible, as they went with him into the Pleroma. Therefore the Church is properly said to have been chosen before the foundation of the world. Indeed, they say, we were reckoned together and manifested in the beginning. Therefore the Saviour says, "Let your light shine," referring to the light which appeared and gave form, of which the Apostle says "which lighteth every man that cometh into .the world," that is, every man of the superior seed. For when man was enlightened, then he came into the world, that is, he ordered himself and put off the passions which were darkening him and were mingled with him. And the Creator who had held Adam beforehand in his Notion, put him forth at the end of creation.

42 The Cross is a sign of the Limit in the Pleroma, for it divides the unfaithful from the faithful as that divides the world from the Pleroma.

Therefore Jesus by that sign carries the Seed on his shoulders and leads them into the Pleroma. For Jesus is called the shoulders of the seed and Christ is the head. Wherefore it is said, "He who takes not up his cross and follows me is not my brother." Therefore he took the body of Jesus, which is of the same substance as the Church.

43 So they say that those on the right knew the names of Jesus and Christ even before the Advent, but they did not know the power of the sign. And when the Spirit gave all power, and the Pleroma united in praise, he is sent forth, "as the angel of the counsel" and becomes the head of the whole after the Father. "For all things were created by him, things visible and invisible, thrones, dominions, kingdoms, divinities, services." "So God also exalted him and gave him a name which is above every name that every knee should bow and every tongue confess that Jesus Christ, the Saviour, is the Lord of Glory." "He who ascended also descended. That he ascended, what does it imply but that he descended? He it is who descended into the lower parts of the earth and ascended above the heavens."

44 When Wisdom. beheld him she recognized that he was similar to the Light who had deserted her, and she ran to him and rejoiced and worshipped and, beholding the male angels who were sent out with him, she was abashed and put on a veil. Through this mystery Paul commands the women "to wear power on their heads on account of the angels."

45 Straightway, therefore, the Saviour bestowed on her a form that was according to knowledge and a healing of passions, exhibiting the contents of the Pleroma and stages of emanation down to her own, from the unbegotten Father. And, having taken away the passions of her who had suffered, he made her impassible, and, having separated the passions, he kept them and they were not distinguished as from those within, but he brought into being both them and the elements of the second rank. Thus through the appearance of the Saviour, Wisdom came into being and the elements without were created. "For all things were made by him and without him was not anything made."

46 First, therefore, he drew these things from immaterial passion and chance and transformed them into matter still incorporeal, then in a similar manner into compound substance and bodies. For it was not possible for passion to be brought into being by a single process and he endowed the bodies with properties suitable to their nature.

47 Now the Saviour became the first universal creator. "But Wisdom," the second, "built a house for herself and hewed out seven pillars" and first of all she put forth a god, the image of the Father, and through him she made heaven and earth, that is "heavenly things, and the earthly"—the things on the right hand and on the left. This, as an image of the Father, then became a father and put forth first the psychic Christ, an image of the Son, then the archangels as images of the Aeons, then the angels of the archangels from the psychic and luminous substance to which the prophetic word refers, "And the Spirit of God was superimposed upon the waters," declaring that in the combination of the two substances, made for him, the simple was superimposed but the heavy and material substance is borne under, the thick and coarse. But it is even suggested that this was incorporeal in the beginning when it is called "invisible." Yet it was never invisible to any man that ever lived nor to God, for he made it. But he has somehow declared its absence of form, shape and design.

48 Now the Creator divided the refined element from the coarse, since he perceived the nature of each, and made light, that is, he revealed and brought it to light and form, for he made the light of sun and heaven much later. And of the material elements he made one out of grief, which gives substance to the "spiritual things of

evil with whom is our contest" (and therefore the Apostle says, "And do not grieve the Holy Spirit of God, by whom ye were sealed"), and another he made from fear, the wild beasts, and another from terror and need, the elements of the world. And in the three elements fire drifts about and is disseminated and lurks, and is kindled by them and dies with them, for it has' no appointed place of its own like the other elements from which the compound substances are fashioned.

49 And since he did not know her who acted through him and thought he created by his own power, for he was naturally fond of work, therefore the Apostle said: "He was subject unto the vanity of the world, not willingly, but by reason of him who subjected it, in hope that it also will be set free," when the seeds of God shall be assembled. And a special proof of his unwillingness is his blessing the Sabbath and the warm welcome he gave to rest from labour.

50 "Taking dust from the earth": not of the land but a portion of matter but of varied constitution and colour, he fashioned a soul, earthly and material, irrational and consubstantial with that of the beasts. This is the man "according to the image." But the man who is "according to the likeness" of the Creator himself, is he whom he has breathed into and inseminated into the former, placing in him by angels something consubstantial with himself. Inasmuch as he is invisible and immaterial, he called his substance" the breath of life," but that which was given form became a "living soul," and he himself confesses that it is so in the prophetic writings.

51 Therefore man is in man, "psychic" in "earthly," not consisting as part to part but united as whole to whole by God's unspeakable power. Therefore he was created in Paradise in the fourth heaven. For there earthly flesh does not ascend but it was to the divine soul as material flesh. This is the meaning of "This is now bone of my bones,"—he hints at the divine soul which is hidden in the flesh, firm and hard to suffer and very potent,—and "flesh of my flesh"—the material soul which is the body of the divine soul. Concerning these two also, the Saviour says, "That is to be feared which can destroy this soul and this body, the psychic one, in hell."

52 This body the Saviour called an "adversary" and Paul said a "law warring against the law of my mind" and the Saviour advises us "to bind it" and to "seize its possessions" as those of "a strong man" who was warring against the heavenly soul, and he also advises us to be "reconciled with him on the way lest we fall into prison" and punishment, and similarly to "be kind to it" and not to nourish 'and strengthen it by the power of sin but to put it to death here and now, and manifest it as extinct in the domain of wickedness in order that at its dissolution it may secretly be separated and breathed away, but not gain any existence of its own, and so have power by itself in its passage through the fire.

53 This is called a "tare" which grows up with the soul, the good seed, and is also a seed of the devil, since it is consubstantial with him, and a "snake" and a "biter of the heel" and a "robber" attacking the head of a king. And Adam without his knowledge had the spiritual seed sown in his soul by Wisdom. He says, "Established through angels by the hand of a mediator. And the mediator is not of one but God is one." Therefore the seeds put forth into "becoming" by Wisdom are ministered to so far as they can come to being by the male angels. For just as the Demiurge, moved by Wisdom without his knowledge, thinks that he is a free agent, so also do men. So Wisdom first put forth a spiritual seed which was in Adam that it might be "the bone," the reasonable and heavenly soul which is not empty but full of spiritual marrow.

54 From Adam three natures were begotten. The first was the irrational, which was Cain's, the second the rational and just, which was Abel's, the third the spiritual, which was Seth's. Now that

which is earthly is "according to the image," that which is psychical according to the "likeness" of God, and that which is spiritual is according to the real nature; and with reference to these three, without the other children of Adam, it .was said, "This is the book of the generation of men." And because Seth was spiritual he neither tends flocks nor tills the soil but produces a child, as spiritual things do. And him, who "hoped to call upon the name of the Lord" who looked upward and whose "citizenship is in heaven"—him the world does not contain.

55 On Adam, over the three immaterial elements, a fourth, "the earthly," is put on as "the leathern garments." Therefore Adam neither sows from the spirit nor, therefore, from that which was breathed into him, for both are divine and both are put forth through. him but not by him. But his material nature is active toward seed and generation, as though mixed with seed and unable to stand apart from the same harmony in life.

56 Therefore our father Adam is "the first man of the earth, earthy" and if he had sown from psychic and spiritual as well as from material substance, all would have become equal and righteous and the Teaching would have been in all. Therefore many are material, but not many are psychic, and few are spiritual. Now the spiritual is saved by nature, but the psychic has free-will, and has the capacity for both faith and incorruptibility, as well as for unbelief and corruption according to its own choice; but the material perishes by nature. When, therefore, the psychic "are engrafted on the olive tree" into faith and incorruptibility and share "the fatness of the olive tree" and when "the Gentiles come in," then "thus shall all Israel." But Israel is an allegory, the spiritual man who will see God, the unlawful son of the faithful Abraham, he who was born of free woman, not he who was according to the flesh the son of the Egyptian bondwoman.

57 Therefore from the three species a formation

of the spiritual element happens to one and a change of the psychic from slavery to freedom happens to the other.

58 Then after the Kingdom of Death, which had made a great and fair promise, but had none the less become a ministry of death, Jesus Christ the great Champion, when every principality and divinity had refused, received unto himself by an act of power the Church, that is, the elect and the called, one (the spiritual) from the Mother, the other (the psychic) by the Dispensation; and he saved and bore aloft what he had received and through them what was consubstantial. For "if the first fruits be holy, the lump will be also; if the root be holy, then will also the shoots."   .

59 First, then, he put on a seed from the Mother, not being separated but containing it by power, and it is given form little by little through knowledge. And when he came into Space Jesus found Christ, whom it was foretold that he would put on, whom the Prophets and the Law announced as an image of the Saviour. But even this psychic Christ whom he put on, was invisible, and it was necessary for him when he came into the world to be seen here, to be held, to be a citizen, and to hold on to a sensible body. A body, therefore, was spun for him out of invisible psychic substance, and arrived in the world of sense with power from a divine preparation.

60 Therefore, "Holy Spirit shall come upon thee" refers to the formation of the Lord's body, "and a Power of the Most High shall overshadow thee" indicates the formation of God with which he imprinted the body in the Virgin.

61 That he was other than what he received is clear from what he professes, "I am the Life, I am the Truth, I and the Father are one." But the spiritual nature, which he received, and the psychic he thus indicates, "And the child grew and advanced greatly." For the spiritual nature

needs wisdom but the psychic needs size. But by the flowing out from his side he indicates that the substances having become free from passion have been saved by the flowings out of the passions from those who shared in them. And when he says "The Son of Man must be rejected and insulted and crucified," he seems to be speaking of someone else, that is, of him who has passion. And he says, "On the third of the days I will go before you into Galilee." For he goes before all and indicated that he will raise up the soul which is being invisibly saved and will restore it to the place where he is now leading the way. And he died at the .departure of the Spirit which had descended upon him in the Jordan, not that it became separate but was withdrawn in order that death might also operate on him, since how did the body die when life was present in him? For in that way death would have prevailed over the Saviour himself, which is absurd. But death was out-generalled by guile. For when the body died and death seized it, the Saviour sent forth the ray of power which had come upon him and destroyed death and raised up the mortal body which had put off passion. In this way, therefore, the psychic elements are raised and are saved, but the spiritual natures which believe receive a salvation superior to theirs, having received their souls as "wedding garments."

62 Now the psychic Christ sits on the right hand of the Creator, as David says, "Sit thou on my right hand "and so on. And he sits there until the end "that they may see him whom they pierced." But they pierced the appearance, which is the flesh of the psychic one, "for," it says, "a bone of him shall not be broken," just as in the case of Adam the prophecy used bone as an allegory for the soul. For the actual soul of Christ deposited itself in the Father's hands, while the body was suffering. But the spiritual nature referred to as "bone" is not yet deposited but he keeps it.

63 Now the repose of the spiritual elements on the Lord's Day, that is, in the Ogdoad, which is called the Lord's Day, is with the Mother, who keeps their souls, the (wedding) garments, until the end; but the other faithful souls are with the Creator, but at the end they also go up in the Ogdoad Then comes the marriage feast, common to all who are saved, until all are equal and know each other.

64 Henceforth the spiritual elements having put off their souls, together with the Mother who leads the bridegroom, also lead bridegrooms, their angels, and pass into the bride chamber within the Limit and attain to the vision of the Father,—having become intellectual Aeons,— in the intellectual and eternal marriages of the Syzyge.

65 And the "master" of the feast, who is the "best man." of the marriage, "and friend of the bridegroom, standing before the bride chamber and hearing the voice of the bridegroom, rejoices greatly." This is "the fulness of his joy" and his repose.

66 The Saviour taught the Apostles at first figuratively and mystically, later in parables and riddles, and thirdly clearly and openly when they were alone.

67 "When we were in the flesh" the Apostle says, as if he were already speaking without the body. Now he says that he means by flesh that weakness which was an offshoot of the Woman on high. And when the Saviour says to Salome that death will reign as long as women bear, he does not speak in reproach of birth since it is necessary for the salvation of the believers. For this birth must be until the previously reckoned seed be put forth. But he is alluding to the Woman on high whose passions became creation when she put forth those beings that were without form. On her account the Saviour came down to drag us out from passion and to adopt us to himself.

68 For as long as we were children of the female only, as if of a base intercourse, incomplete and infants and senseless and weak and without form, brought forth like abortions, we were children of the woman, but when we have received form from the Saviour, we have become children of a husband and a bride chamber.

69 Fate is a union of many opposing forces and they are invisible and unseen, guiding the course of the stars and governing through them., For as each of them arrived, borne round by the movement of the world, it obtained power over those who were born at that very moment, as though they were its own children.

70 Therefore through the fixed stars and the planets, the invisible powers holding sway over them direct and watch over births. But the stars themselves do nothing but display the activity of the dominant powers, just as the flight of the birds (for omens) indicates something but effects nothing.

71 Now the twelve signs of the Zodiac and the seven stars which follow them rising now in conjunction, now in opposition, . . . these, moved by the powers, show the movement of substance toward the creation of living beings and the turn of circumstances. But both the stars and the powers are of different kinds: some are beneficent, some maleficent, some right, some left, and that which is born shares in both qualities. And each of them comes into being at its own time, the dominant sign fulfilling the course of nature, partly at the beginning, partly at the end.

72 From this situation and battle of the powers the Lord rescues us and supplies peace from the array of powers and angels, in which some are arrayed for us and others .against us. For some are like soldiers fighting on our side as servants of God but others are like brigands. For the evil one girded himself, not taking the sword by the side of the king, but in madly plundering for himself.

73 Now because of the opponents who attack the soul through the body and outward things and pledge it to slavery; the ones on the right are not sufficient to follow and rescue and guard us. For their providential power is not perfect like the Good Shepherd's but each one is like a mercenary who sees the wolf coming and flees and is not zealous to give up his life for his own sheep. And besides man, over whom the battle rages, since he is a weak animal, is easily led toward the worse and captured by those who hate him. Whence also he incurs greater evil.

74 Therefore the Lord came down bringing the peace which is from heaven to those on earth, as the Apostle says, "Peace on the earth and glory in the heights." Therefore a strange and new star arose doing away with the old astral decree, shining with a new unearthly light, which revolved on a new path of salvation, as the Lord himself, men's guide, who came down to earth to transfer from Fate to his providence those who believed in Christ.

75 They say that the results prophecied show that Fate exists for the others and the consideration of calculations is a clear proof. For example, the Magi not only saw the Lord's star but they recognized the truth that a king was born and whose king he was, namely of the pious. At that time only the Jews were noted for piety; therefore the Saviour going down to the pious, came first to these who at that time were carrying fame for piety.

76 As, therefore, the birth of the Saviour released us from "becoming" and from Fate, so also his baptism rescued us from fire, and his Passion rescued, us from passion in order that we might in all things follow him. For he who was baptised unto God advanced toward God and has received "power to walk upon scorpions and

snakes," the evil powers. And he commands the disciples "When ye go about, preach and them that believe baptise in the name of the Father, and of the Son and of the Holy Spirit," in whom we are born again, becoming higher than all the other powers.

77 Therefore baptism is called death and an end of the old life when we take leave of the evil principalities, but it is also called life according to Christ, of which he is sole Lord. But the power of the transformation of him who is baptised does not concern the body but the soul, for he who comes up <out of the water> is unchanged. From the moment when he comes up from baptism he is called a servant of God even by the unclean spirits and they now "tremble" at him whom shortly before they obsessed.

78 Until baptism, they say, Fate is real, but after it the astrologists are no longer right. But it is not only the washing that is liberating, but the knowledge of who we were, and what we have become, where we were or where we were placed, whither we hasten, from what we are redeemed, what birth is and what rebirth.

79 So long, then, they say, as the seed is yet unformed, it is the offspring of the female, but when it was formed, it was changed to a man and becomes a son of the bridegroom. It is no longer weak and subject to the cosmic forces, both visible and invisible, but having been made masculine, it becomes a male fruit.

80 He whom the Mother generates is led into death and into the world, but he whom Christ regenerates is transferred to life into the Ogdoad. And they: die to the world but live to God, that death may be loosed by death and corruption by resurrection. For he who has been sealed by Father, Son and Holy Spirit is beyond the threats of every other power and by the three Names has been released from the whole triad of corruption. "Having borne the image of the earthly, it then bears the image of the heavenly."

81 The material element of fire lays hold of all material things, and the pure and immaterial element lays hold of immaterial things such as demons, angels of evil and tbe devil himself. Thus the heavenly fire is dual in its nature, belonging partly to the mind, partly to the senses. By analogy, therefore, baptism. is also dual in its nature, the sensible part works through water which extinguishes the sensible' fire, but the intellectual through Spirit, a defence against the intellectual fire. And the material Spirit when it is little becomes food and kindling for the sensible fire, but when it has increased it has become an extinguisher, but the Spirit given us from above, since it is immaterial, rules not only over the Elements, but over the Powers and the evil Principalities.

82 And the bread and the oil are sanctified by the power of the Name, and they are not the same as they appeared to be when they were received, but they have been transformed by power into spiritual power. Thus, the water, also, both in exorcism and baptism, not only keeps off evil, but gives sanctification as well

83 It is fitting to go to baptism with joy, but, since unclean spirits often go down into the water with some and these spirits following and gaining the seal together with the candidate become impossible to cure for the future, fear is joined with joy, in order that only he who is pure may go down to the water.

84 Therefore let there be fastings, supplications, prayers, raising of hands, kneelings because a soul is being saved from the world and from the "mouth of lions." Wherefore there is immediate temptation for those. who long also for the things from which they have been separated, and even if one has fore-knowledge to endure them, yet the outward man is shaken.

85 Even the Lord after baptism was troubled like as we are and was first with beasts in the desert. Then when he had prevailed over them and their ruler as if already a true king, he was already served by angels. For he who ruled over. angels in the flesh was fittingly served already by angels. Therefore we must put on the Lord's armour and keep body and soul invulnerable—armour that is "able to quench the darts of the devil," as the Apostle says.

86 In the case of the coin that was brought to him, the Lord did not say whose property is it, but, "whose image and superscription? Caesar's," that it might be given to him whose it is. So likewise the faithful; he has the name of God through Christ as a superscription and the Spirit as an image. And dumb animals show by a seal whose property each is, and .are claimed from the seal. Thus also the faithful soul receives the seal of truth and bears about the "marks of Christ." These are the children who are now resting in bed and "the wise virgins," with whom the others, who are late, did not enter into "the goods which have been prepared, on which the angels desire to gaze."

NOTES

This was transferred into electronic format by Andrew Criddle, hosted on the Internet by Stephen Carlson at http://www.hypotyposeis. org/papers/theodotus.htm and included in *The Gnostic* with the agreement of Andrew Criddle. His notes on the source follow.

This is the English text of the Greek-English version of the *Excerpta Ex Theodoto* prepared by the late Robert Pierce Casey. It was published in 1934 as No. 1 in the Studies and Documents series, under the Editorship of Kirsopp and Silva Lake. American copyright was not renewed in the 1960's and it appears to be now out of USA copyright.

It is a collection of notes made by Clement of Alexandria mainly dealing with the teachings of the Valentinian Theodotus, but also covering other Valentinian and orthodox speculations.

It has not previously been available online. The online text called "Extracts from Theodotus" is a quite separate work by Clement of Alexandria, more accurately known as "Selections from the Prophetic Scriptures" or "Prophetic Eclogues."

Jeremy Puma

Perfect Day Living: Life as a Contemporary Gnostic
The Temple and the Bridal Chamber

God never really asked for a Temple to be built in his name. Really, it's right there in 2 Samuel 7. King David (a real jerk, by the bye) has a palace built of cedar for himself (which was a pretty huge deal: a King in a Palace in a City– what a change from a tent and rule by Judges!), and gets it in his mind that God needs a house, too. Essentially, he wants to "civilize" God by constructing a Temple. God isn't terribly amused:

Are you the one to build me a house to dwell in? I have not dwelt in a house from the day I brought the Israelites up out of Egypt to this day. I have been moving from place to place with a tent as my dwelling. Wherever I have moved with all the Israelites, did I ever say to any of their rulers whom I commanded to shepherd my people Israel, "Why have you not built me a house of cedar?" (2 Sam. 7:5-7)

God's basically saying, "look, you expect me to live in this big building? I'm EVERYWHERE!" Still, this isn't good enough for David. Alas, the good king comes to a (well-earned– read the stories) ignominious end, and the desire for a Temple passes along to his son Solomon.

It's interesting, what's happening during this part of the story. See, here's the thing: during the time, every god had a temple in which he or she lived. Every pagan deity and his or her brother had a massive stone edifice in which to put up his or her feet. Solomon's temple was really nothing special for the era; indeed, compared to other similar structures in Egypt and Mesopotamia, it was pretty much par for the course. Until this point, God had been a God of the desert, not a God of civilization. By constructing a "house" for God, David and Solomon essentially civilized Him, reduced Him to the stature of a local God instead of the God of and In Everything.

God, however, changes his mind once Solomon finishes the construction of the First Temple. It helps that Solomon issues a rather cloying plea at the Temple's dedication, acknowledging (unlike his father) that God is too big to contain in a building:

But will God really dwell on earth?

The heavens, even the highest heaven, cannot contain you. How much less this temple I have built! Yet give attention to your servant's prayer and his plea for mercy, O LORD my God. Hear the cry and the prayer that your servant is praying in your presence this day. May your eyes be open toward this temple night and day, this place of which you said, 'My Name shall be there,' so that you will hear the prayer your servant prays toward this place. Hear the supplication of your servant and of your people Israel when they pray toward this place. Hear from heaven, your dwelling place, and when you hear, forgive. (2 Chron. 6: 18-21)

God agrees, declaring he'll dwell in the Temple as long as Solomon and his people "walk before me in integrity of heart and uprightness." He agrees to become "civilized," so long as His people agree to obey his Law, and to refrain from the worship of other Gods (a promise that Solomon breaks almost immediately by building additional temples to Pagan deities a few years later).

So what's with the Temple, anyhow? First of all, it was a massive complex with a series of courtyards and a number of different gates. Access to the various areas in the Temple were dependent upon varying proscriptions (i.e. sacrificants here, women here, foreigners here), but what concerns us is the actual dwelling place of God, the Holy of Holies. The most important part of the Temple, surrounded by this entire complex, was a room about the size of a closet which contained (until its mysterious disappearance) the Ark of the Covenant. This room was entered once a year, on Yom Kippur, and could only be entered by the High Priests.

Now, this dwelling place of God, including the Holy of Holies, was twice destroyed by empires. Solomon's Temple came to an end when the Babylonians invaded, but not before the entire complex fell into terrible disrepair. The post-Solomonic kings of Jerusalem were a mixed lot, but more than a few took insane liberties with the Temple, bringing in pagan altars, looting the golden decorations, etc. By the time of the Babylonian Exile, the Temple had lost much of its essential meaning.

The Second Temple was essentially a massive renovation of the remains of the First, undertaken by King Herod (only marginally worse than David). Herod unabashedly intended the Second Temple to impress foreigners, most notably the Romans, to whom he especially kowtowed by erecting a massive golden eagle over the Temple gates (when a pair of Zealots tore the eagle down, he had them burned alive). This is, of course, the Temple into which Jesus marched and turned over the tables of the merchants. After studying the history of the Temple a bit, we have to wonder whether the merchants were really the cause for his ire, or if he was protesting the desecration of the Temple

that started about ten years after the First one was constructed by Solomon. Jesus, you see, not only kicks the merchants out of the Temple, but declares that he intends to destroy the Temple in such a way that it can never be rebuilt!

We find Jesus promising to destroy the Temple in all of the Canonical Gospels, and the *Gospel of Thomas*, so it seems fairly likely he actually said it. Of course, in Mark's Gospel he is said to have claimed, "I will destroy this man-made temple and in three days will build another, not made by man," and in Thomas he says, "I will destroy this house, and nobody will be able to rebuild it."

It seems to me that in calling for the destruction of the Temple, Jesus is accomplishing two things. To begin, he's returning to the original protest against the Temple by God himself, when David originally came up with the idea. God didn't think it was the best idea, as He couldn't be contained in a stone building. Still, Solomon went ahead with it, and as God predicted, the Temple was a drastically failed experiment. Jesus is telling us, "look, this Temple is nice and all, and if God lives here, it doesn't deserve to be desecrated by moneylenders and merchants. But listen: you don't need it. There's a spiritual Temple that's far nicer."

For Gnostics, the correlative can be found in the *Gospel of Philip*:

At the present time, we have the manifest things of creation. We say, "The strong who are held in high regard are great people. And the weak who are despised are the obscure." Contrast the manifest things of truth: they are weak and despised, while the hidden things are strong and held in high regard. The mysteries of truth are revealed, though in type and image. The bridal chamber, however, remains hidden. It is the Holy in the Holy. The veil at first concealed how God controlled the creation, but when the veil is rent and the things inside are revealed, this house will be left desolate, or rather will be destroyed.

The Temple itself is representative of the "manifest things of Creation." As we know, the Temple, surrounded by a "veil," contains the Holy of Holies. The Temple, as a giant, magnificent stone building located in beautiful downtown Jerusalem, means absolutely nothing without the Holy of Holies contained therein. The "veil" represents the veil of illusion that covers the World of Forms, and the Holy of Holies is the spirit within the body, the Pleroma and fullness of God within the individual and the world.

According to Judaic Law, only the High Priest was ever allowed to enter the Holy of Holies, and only on certain days. What Jesus wants to do, however, in destroying the "Temple," is to remove this veil and make the essence within available to all seekers on every day, not just those who are somehow better because they are priests. Of course, instead of thinking of this as "Jesus wants to do away with the High Priest and Holy Days," the Gnostic might think of it instead as "Jesus wants to make everyone High Priests and every day Holy." Jesus wants everyone to realize that the external appearance of the Temple, and thus the world and the body are nothing compared to what exists within. In doing so, he destroys the Temple, meaning he destroys the illusion of strength presented by the insane delusions of the Universe. By telling us that he wants to destroy this house, Jesus refers not to some kind of physical destruction, but an end to the false power structures that prevent each and every one of us from entering our own Holy of Holies.

Essentially, Jesus is telling the people that God doesn't need a house or a structure, nor is access to Him restricted to certain people or certain days of the year. It's always available, any time. As soon as the house is built, it becomes subject to the imperfection of the World of Forms. Even those with the most noble intentions– like King Solomon– cannot succeed when attempting to limit God to a particular segment of space and time.

Now then, where am I going with all of this? Believe it or not, I'm continuing the eternal discussion Gnostics like to have on definition versus inspiration. When discussing Gnosticism, how much definition is too much? When do the lines become so defined that instead of a religion, we have a fundamentalism? And yet, how can we explain our spirituality in a way that allows it its own context and keeps it from becoming a meaningless abstraction?

It strikes me that what we have here might be a false dichotomy, a conflation of the exoteric and esoteric. In modern Gnostic circles, the canonical scriptures are generally considered exoteric, designed to teach us about Law, morality, ethics, interaction with the physical world in which we live. The Gnostic scriptures, however, are considered esoteric teachings, teachings concerning the inner life, mystical experience, etc. For much of modern history, these two different approaches to religion have seemed at odds to many interested in spirituality and religion. The overused—and elitist—trope is that the exoteric teachings were for the masses, the esoteric for the initiated few, that the exoteric teachings (the Temple) contained the esoteric teachings (the Holy of Holies), which in turn contained God.

In essence, let's think of the exoteric teachings as the temple compound, the courtyards, etc. Let's think of the esoteric teachings as the Inner Sanctum, the Holy of Holies. If the exoteric teachings surround, or house the esoteric teachings, then only a few individuals can access the inner life, and average individuals are restricted to the courtyard. As God only dwells in the Holy of Holies, only those who have access to the esoteric teachings have access to God.

According to Jesus, this misses the point, and, here's why: God cannot be contained. Jesus knew his scriptures, especially the parts about King David. He would have known that the very first time David came up with the idea of a temple, God told him it was a bad idea. Instead of esoteric teachings contained in exoteric proscription–

the Holy of Holies contained within the Temple, Jesus says that both the exoteric and esoteric house God, and are accessible to everyone. In addition, the Temple as a physical building, as the House of God, exists within the world of forms and is therefore imperfect, and always has been.

Just as God dwells in the wilderness, not in the Temple, God dwells in both the exoteric and the esoteric, the inner and the outer (as Jesus says, when you make the outside like the inside, the Kingdom will be yours). The two are not at odds; according to Jesus, all of the teachings of God are available to everyone. Jesus, for this reason, was a great spiritual equalizer in his own right, and intended with this analogy to do for his spiritually segmented culture what the Buddha tried to do for the Hindu caste system.

In my opinion, this false dichotomy between the esoteric and exoteric is responsible for the contention we find when discussing whether Gnosticism can be defined by its scripture (the Nag Hammadi library, etc.). Using Gnostic Scripture to define modern Gnosticism is a dangerous game. God cannot be contained in scripture, just as He cannot be contained in a Temple. God needs no houses built to contain him.

However, we need both the exoteric and the esoteric, the canonical books that made it into the Bible, the apocryphal books that did not (The Acts of Thomas, The Acts of John, etc.)– these are as much our legacy as the Nag Hammadi library. They are our Temple Complex. But, we get more. The Nag Hammadi Scriptures, the esoteric teachings, these are our Holy of Holies, our inner teachings. We can't have one without the other. We're not a rebellion against the canonical tales of Jesus, we're a supplement. And, as many modern scholars are now concluding, the creation myths found in the Nag Hammadi collection aren't meant to replace the canonical texts, but to comment on them.

To summarize up to this point: to God, the Temple was completely unnecessary. He told King David he preferred camping out in a tent, after all. He's the God of everything– why would he need the same kind of building as the other Gods of the area? Consider this idea the "Holy of Holies" of this discussion. My post, until this point, focuses on the esoteric. Let's go a little exo- and hopefully where I'm coming from will be a bit clearer.

Now, we know the Temple was no biggie to God, but what did the Temple mean exoterically? What did it mean to the Jewish people? Let's remember that even though God was originally not too keen on the Temple, he did agree to hang out there as long as the people kept their promise to him to live with integrity and uprightness. The Temple became an exceptionally powerful symbol for Judaism, so powerful that when Jesus did threaten its metaphorical destruction, it was tantamount to terrible blasphemy.

After the destruction of the Second Temple by the Romans, the Jewish people were forbidden from the Old City of Jerusalem, and would gather to mourn the loss of the Temple on the Mount of Olives. It wasn't until the Turks conquered Jerusalem in the Sixteenth Century that the Jewish people were allowed by them to return to the Temple complex and mourn the Temple's destruction at the Western Wall. The Temple hasn't existed in almost two thousand years, except as a symbol of the Jewish people, a reminder of God's presence on Earth and in Jewish Culture. Just because God cannot be contained within the Temple, doesn't mean that He's not there anyhow. But this is what it's all about: Culture.

No, God cannot be contained, that's the esoteric part of the story. But, the exoteric part of the story is that God Dwells Among Us In Our Culture. Indeed, the Temple has been transformed into a Spiritual Temple that can no longer be destroyed by humans, and with this marriage of the eso- and exoteric, God has indeed come to dwell within the Holy of Holies symbolized by the Temple, for generations of Jews, and likely for their descendants.

This is the place scripture can have in

Gnosticism. We know God doesn't literally dwell within the Nag Hammadi library. We know scripture cannot define us, any more than a physical building can define a people. Gnostic scripture, however, can provide all contemporary Gnostics with an underlying sense of culture.

How do those of us who see ourselves as Gnostic establish an identity, especially in light of the evidence that the "Gnostics" never existed as a monolithic group per se? What can we use as this Temple that doesn't house God, but helps us remember that He is contained in everything, that the Holy of Holies is available to everyone? Do we say gnosis? Gnosis is our aim and goal, but it's rather abstract to use to establish a cultural identity. We also need to take into consideration the fact that Gnosticism isn't just for people who have experienced gnosis, it's also for those who are interested in cultivating the experience but haven't yet.

So, what do we have? Right now, we have the Nag Hammadi scriptures. Above and beyond anything else, above and beyond the tradition of Apostolic succession, to which many of us do not ascribe, above and beyond abstractions and lineages and various sacramental forms, we have these amazing and inspirational scriptures that give us an identity which transcends Gnostic "flavors" in the same way that the Temple, as a symbol, transcends the various branches of Judaism. They are what we can return to, what we can rebuild, and what can help us relate to one another in spite of our different approaches. It's true, they were only discovered recently within the context of Gnostic history, but that's an even better reason to use them as a starting point.

Take them literally? Never—God is not restricted to the Temple. Remember them as a legacy of our culture? Absolutely. Our culture is a desert culture, but one which has infiltrated our cities and become urban. It is a wild culture in which God is everywhere, a culture of outsiders that has seen persecution. It has lain fallow, housing living information from a number of different traditions, syncretic, sacramental.

And, it was rediscovered and revivified in the Modern Era and is evolving at an unprecedented rate. It's all there in the Nag Hammadi library–the history of these documents is the history of Gnosticism itself. It's ours, and nobody can take it from us.

That's the exoteric story, just as full of God as the mystical.

Reginald Freeman

A Reader Response to Jeremy Puma's
Perfect Day Living column,
'Keeping Gnosticism Real' in The Gnostic 2:

Firstly, I must state how much I enjoy Jeremy Puma's writings, and that I find his column, Perfect Day Living, to be a refreshingly honest and sober approach to modern Gnosticism. When I read his point-of-view material, I find myself nodding along, saying to myself, "Yeah, exactly," the vast majority of the time. But this response would not be very interesting, or in any way necessary, if I merely went through his column point by point, heaping praise upon each sentiment that I too share. Rather, I will go through and offer an additional perspective on certain of his topics that I think are not as clear-cut as he has made them out to seem.

The first statement that I would like to consider is: "The Gnostics were dogmatic." There are two issues to be addressed here. The first issue concerns who, exactly, is being referred to by "the Gnostics." The second issue regards what is meant by "dogmatic." Mr. Puma had already established (rightly) that "There was no monolithic Gnosticism," and that the whole of Christendom, Gnostics included, was "fragmented." But let us, for the moment, set aside the question of who "the Gnostics" were, and examine what is meant by "dogmatic." I think it is important to differentiate between "dogma" and "doctrine." A doctrine is a teaching or principle that is held to be true. And I think there is little doubt that the Gnostic writings are filled with various doctrines concerning the nature of God, Man, the Universe, and how they relate to one another. A dogma, though, is a belief that *must* be accepted and adhered to. Now, I will not say that there is absolutely no dogma in Gnosticism. For instance, there must

be the acceptance of the foundational principle of salvific knowledge, or the designation of "Gnostic" becomes utterly meaningless. But the Gnostic writings in general seem to be more concerned with examining and changing how one views the nature of reality, than dictating dogmatic commandments. That is, the Gnostic doctrines teach one *how* to think instead of *what* to think. I see this as being the over-arching message of Christ and the New Covenant. The Old Law was concerned with dogmatic decrees of imperfect legislation. The Christian theology (and more especially the Gnostic) offers liberation from the fetters of the Law precisely because it is *not* dogmatic. Rather, its doctrines advocate a radically different way of processing information. This is why St. Paul tells us that, "All things are lawful to me, but not all things are beneficial." (1 Cor. 6:12) How could all things be lawful under the demiurgic dogmatism? In other words, the demiurgic Law may contain some sound doctrines, but a dogmatic adherence to the Law may lead to errors greater than those which the Law intended to suppress in the first place. But through the saving grace that we call "gnosis," we may elevate our Soul, that is, our awareness, into the realm of Spirit, wherein any given situation may be seen clearly, thus enabling us to act Wisely because of a perfect Understanding, rather than out of blind obedience required by authoritarian dogma.

Now, Puma states that the "Gnostics were just as dogmatic as the average mainstream Christian sect of the time." I could take this in a couple of ways. If this statement refers to the Western Church, as represented by the likes of Irenaeus, then I would have the same argument as posited above, that Gnosticism was not dogmatic in that way. If, however, we look at the early Eastern Church, we see more nuanced theological debates that do not really seem to have been grasped by the West. In any case, I don't know if any early Christian sect could really be identified as either "average" or "mainstream," unless we are talking about sects that were similar to what would be considered "mainstream" today. But let me move on to the next point.

My next argument concerns Puma's seeming denial of pre-Christian Gnosticism. In order to properly make my points, I will quote the brief paragraph in whole:

"There is virtually no solid evidence for a pre-Christian Gnosticism. This has been proven again and again, but is one of the biggest sticking points. This isn't to say that there absolutely was not a pre-Christian Gnosticism, but literally no evidence exists that this is the case."

The very wording of the above statements, with its logical inconsistencies, seems to raise more doubt about those statements' veracity than it does to convince. His argument begins that "There is virtually no solid evidence." According to the American Heritage Dictionary of the English Language, Fourth Edition, the word "virtually" means "nearly" or "almost but not quite." In other words, what this statement is actually saying is that there is very little solid evidence. Whether or not that is the intention, that is nevertheless what it says. Now, the second sentence begins, "This has been proven again and again..." It is difficult for me to understand what exactly has been proven here. If we are to take the first sentence literally, that little evidence exists, then to draw upon proof of that evidence would seem to be antithetical to the argument as a whole (which seems to be, in spite of its logical fallacies, that there was likely no pre-Christian Gnosticism). If, however, we are to understand that it has been proven that no evidence exists, then the statement is equally problematic. A lack of evidence does not constitute proof of the contrary. And likewise, one cannot "prove"

there to be a lack of evidence. One can make the statement, "there is no evidence," and even use that statement as a premise in an argument. But some sort of evidence is required to formulate a "proof" of any kind. Now, the last sentence states that "literally no evidence exists." This flatly contradicts the first sentence of the paragraph. There cannot (leaving aside quantum physics for the moment) simultaneously be "virtually no... evidence," and "literally no evidence." There is either some or none.

It may seem that I am being overly critical of the semantics of this argument. But logical consistency and semantic clarity should be of the utmost importance in an article that admonishes against the errors of the uncritical. Now, if I am interpreting the context of these statements correctly, then Puma's main argument goes something like this:

The probability of a pre-Christian Gnosticism should be supported by some sort of evidence. Little or no evidence exists. Therefore, there is little or no support for the probability of a pre-Christian Gnosticism.

My structural criticism is not actually my main argument here, but it was necessary to first define terms and identify what exactly was being posited here. My real concern is with a much broader question: How do we define Gnosticism? This question has been debated among both scholars and self-proclaimed Gnostics. There does not yet seem to be a consensus within either group. The scholars have differing criteria, one to the next, of what qualities or characteristics a given group or writing must have to be considered Gnostic; some preferring to discard the term altogether. And the modern Gnostic practitioners are as diverse today as in antiquity. If we define Gnosticism as a specifically Christian movement, then there can be, by definition, no pre-Christian Gnosticism.

If we define as Gnostic only those ancient sects that self-identified as "Gnostic" then we are left with very little. In this case, perhaps only the Mandaeans would qualify, and they are not

Christian at all. Is it then, only those groups who were indiscriminately labeled as "Gnostic" by the heresiologists? Ironically, this last definition may bring us closer to an acceptable answer. That is, if it were not for the heresiologists, we very well may not be using the term "Gnostic" to describe a particular religious philosophy, except maybe that of Clement of Alexandria.

I agree wholeheartedly that Gnosticism cannot mean merely whatever one wishes it to mean. Otherwise, the term becomes completely meaningless. Puma has already established that there was no "monolithic Gnosticism." Therefore, what we refer to as Gnosticism must necessarily describe a number of different doctrines and sets of practices. This view is certainly corroborated by an examination of the Nag Hammadi texts. This diversity which exists among the texts as variations on Gnostic mythology, exegesis, and specific practices, also supports my earlier refutation of dogmatism within these groups. But getting back to our search for the evidence of a pre-Christian Gnosticism, let us look at the philosophic elements that make up the diverse collection of doctrines we call "Gnosticism." In Christian Gnostic texts, the Christian mythos largely serves as a framework to support a combination of Hermeticism, Platonism, Pythagoreanism, and apocalyptic Judaism. So I guess the real question is: Is it only Gnosticism when we bring these elements together? Or does each of these doctrines represent a Gnosticism of its own? I want to quote here the definition of Gnosticism as given in the American Heritage Dictionary:

The doctrines of certain pre-Christian pagan, Jewish, and early Christian sects that valued the revealed knowledge of God and of the origin and end of the human race as a means to attain redemption for the spiritual element in humans and that distinguished the demiurge from the unknowable Divine Being.

I think that this definition represents a sober and reasonable approach to the problem. So if we use this definition as a basis for establishing criteria for what is "Gnostic," then we can certainly find evidence for a pre-Christian Gnosticism; especially in the Hermetic and Platonic doctrines that advocate for a "revealed knowledge of God and of the origin and end of the human race," and that "distinguished the demiurge from the unknowable Divine Being." Not only that, but even within the Christian Gnostic texts, there exists literary evidence of an existing Jewish Gnosticism that had been Christianized. So, in short, I think we have ample evidence for a pre-Christian Gnosticism.

In addition to my comments on dogmatism and the possibility of a pre-Christian Gnosticism, I have one final issue to address. As I was reading this article, I found myself grinning and chuckling a little about the "UFO cultishness of Samael Aon (sic) Weor," and "the moronic pseudo-gnosticism of Sylvia Browne." Then, of course, we come to Doinel's "motley crew" and "historically inaccurate descriptions of channeled Cathar Bishops." Being a spiritual descendant myself of Doinel's Gnostic Church (through episcopal consecration), I could not help but to feel a pang of discomfort. My grin slowly melted into a grimace as I contemplated my treasured spiritual heritage being reduced to New Age buffoonery. My first thought was, "How can he say that!?" "How dare he say that!" I mean, it's one thing to point out the foolishness of those other guys. But he can't talk about *my* tradition like that...right? Well, truth be told, Doinel may have not been the most stable of spiritual leaders. I do have an argument to make in defense of the modern Gnostic traditions that have descended from Doinel's Eglise Gnostique, but I will not attempt to whitewash its history, or try to portray it as something it is not.

To begin with, Jules Doinel does not seem to have been the most well-grounded individual. After having his spiritual visions and establishing his church, he then abdicates the Gnostic Patriarchate and embraces Roman Catholicism. He is later re-admitted into the Gnostic Church, but may have actually left the church once again before he died. The mystical visions and personal flightiness of Doinel may lead one to think of him as a bit of a flake. And this supposition seems perfectly reasonable to me. But do his imperfections invalidate the traditions that have descended from his church? For that matter, does the historical inaccuracy of his visions invalidate the usefulness of those visions? I'm afraid that if we are going to judge the usefulness and validity of a tradition according to its historical accuracy, then we are going to have to throw out pretty much the whole of ancient Gnosticism. We will actually have to discard Christianity altogether. Since it is impossible to reconcile the myriad inconsistencies among the canonical scriptures, and since we cannot possibly know which, if any, of the accounts are factual, shall we dismiss the tradition completely? Of course not. In this sense, I think it could be argued that myth does in fact trump history. The strength of Christian Gnosticism, or even orthodox Christianity, is in the power and efficacy of its mythology, symbolism, and sacramental ritual, not its strict historical veracity. Now, does this mean that factual history should be disregarded, or that a vision should be held to a higher academic standard than recorded history? This is certainly not true either. But we must understand that the practitioner and the scholar, while at times may be one and the same person, have different gauges of valuing the worth of a Gnostic doctrine, writing, or practice. So, while it is unwise for the Gnostic practitioner to insist that mythology represents a literal, historical truth, it is perfectly natural for him to find a transcendent Truth in that same myth that is not dependent upon an historical validation. I think Mr. Puma is saying as much here, but I wanted to emphasize this point because of his apparent ridicule of Doinel's historically inaccurate visions.

I think that the real value of Doinel's church can be seen in the personalities it attracted, and in its sphere of influence, which has touched nearly every major branch of the Western Mystery Tradition. If we look at the formative years of the Eglise Gnostique, we find many occult luminaries among the ranks of the Gnostic Episcopate. One such luminary was that venerable docteur of the occult (and actual medical doctor as well!), Gerard Encausse, better known as Papus. In addition to Papus, we find nearly half of the Supreme Council of l'Ordre Martiniste among the first bishops of the French Gnostic Church. It appears that by 1893, the Church had some formal relationship with the Martinist Order. This is significant in that it now had established a link with the tradition derived from the renowned 18th century Christian mystical philosopher Louis Claude de Saint-Martin (known as Le Philosophe Inconnu, or the Unknown Philosopher), and his spiritual mentor Martinez de Pasqually, founder of a peculiar theurgic order, l'Ordre des Chevalier Macons Elus-Cohen de l'Univers (Order of Knights Masons, Elect Priests of the Universe), which was established throughout France, and into which Saint-Martin had been initiated.

From a purely exoteric view, the French Gnostic Church seems to consist of a series of schisms, the original church lasting no more than about five years or so. But spiritually we must look at these divisions as branches extending from a tree. The various administrative differences, and even doctrinal differences, have led to wonderfully varied expressions of the modern Gnostic tradition. So rather than a weakness, I see this as a strength of the Church, that she has been able to produce so many worthy offspring. Its worthiness may also be seen in that it quickly ceased to be an exclusively French phenomenon, extending throughout Europe, the U.K., and the Americas. As early as 1899 we can find the tradition in the Americas. In this year, the Haitian Lucien-Francois Jean-Maine (who is said to have been an Elus-Cohen initiate from Temples established by Pasqually in Haiti, which is where Pasqually died in 1774) is consecrated by Tau Synesius (Leonce-Eugene Joseph Fabre des Essarts), Doinel's successor, as well as by Paul Pierre de Marraga, which brings the succession of Bernard Raymond Fabré-Palaprat's Johannite Church, which in spite of its contrived Templar lineage, seems to have had a separate valid Apostolic Succession from the Roman Catholic Church. By 1908, Theodore Reuss (institutor of the Ordo Templi Orientis) had received episcopal consecration by Papus. Arnoldo Krumm-Heller later brings a version of the Church to South America. These are just a few of the individuals who were directly involved with some branch of the Church. We could go on for pages listing all of the peripheral figures involved, which would include nearly everyone associated with Martinism, Rosicrucianism, and esoteric Freemasonry. My point is that while it may seem easy to make a mockery out of Doinel and his "motley crew," I think it is clear that the fruits of his efforts have proved the worthiness of the vine.

Having said all of this, I must repeat my earlier sentiment that I am in agreement with Puma's statements on most topics, and with his call to historical honesty and academic responsibility. I do not see, however, the dogmatism that he claims to find in Gnostic literature. The fact that there are *doctrines* present within the texts, does not necessarily suggest the authoritarianism characteristic of *dogma*. In regards to pre-Christian Gnosticism, this is a difficult issue to address because of the lack of a universally accepted definition of Gnosticism. But if we look at the core principles of the Christian Gnostics, we can see echoes of the Hermeticism that emerged in Hellenized Egypt in the 3rd to 2nd century BC, as well as apocalyptic Judaism and Pythagoreanism, both having roots even earlier in the 6th century BC. And finally, in the matter of the struggle between myth and historical accuracy, I agree with the author as regards not misrepresenting fact. Myth and symbol should never be mistaken for literal fact, any more than they should be mistaken for the ineffable principles they represent. These are the great fallacies of fundamentalism. But whether to place a greater value on either myth or history depends greatly upon what type of truth one is seeking. For the academic researcher, factual data is of utmost importance,

as is putting that data into the proper historical context. But for the Gnostic seeking Truth in the sense of a transcendental awareness, or a path of initiation that liberates the consciousness from the dictates of the temporal passions, myth and symbol are the working tools with which one navigates the uncharted landscape of the human soul. Thankfully, one does not have to make that terrible choice of placing one over the other. I merely want to emphasize that dismissing mythology or revelatory visions because they are not historically accurate can be just as detrimental to the modern Gnostic traditions as ignoring the factual history of ancient Gnosticism; especially considering that factual history consists largely of mythology and revelatory visions.

Andrew Phillip Smith

Into the Bridal Chamber: 1, 2, 3...

In the beginning there was only unity, the true God, the Father, the One. But the Father wanted to know himself or make an image of himself, and as a result the aeons were emanated and the Pleroma came into existence. Note that we now have two things, God and the Pleroma, God and his image, though they still form a connected unity. But then at the edge of the pleroma, the last of the aeons illegitimately tried to know the Father, or to explore beyond the Pleroma, and we have the Fall. (As an aside, if God wanted to know himself and emanated out, is it any surprise that Sophia did the same? Was Sophia's transgression a natural result of God's own activity? Surely, if the implications of God's first act are carried through, the current situation of mankind is a direct result of God's action.)

Then we have the birth or abortion of a second God, the demiurge, and a world outside the Pleroma. Are there now two gods? Well, not really. In what way is the demiurge a God in comparison to the true God? Is this a duality? He may consider himself to be the true God, and humanity at large might be deceived by him and take him to be the true God, but in actuality he is no God. From the point of view of humanity, there is a dualism and a choice; for the pleroma it is merely an unfortunate accident. To a certain extent. The Pleroma has been ruptured, and there is now an intelligent, though limited, force outside the Pleroma. But there is no influence of the demiurge and the created world on the Pleroma. Sophia, or in some versions, the lower Sophia, is trapped outside the Pleroma.

G.I. Gurdjieff introduced a complex and beautiful cosmology in which the universe is structured according to two cosmic laws, the law of three and the law of seven. The law of seven or law of octaves uses the western major scale, with its seven stages and semitone intervals between Mi and Fa, the third and fourth notes and Si and Do, the seventh and eighth notes, the latter of which is the reaffirmation of the first note on a higher level, with twice the number of vibrations, to describe the development of a process, the discontinuity between Mi and Fa and Si and Do meaning that processes would deviate without additional 'shocks' at those points to keep them on track. The law of three specifies that any new arising or phenomenon needs three aspects. Gurdjieff termed these Holy Affirming, Holy Denying and Holy Reconciling, or the active, passive and neutralising forces. His pupil J.G. Bennett, drawing on hints given by Gurdjieff in a talk recorded by P.D. Ouspensky, realised that all of the whole numbers could be used to describe systems, and described the characteristics of systems with one term, two terms, three, four terms and on up to 12 terms and then many-term systems.

Dualism is a system with two terms. But where there is only light and dark, or spirit and matter, nothing happens. Only opposition is possible. It is only when there is some mixing or relation that the story truly begins. This can be seen clearly in the absolute or radical dualism of the Manichaeans. Light and dark are coexistent. It is in fact the darkness that takes the initiative, invading the light and mixing with it. The earth and humanity, through a variety of stages, emerge as a method of separating the light from the darkness and liberating the imprisoned light so that it can return, via the transmitting apparatus of the Milky Way, to the kingdom of light. The earth and humanity are a third term that introduces action, dynamism and transformation into the universe. There is clearly a difference between this evolving situation and the original coeternal dualism of two competing powers. In absolute dualism there are two principles contending with each other from the beginning. In moderate or mitigated or monarchian dualism the second principle appears later. The other distinctions are whether the dualism is temporary, i.e. light will eventually win and the darkness disappear, and whether the physical world and matter are seen as a good creation (cosmic) or an evil creation (anti-cosmic).

As we have seen, the situation is not so simple in what is usually designated the moderate, mitigated or temporary dualism of the Sethians and Valentinians. In the cut-down myths of the Exegesis on the Soul and the Authoritative Discourse, there is a clear choice between two influences: remain in the misery of an attachment to the body and matter or return to the Father. The options available are very dualistic. However, there are three elements in the story: the Pleroma, the soul and the material world.

According to Yuri Storyanov, author of *The Other God,* the definitive modern work on dualism, true dualism requires both principles being involved in cosmogony and anthropogony, the creation of the world and mankind. Without the mixing of these influences in humanity, nothing happens. In the *Hypostasis of the Rulers*, Adam remains inert on the ground until endowed with spirit.

Perhaps duality only arises with the creation of humanity. According to some texts, humanity is created by the demiurge (the soul) and his archons (the body). The aeons take advantage of this to endow humanity with spirit, a spark of light from the Pleroma. Do we now have a duality? No, we have a trichotomy, a tripartite division of humanity into body, soul and spirit. We have three things, not two.

Without the human drama there is no progress and no relationship. No dualism that insists on "an impermeable divide between good and evil, light and dark" (to refer to a claim in a recent article for a popular audience by Bruce Chilton, http://www.bibleinterp.com/opeds/chilton5357919.shtml.) If that was the case there could be no story: light and dark would be in opposition and that would be the end of it. In the absolute dualism of the Manichaeans the whole point of the existence of the world and humanity is that light and dark are mixed and the world is a transforming apparatus to separate the light from the darkness and return it to its source.

Sophia and the soul mirror each other. The fall of Sophia is a grander version of the descent of the soul. Sophia is trapped in matter and Sophia, like the soul, which typifies humanity, is a mediating force.

What we call dualism is actually a three-term system. There is the spiritual and the material, or the light and the dark, and then there is the human creation mediating between the two. Without the mediation or the mixing there is no story. Without the story there is no role for humanity. Without humanity there is no one to tell the story, no one to develop the myth, and without the myth there is no dualism.

Book Reviews

Planetary Types: The Science of Celestial Influence, Tony Cartledge, Foreword by A.T. Mann, Bardic Press, 248 pp, $19.95, £11.95.

When I began my study of astrology over forty years ago, I sought an answer to the most basic question of all: "How does it work?" The whole edifice seemed to rest on the most insubstantial of foundations. The influence of the sun and moon upon terrestrial life was obvious and demonstrable, but planetary "influence" was another matter altogether. How could these bodies – much smaller than the sun, much further away from us than the moon – possibly affect us? What occult rays did they emit that were able to determine the character and destiny of a human being? I remember hearing Patrick Moore the BBC's astronomer saying that the midwife's gravitational pull upon the newborn child was stronger than that of any of the planets, and this fact, he said, should put paid to the preposterous theories of the astrological charlatans. And yet, not only did astrology postulate the existence of such planetary influences, it even ascribed influences to non-substantial entities like the zodiac, the moon's nodes and certain angular distances between planets. Some astrologers, alert to the problems associated with planetary influence, opted to explain things in less physical terms. The doyen of 20th century astrology, Dane Rudhyar, for example, described astrology as "the algebra of life," and many offered the vague suggestion that "symbolism" or Jungian synchronicity could somehow account for the phenomena.

These foundational problems are addressed by Tony Cartledge in this intriguing book, and his conclusions are quite astonishing and eminently plausible: it's not a matter of "influence" or of "symbolism" but of "resonance". The "harmony of the spheres" of Pythagoras and later of Kepler is not just poetic metaphor: the universe sings its song, and the resonances of the individual planetary notes are picked up by the ultra-sensitive glandular system of the new-born child.

However, Cartledge is no apologist for astrology, which, he says, has failed every scientific test it has been subjected to. Instead, following the lead of the redoubtable French investigator, Michel Gauguelin, whose work he describes in some detail, Cartledge rejects most of the astrological tradition – including the zodiac and the astrological houses – but hangs on to the ancient theory of "planetary types" which, he says, has been proved statistically by Gauguelin's exhaustive work with thousands of accurately timed births. What is more, says Cartledge, numerous attempts by sceptics to undermine Gauguelin's conclusions have been in vain: it would indeed seem that "martial" people tend to be born when the planet Mars is either rising in the east or culminating directly overhead, and the same applies to the saturnine, the jovial and the rest.

Cartledge then goes on to describe these planetary types, detailing their physical and psychological characteristics and illustrating them with photographs and planetary data of numerous celebrities. This is the most enjoyable part of the book, and I now find myself almost obsessively categorising my friends, acquaintances and television personalities according to Cartlege's scheme! I am undoubtedly a Jupiterean. In my natal chart, Jupiter is close to the ascendant and making square (90 degree) aspects to four planets and the midheaven. Consequently, I am "intelligent, creative, discriminating.... flamboyant, gregarious and entertaining" as well as "vain and self important!" I am also completely bald, which, says Cartledge, is almost a defining characteristic of the male Jupiterean. He deals similarly with martial, mercurial, saturnine, venereal, solar and lunar types, along with sub categories such as Jupiter/Moon, Saturn/Mars.

This book is no coffee-table astrological primer. It is a serious attempt to establish the foundations of SCI, the Science of Celestial Influence, free from the restrictions imposed by what the author sees as the debilitating weight of unscientific astrological tradition, and from the prejudices of the scientific community which rejects *a priori* all talk of correspondence between celestial and terrestrial phenomena. It describes the work of Pythagoras, Kepler, Gurdjieff, Ouspensky, Rodney Collin, and Percy Seymour, and it examines musical theory and the physiology of the human glandular system in some depth. The author is scrupulously fair. He acknowledges the inadequacies of his own attempts at putting his ideas to statistical tests, and even anticipates the objections that members of the scientific community might bring against his theories. He's not trying to pull the wool over anyone's eyes, or to sidestep criticism; he's simply trying to find what is worth salvaging from what he considers the confused jumble of unscientific ideas which comprise contemporary astrology.

I found some parts of the book heavy going. The chapters on musical theory and on glandular structures found me skimming a little, and I would have liked a comprehensive appendix giving the birth data (date, time, place) of all the celebrities mentioned in the book, so that I could check Cartledge's findings for myself. But these are minor complaints. The book is well researched, well written, honest, enlightening and entertaining. It is beautifully produced, well illustrated and comprehensively indexed. I strongly recommend it.

Bill Darlison

The Power of Coincidence: The Mysterious Role of Synchronicity in Shaping Our Lives, **Frank Joseph, Arcturus Books, 208pp, £9.99.**

Chiefly a writer on ancient history and aviation, Frank Joseph became fascinated with coincidence, began to record his own synchronicities and to interview one hundred people from disparate backgrounds on their own experiences. All but three of the one hundred felt that meaningful coincidences had played an important part in their own lives.

This book is filled with anecdotes, stories of meaningful coincidences of various strengths and degrees of likelihood. Joseph divides coincidences into 17 categories—for example, precognition, dreams, guidance, telepathy, parallel lives, warnings, etc.—and goes on to elaborate these in separate chapters, with many enjoyable examples from his own life, from his interviewees and historical anecdotes. These categories overlap considerably with each other, as Joseph admits, and I found them to be too diffuse to have much explanatory power. The entire book may be said to suffer from the same problem: it illustrates but doesn't explain.

Still, this is justified somewhat by the author's approach. He considers that, while synchronicities should be analysed and pondered, this should be done on the event's own terms. We should seek to understand the symbolism implicit in the coincidence, relate its meaning to our own lives, and feel the awe and wonder that goes along with strange synchronicities. The author feels that intepreting coincidences and acting on them can make you more successful, give a greater sense of wholeness in your life and even offer a key "to unlock the reality of spiritual existence."

While this is surely an oversimplification, and it reminds me of a book by Deepak Chopra, *Synchrodestiny*, which claimed that the only two signs of enlightenment were that you stop worrying and experience more synchronicities (surely he left out the third and most important sign of enlightenment, that you make lots more money) I do agree with the author that there is certainly a deep satisfaction in recognising coincidences and that acting on them and understanding them can lead to an invigorating and meaningful life. Whether you feel that the source of coincidence is hidden dimensions, the web of the universe, authoritarian divinities or merely the pattern-finding capacity of the human mind surely has some bearing on the experience. Also there is no attempt to weed out the less meaningful coincidences that will occur by chance alone. Karl LeMarks has illustrated these with his Kangaroo Paradox. Listen out for the word "kangaroo" for the next week. You'll come across the word more often than you expect.

Despite the lack of useful analysis or perceptive theory, *The Power of Coincidence* made me more aware of synchronicty and convinced of its importance, and a book that can achieve this is worth reading.

Andrew Phillip Smith

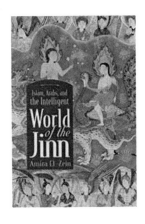

Islam, Arabs and the Intelligent World of the Jinn,

Amira El-Zein, Syracuse University Press, 215pp, $39.95/£35.50.

Amira El-Zein has unquestionably produced the definitive book on the Jinn. Meticulously researched and extremely well written, this tome is truly one for the ages. This study is long overdue in the realms of Islamic and paranormal studies as most works in this field are either scanty or possess a somewhat embarrassed tone concerning this integral part of Muslim theology . El-Zein covers the essential elements of who and what the Jinn are in the spiritual and literary dimensions of Arabic civilization..

Jinn are far more complex beings than are depicted in popular culture or even academic examinations. The author's pithy introduction is a pleasure for both the novice and the expert because it clearly outlines the religious themes and historical framework of these metaphysical beings. The proceeding chapters cover such Jinn related topics as magic, possession, divination, diseases, curses, shape-shifting, romance and even poetic inspiration! On top of this World of the Jinn is by far the best study of Islamic cosmology in the English language. It is the Muslim parallel to C.S. Lewis's Christian classic *The Discarded Image* and cogently expresses the Koranic world-view in an erudite yet reader friendly style.

I highly recommend this marvelous journey into the historical and mystical realm of the Jinn!

William H. Kennedy

Sacred Space, Sacred Sound, Susan Elizabeth Hale, Quest Books, 286pp $23.95/£23.

It's an unusual concept. After all, one doesn't primarily associate stone age monuments and Egyptian temples with their sounds. Cathedrals, with their echoing spaces and choirs, yes, but not abandoned ancient monuments. The obvious difference is that the human component has disappeared from the more ancient sites and they are no longer living sacred spaces. Celebrants have been replaces by tourists, and the occasional pagan revivalist. The author, a music therapist and sound healer, rediscovers the acoustic possibilities of these sites through the simple joy of singing once again in these places. For her, sound has pleasure, meaning and significance in itself, and luckily she is able to translate her aural experience into the silent medium of words on a page.

This is a book based on wide-ranging experience. Haler has charmed her way into many ancient sites which are inaccessible to the ordinary tourist. The variety of her friends and acquaintances is as dizzying as the range of sacred spaces she has sung in. She knows, and sings with, Freemasons, native American Catholics, Scottish seers, Tibetan Buddhists from New Mexico, Anglican choristers, and Egyptologist John Anthony West. She sings or hums in Lascaux (the original cave, not the tourist replica), Newgrange, Rosslyn Chapel, Chartres Cathedral, Avebury and Stonehenge, in American national parks, in Egyptian temples and pyramids.

Each chapter focuses on a specific site, or type of site, relates her experience and any other anecdotes that come to mind, and draws in a good amount of standard historical information plus stimulating speculation and alternative history theories. Importantly, she relates her impressions of the acoustic properties of each of these sites.

Despite giving the impression of being very slightly ditzy occasionally (only very, very, very slightly and only occasionally), Hale is an honest reporter of her experience. For example, to her chagrin she finds the Newgrange burial mound in Ireland to be acoustically dead. She is refused permission to conduct an acoustic experiment there (i.e., singing in the chamber). Yet she is straightforward here about her lack of success and her optimism is not dampened. She even has a chapter on "Desecration", discussing the ways in which the sites have been mistreated over the centuries and the obnoxious and insensitive reactions of tourists (and, yes, all of us are tourists when we visit these places.) Another, "Dissonance" looks at the noise of modern human life, but she is too much of an optimist to end there, and in the final couple of chapters she looks at the possibilities of new forms of sacred sound architecture, and even creates a Cretan labyrinth of her own.

This is a charming book.

Andrew Phillip Smith

The Deeper Secret: What Does Life Want From You?, Annemarie Postma,

Watkins Publishing, 230 pp, £12.99

Whenever I come across a book such as this, I'm reminded of the comment made many years ago by British comedian Alexei Sayle: "There are these women with row after row of self-help books on their shelves, and they're still fucking barmy!"

But Alexei was being a little unkind—and terribly male! No doubt these books are sold mainly to women, and mainly to women who are dissatisfied with their lot. No doubt, too, this particular book has been published in an attempt to capitalise on the phenomenal success of *The Secret* by Rhoda Byrne—same shape volume, same look, same quality paper, same feel. However, despite the female focus and the cynical marketing, *The Deeper Secret* is quite surprising. It's reasonably well written, with plenty of interesting personal anecdotes which help to illustrate the author's argument. What's more, there's no implied guarantee that love, riches and success will attend the reader who puts its principles into practice. Just the opposite: Annemarie Postma promises nothing. She explains that simply "wishing," even "wishing fervently," even "believing in your heart that you will get what you want," (which seem to be the techniques recommended by *The Secret*), are not enough to transform one's life, and in employing them one is really only setting oneself up for disappointment and failure. While agreeing with Rhoda Byrne *et al* that a "law of attraction" exists in the universe, Postma says that much more than wishing is required in order to make it work to our advantage. The book outlines what that "more" is.

The reader, says Postma, has to be aware that there are Twelve Laws of Creation. Law 1, for example, is *Release your Will*. By this she means, "instead of imposing your will on reality to get what you want, learn to want what appears.... .... You don't get what you want; you get what you need for your inner growth." She reminds the reader that sometimes, with hindsight, one can be very grateful that one didn't get what one wished for. Other laws include, Law 3: *Know why you want what you want*; and Law 11: *Give what you want to receive*. Analysis of this latter "law" constitutes one of the book's most interesting chapters, and provides a useful corrective to those who, inspired by *The Secret*, feel that the universe exists simply to satisfy our selfish desires.

Each chapter explores one of these twelve laws, and is followed by a summary, some suggestions for putting the law into practice, and an "affirmation" which encapsulates the chapter's basic idea. The book concludes with a meditation in which the reader is encouraged to "focus on whatever constructive goal" he or she has chosen.

This is a much more realistic, and a much more sensible book than *The Secret*, probably because its author is no stranger to adversity. An untreated tick bite in childhood left her paralysed, but she went on to study law and she eventually became a model, appearing in *Playboy* in 1995. Convinced by her own experience of the powerful connection between our thoughts and our health, she tries to pass this message on to her readers.

This, I think, is the importance of books like this. We can all sneer with Alexei Sayle, but the fact that these books sell in such huge quantities demonstrates that there is a great deal of unhappiness around, caused in no small part, I fear, by the feelings of insignificance and powerlessness which have been systematically instilled in us all by our materialistic culture, which would have us believe that there is very little we can about anything beyond complaining about our lot as we try to change the external circumstances of our life. Annemarie Postma and the rest revive the currently unfashionable idea that we live in a responsive, ordered universe, and that we are not simply the chance outcome of purposeless, chemical combinations. They remind us, too, of the age old spiritual principle which tells us that life is lived from the inside out, that we create our own reality, and that by changing our thoughts we can change our life. It's not as easy to do as these authors suggest, but since our churches rarely preach this message – even though it is clearly taught in the Christian scriptures (see, for example, Mark 11:12-25), and since it doesn't seem to be readily available anywhere else, we should be glad that a simplified and diluted version of it is being disseminated via the Body Mind and Spirit section of the bookstore.

Bill Darlison

Indra's Net: Alchemy and Chaos Theory as Models for Transformation, Robin Robertson, Quest Books, 196pp, $16.95/£16.50

Quantum physics has provided fertile ground for spiritual speculation. Works like the *Tao of Physics* and the *Dancing Wu Li Masters* and a host of successors have drawn on the role of the observer, and thus of consciousness, in quantum physics experiments, and the decidedly un-clockwork approach to matter that emerges, to make comparison to spiritual tradition. Now, Robin Robertson draws analogies between chaos theory, alchemy and modern spiritual transformation, particularly based on Jungian psychology in *Indra's Net.*

Robertson sees connections between alchemy and chaos science in the repetition of alchemical processes, the tail-swallowing Ouroboros and the fundamental importance of feedback in chaos science.

Robertson has a deft touch. His descriptions of both alchemy and chaos science are extremely clear. He manages to delineate each discipline clearly without compromising the dignity of either the ancient or modern science. As the subtitle suggests, these are treated as models, not as fundamental truths, and Robertson is able to use each of them as paradigms of transformation without resorting to any kind of dishonesty. His account of the essentials of chaos theory is elegant and to the point and is the clearest I've encountered. Likewise, his summation of the various operations, stages and materials of the alchemical process is sketched out beautifully. He clarifies without simplifying. For instance, he acknowledges that various alchemical texts give different sequences of operations and stages.

The personal spiritual aspect of the book is very much focused on Jungian psychology. The book's title, *Indra's Net*, is used only for a single example and seems the least necessary aspect of the book. But the image of a net of jewels, each of which reflects the other jewels on its polished surface, is again used clearly and honestly.

In short, this is a beautiful and insightful book, and in itself a model of how to make use of science as an analogy to spirituality with integrity.

Andrew Phillip Smith

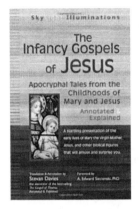

The Infancy Gospels of Jesus: Apocryphal Tales from the Childhoods of Mary and Jesus--Annotated & Explained, Skylight Illuminations, 180pp, $16.99/£14.99.

Sex Texts from the Bible: Selections Annotated & Explained, Teresa J. Hornsby, Skylight Illuminations, 171pp, $16.99; £14.99.

Renowned for his work on the Nag Hammadi *Gospel of Thomas*, Stevan Davies now turns his attention to the other *Gospel of Thomas*, widely known as the *Infancy Gospel of Thomas*, and two other gospels that tell stories of the childhood of Jesus, the *Gospel* (or *Protoevangelion*) *of James* and the ("Arabic") *Gospel of the Infancy*.

As Davies points out in the introduction, "No one will say that the infancy stories are historically factual, and hardly any one will argue that they are crucial to Christian belief." Davies sees them as the result of folk religion, the Christianity of the ordinary people of the early centuries AD. Though popular in medieval Christendom, stories from the infancy gospels received their greatest exposure, though uncredited, in the Qur'an. The quranic tales of Mary being fed by angels, of the baby Jesus speaking aloud the gospel and of the young Jesus making clay birds come to life are all derived, if indirectly, from the infancy gospels. As Davies points out, as Muhammad was illiterate he would have discovered the stories through oral tradition.

The reader will have to go through these texts with a toothcomb to find profundities, but there is plenty of oddness and small beauties emerge. For instance, Jesus is born in a cave rather than a stable. The cave is surrounded by so many shepherds and singing angels that it is said to resemble the Temple of God in Heaven; an old woman thanks God for letting her see the birth of the Saviour. We discover later, in a humorous passage, that Joseph was a very bad carpenter so Jesus had to magically alter the length of each piece of wood that Joseph cut in order to make it fit.

Davies' annotations have a pragmatic, commonsense flavour to them. In all of his writing he has a talent for pointing out those seemingly obvious features that would otherwise go unnoticed, With regard to the star followed by the Magi to Bethlehem: "It is curious that people find it so easy to imagine following a star to a particular destination. Just try it! A star might, at best, point to a particular direction at a particular period of the nighttime, but simple observation will reveal that stars move across the sky all night." (p.52)

The Infancy Gospels of Jesus is recommended to anyone interested in apocryphal gospels.

Teresa J. Hornsby's *Sex Texts from the Bible: Selections Annotated & Explained* in the same series gives us a new view of familiar material rather than the exposure to exotic or little-known texts that is typical of this series. It is chiefly, but not wholly, the Old Testament or Hebrew Bible that is excerpted here. The introduction and annotations allow us to uncover the sexual assumptions and decode the allusive and metaphorical language of Bible eroticism. Hornsby gives us a window into another world, and what an utterly foreign world it is. The Old Testament has precious little in it that can justify the sexual morality of modern Christianity. Hornsby explains, "It is surprisingly non-judgmental on topics we think it should be adamant about—for example, visiting prostitutes, having more than one wife at a time, and having sex with your daughter—and it complicates topics we may be indifferent about, like how soon a person can have sex after childbirth." (p. Xvi.) Further "there is no biblical Hebrew or Greek word for 'homosexuality.' There is no word for 'abortion.' In fact, in biblical Hebrew there is no word for 'marriage..'"

"Sometimes a marriage, especially of a second or lesser wife, was no more than a presentation of a gift from man to man. Not very romantic... The man who has sex with another man's wife, future wife or virgin daughter is basically a thief. He is taking something that isn't his, and, in the case of the virgin, he reduces her value; she is essentially damaged goods."

With sections on euphemisms, interracial marriage, cheating, multiple partners, sexual orientation, masturbation, menstruation, illegitimacy and violence, there is something here to rock everyone's pre- and misconceptions. I found myself plunged into a culture of utterly strange (and largely repellant) sexual conditions, less familiar to me even than those of the ancient Greeks or Celts.

Andrew Phillip Smith

 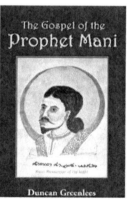

The Gospel of the Gnostics, Duncan Greenlees, The Book Tree, Arcturus Publishing, 330pp, $29.95/£17.95

The Gospel of the Prophet Mani, Duncan Greenlees, The Book Tree, Arcturus Publishing, 378pp, $59.95/£34.95

The discovery of the Nag Hammadi library changed our view of the Gnostics forever. Where previously we had only a handful of Gnostic texts and the hostile acounts of the church fathers, suddenly we had dozens of genuine, major Gnostic works. But the earlier pieces tended to be swept away by the new broom. Now the Book Tree has reprinted Duncan Greenlees' *The Gospel of the Gnostics* and *The Gospel of the Prophet Mani*, two volumes from a series originally published by the Theosophical Society in India in the 1950s.

The Manichaean volume is particularly useful as collections of Manichaean literature are still quite rare, and this is one of only two or three nonspecialist collections of Manichaean material.

The Gospel of the Gnostics highlights the pre-Nag Hammadi material, but is slightly less essential than the Manichaean volume and certainly shouldn't be anyone's first (or second or third) book on Gnosticism. Yet it certainly has some appeal for the dedicated reader. The original introductions and a foreword by publisher Paul Tice are included in both volumes. The material is ordered thematically, consisting mostly of meaningful excerpts rather than complete texts, although some material, such as the *Hymn of the Pearl* and the Gnostic sections of the *Acts of Thomas*, is included in its entirety. The selection and arrangement makes even the better known material seem unfamiliar and refreshing, and it's a useful device. In addition to the extracts from the Bruce and Askew codices and material preserved by the heresiologists, such as the Naasene hymn and psalm, there are fragments that I have never come across before, even if the Gnostic attributes of some of them might be questionable, such as a Gnostic prayer from a Turin papyrus. All in all, these reprints are a welcome addition to the library of the dedicated Gnostic.

Andrew Phillip Smith

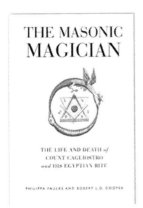

The Masonic Magician: The Life and Death of Count Cagliostro and His Egyptian Rite Philippa Faulks and Robert L.D. Cooper

Watkins Publishing 317pp, $24.95/£16.99.

There are few characters in Masonic history as interesting, controversial, and enigmatic as the Comte de Cagliostro. His very name evokes images of mystery and intrigue. Touted as a Master of alchemy and theurgy by his admirers, he is also believed by many to have been a cunning charlatan by the name of Giuseppe (Joseph) Balsamo. The present work, however, falls firmly on the side of admiration, upholding the nobility of Cagliostro, and strongly denouncing suggestions of fraud. While the authors do not outright deny that Cagliostro and Balsamo were the same person, neither do they give credibility to the claim. But the purpose of this work is not to re-examine old controversies. Rather, the authors here are presenting the first full English translation of Cagliostro's Egyptian Rite of Freemasonry. The structure of the book is divided into three principal parts, titled: "The Life and Times of Cagliostro," "The Origins and History of Freemasonry," and "Cagliostro's Egyptian Freemasonry."

"The Life and Times of Cagliostro" introduces the reader to many of the landmark events and meetings in the life of the Count, and attempts to put them into an historical context by describing the prevailing customs, mores, and philosophies of the time. While not comprehensive, the authors give us a taste of the unique dynamics of the Enlightenment era, with a Church that is still steeped in superstition, and fearful of the rational and mystical philosophies emerging out of the resurgence of Hermeticism and Neoplatonism. We are also introduced to some of the major personalities of esoteric Freemasonry such as, Martinez de Pasqually, Louis-Claude de Saint-Martin, Friedrich Joseph Wilhelm Schroeder, Franz Anton Mesmer, Emanuel Swedenborg, Dom Antoine Joseph Pernety, and other contemporaries of Cagliostro, some of whom must have undoubtedly influenced the Egyptian Rite.

This first section of the book succeeds in giving a basic outline of Cagliostro's life, and some of the Hermetic, Alchemical, and Theurgic principles he espoused. However, it must be kept in mind that the purpose of this section is largely to provide context for the third section of the book, which deals with the Egyptian Rite itself. This is affirmed by the authors, who state on page xv of the Introduction, "One book could never contain everything about Cagliostro, and so our aim is to concentrate on the Count's Masonic and spiritual work that in turn will reveal the teachings of Egyptian Freemasonry." So, for the reader who wishes to delve deeply into the events of Cagliostro's life, this hundred-page introduction may not suffice. There are, however, several excellent works on the subject, such as the old Trowbridge work (*Cagliostro*, 1910), or more recent works such as Iain McCalman's *The Last Alchemist* (2003).

The second section of the book, "The Origins and History of Freemasonry," follows along much as one might expect for the most part. It begins with Schaw's work in the late 16th century, and touches upon the usual cast of characters: Ashmole, Moray, Anderson, etc. Concerning the exoteric historical elements here, these names, dates, and facts have been recorded so often, in so many voluminous works, that it is not even necessary to comment upon them here. For the reader who knows little to nothing of the Craft, there will be some important background information, but the serious Masonic researcher should not expect to find any fresh material here. Though, I did find it significant that the authors gave considerable attention to the persecution of Freemasons in 1930s and 40s Germany and Italy. For instance, it is not widely known that Freemasons in Nazi Germany had been forced to wear a unique identifying mark (a red triangle, point down). In short, this section, like the first, is really just framework and set-up for the exposition of the Egyptian Rite.

As I began reading Part Three of this work, I was eagerly anticipating the study of the Egyptian Rite in its entirety. This section begins with a twenty-page introduction to the text of the Rite. After nearly 200 pages of historical material that I was, for the most part, already familiar with, I was ready to delve into the ritual itself, which is surely the raison d'être of the whole work. I had managed up until this point to not simply skip ahead and dig right into the main course. No, I had taken the bits as they were doled out to me. I had caught a glimpse of it though, as there is a photographic reproduction of a portion of the title page of the original French document, which is included in a sixteen-page glossy insert that contains thirty-five plates. As I began reading the translation of the ritual, I became somewhat concerned about its accuracy. On page x, in the Acknowledgement pages, the authors write: "Gratitude to the team at TRANSCEN, Middlesex University Translation Institute, who did a superb and precise job in translating..." However, based on the brief passages reprinted here of the original text, if the translation they offer of this brief selection is indicative of the quality of the work as a whole, then I am afraid that the job may be neither "superb" nor "precise." Let me give a few examples to illustrate.

In the first line of text (after the title and a listing of various virtues, such as Glory, Wisdom, Union, Prosperity, etc.) we find the French, "Nous Grand Cophte Fondateur et Grand Maitre..." This is translated by them as, "You, Grand Copht, Founder and Grand Master..." But it should read, "We, Grand Copht, Founder..." In other words, they have mistaken the French "nous" for "vous" meaning "you." In the photograph it is quite clearly "nous" and not "vous." Cagliostro is addressing the reader here, not the other way around! And we don't

get through more than a few words before we find an omission of the words "oriental and occidental." Even "eastern and western" would have sufficed. The opening sentence, as they have translated it, reads thus: "You, Grand Copht, Founder and Grand Master of High Egyptian Freemasonry in all corners of the globe." My reading of the sentence is as follows: "We, Grand Copht, Founder and Grand Master of High Egyptian Masonry in all oriental and occidental (or eastern and western) corners of the globe." So, you see here that we have both an error and an omission. One final note on the translation concerns not so much an error, but what I find to be a poor choice of wording. The last words visible on the photographic reprint are, "le desir ardent." They have this translated as "the strong desire." Now, while that is certainly not a mistranslation, it would seem preferable to simply state, "the ardent desire," which would be a more straightforward translation, and help to preserve the literary style of the original.

So, unfortunately, if the rest of the document is given the same treatment as the very brief section that I've been able to view (of the original), then I don't know how reliable we may consider it. That is not to say that the text of the Rite is wholly without value. But throughout the reading of it, I could not help but to find myself questioning certain words and phrases along the way. I would like to see in the future a publication of the entire French text, or a side by side translation for easy comparison. Regardless, in spite of its flaws, the ritual is a precious gem nonetheless. Freemasons, Martinists, Rosicrucians, and all other students of Hermeticism and alchemy will appreciate the rich symbolism present in the discourses, numerology, vestment colors, and other aspects of the Rite. It does seem, though, that this version of the Rite may be missing certain elements. For instance, there is no Second Degree Catechism, but those of the Apprentice and Master are included. The authors, in fact, comment on this absence, and speculate as to the possible content of the Companion's Catechism.

The "Commentary on Cagliostro's Egyptian

Ritual" is intriguing and thought provoking in many parts, but does not ever delve too deeply into the profound theurgical and alchemical properties of the Rite. The authors seem satisfied to give a philosophical treatment without really doing more than skimming the mystical. To be sure, the mysticism of the Rite is mentioned and commented upon. But its depths are merely hinted at. A deep and thoughtful exposition is never forthcoming. I cannot speculate as to whether this is because of a lack of insight on the part of the authors, or if they have merely chosen to leave a deeper interpretation to the individual student of this Rite.

In conclusion, I must admit that I have mixed feelings about this book. As I stated previously, if you are looking for a book on the life of Cagliostro, or a serious work on Masonic history, the brief considerations given in this volume are sure to disappoint, and you would do well to seek those studies elsewhere. But, an in-depth exploration of these topics is surely not intended here. Truly, the background material, as well as the commentary, is really just padding for the thirty-nine pages of text that comprise the ritual itself. And here again is another reason for me to have mixed feelings about the work. As grateful as I am to have an English translation of the Rite, the errors that are apparent in the first few lines of text make me extremely skeptical about the accuracy of the remainder.

This work is not without value, but it is difficult to determine who, exactly, the intended audience is. The subject matter is too specialized for general interest. But many researchers and students of the esoteric arts and sciences may find the waters a bit shallow. For the avid Masonophile, though, this book will be a must-have. Likewise, all English-speaking enthusiasts of 18th century French occultism will want to review the contents of the Egyptian Rite, in spite of its questionable translation. If you fall into one of those two categories, I will recommend this book. My own expectations of this work were rather high, and I found myself often disappointed. So it will be better for you to approach the work with lowered expectations, for then you may be pleasantly surprised at times.

Reginald Freeman

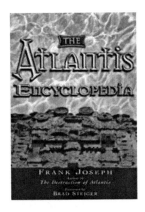

The Atlantis Encyclopedia, Frank Joseph, New Page Books 312pp, $19.99/£13.99.

The vast majority of books on Atlantis are either dismissive academic studies or the metaphysical ramblings of New Age crack pots. However, Frank Joseph's Atlantis Encyclopedia is a rare gem that gathers together all the disparate aspects of the lost continent in a highly organized and factual manner. This exhaustive study covers such diverse subjects as astronomy, folk traditions, classics, geology, mythography, anthropology and history to forge a panoramic view of this highly alluring and even charming topic. Joseph traveled the world and tracked down the most remote references to the antediluvian epoch which saw the rise and fall of a great civilization written about by intellectual giants like Plato and Francis Bacon.

This 316 page masterpiece explores the entire gambit of Atlantean studies and examines the origin of the Atlantis myth and the possible influence it may have had on the seemingly mutually exclusive cultures of Egypt, the Mayans and even the Chinese. Joseph also examines the effect the lost continent has had on the modern occult movement and reviews the careers of Madame Blavatsky, Edgar Casey and Paul Lecour among many others in the context of Atlantean studies. The Atlantis Encyclopedia also takes into consideration the ancient astronaut theory and current UFO phenomenon in relation to the lost continent. Joseph's profound opus is a must read for anyone interested in paranormal studies and/or ancient history -- open to any page and you find hard facts intertwined with profound wisdom.

William Kennedy

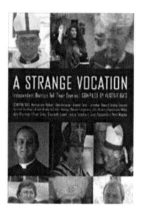

A Strange Vocation: Independent Bishops tell their Stories, **Compiled by Alistair Bate,**

Apocryphile Press, 212pp, $16.95.

I came to this book with a sense of amusement. I'd read about the "independent bishops" and the "wandering bishops," those renegades from Roman Catholicism (generally) who like to dress up in clerical garb and to ordain all and sundry into their meticulously researched lines of apostolic succession. I'd always thought that they represented the weirder wing of Christianity, an opportunity for men to bypass rigorous seminary training, or to escape from canon law condemnations of homosexuality, while enjoying some kind of clerical status and the opportunity to indulge their somewhat baroque liturgical tastes.

I was disabused of these unkind and totally unwarranted opinions by this volume. Edited by Alistair Bate, himself a bishop in the Liberal Catholic Apostolic Church, it is a compilation of autobiographical essays in which seventeen Independent Catholic Bishops give an account of their turbulent and somewhat circuitous spiritual journeys. The essays are unfailingly interesting, moving, and

well written. They are by men and women of genuine intellectual stature (Elizabeth Stuart is a university professor), most of whom have felt a call to priesthood from their earliest years, but who have been denied the right to assume it or to exercise it by the petty strictures of the institutional church.

One of these petty strictures is, of course, to do with homosexuality. We all know that the Anglican and Catholic priesthoods have more than their fair share of homosexuals, but the official teaching of both bodies excludes "practising" homosexuals from ministry. Nine of the contributors to this book are openly gay, and have therefore come into conflict with church hierarchies, but have bravely and at times almost recklessly decided to remain faithful both to their vocation and to their sexuality by leaving the major church organisations behind and striking out on their own. These are men and women on the margins, but they seem perfectly content to be there, inspired by the example of Jesus who was himself an outcast, and whose ministry was to those who felt themselves rejected and even despised by the conventionally religious people of first century Palestine. In one particularly moving essay, Bishop River Sims of the Society of Franciscan Workers outlines the nature and scope of his ministry:

> My spiritual director once pointed out: "The people you are serving are sitting in the middle of the highway with different trucks aimed at them—all the stereotypes the biases of our society: drug addict, prostitute, thief, murderer, queer, transgender, bisexual, are aimed towards them and because you stand with these kids those trucks are aimed at you as well.' So I am identified with them, and treated as they are." (Page 154)

Many of the contributors seem well aware of the drawbacks to this kind of loose church organisation. "There are a lot of asshole bishops out there in the Independent Catholic Movement, as well as the larger communions," says Bishop John Mabry of the Old Catholic Order of Holy Wisdom, and Archbishop Ronald Langham of the United Ecumenical Catholic Church writes darkly of "delusional self-made Patriarchs and alternative popes," but the impression given by the contributors to this book is of men and women trying their best to bring the beauties and consolations of sacramental worship to those who have been deprived of it by "latter day Sadducees."

This book provoked me to think seriously about my own spiritual journey from Roman Catholicism to Unitarianism, and for that inspiration I am extremely grateful. But I saw something else shining through the pages: for all that these bishops represent tiny organisations, some with ludicrous names, some with only a handful of members and most of those ordained, these people are showing, in the words of Bishop John Plummer, "new, flexible, portable, ways of being church." These new ways are, in fact, the old ways, the old Gnostic ways, which existed before the institutional church emerged to impose structure and uniformity and to construct barriers against the Holy Spirit. These bishops represent contemporary Christian Gnosticism, a chaotic, disorganised, turbulent, perhaps even dangerous vehicle for what R.S. Thomas calls "a fast God," who is "always ahead of us, always leading and teasing us on."

Bill Darlison

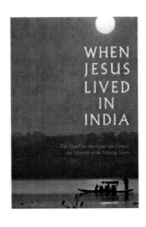

When Jesus Lived in India, Alan Jacobs, Watkins Publishing, 216pp, £10.99

Where was Jesus between the ages of 12 when, according to Luke he travelled to the Jerusalem Temple, and 30 when he began his ministry? According to Nicholas Notavitch, a nineteenth century journalist explorer, and an Orthodox convert from Judaism, Jesus travelled to India, and the Pali manuscript he came across in the Tibetan monastery at Hemis proved it.

Jacobs feels that Jesus must have been doing something in those missing years, and offers time spent with the Essenes or the Theraputae as an alternative. He makes little reference to the standard academic historical-critical dismantling of the canonical gospels, through which lens much of the gospel story is seen to be historically questionable at best. Indeed, as Jesus' visit to the Temple at the age of 12 is found only in Luke 2, 41-52, and is definitely a historically questionable episode. Thus the missing or lost years of Jesus might extend from his circumcision when he was eight days old, up until his meeting with John the Baptist. In the *Life of Saint Issa*, Jesus goes off on his travels at the age of 14, returning conveniently at the age of 29, which surely shows dependence on the Gospel of Luke.

Jacobs provides extensive and useful summaries of the *Aquarian Gospel of Jesus Christ* and the *Life of Saint Issa*. The *Aquarian Gospel* in particular is a long and often tedious text. The Jesus of the *Aquarian Gospel* was an extensive traveller, visiting Persia, Assyria, Greece and Egypt in addition to India and Tibet. The *Aquarian Gospel* was dictated directly from the Akashic Records, a mode of composition that, in my opinion, is also likely to be the method of choice of Notavitch's "discovery".

Jacobs provides chapters on the parallels between Christianity, Hinduism and Buddhism, on Jesus in Islam, and on the problem of resurrection or Jesus surviving the crucifixion. There is no mention of *The Acts of Thomas*, in which the apostle Thomas travels to India, in Jacobs' book, though it would have provided an interesting comparison, and, while the account is surely legendary, it is considerably older than any of the sources that propose that Jesus was in India.

It isn't until the final chapter of the book that Jacobs assesses the authenticity of the Jesus in India legend. He is always willing to give the benefit of the doubt to the various characters who are involved with the *Life of Saint Issa* text, stressing their moral uprightness and personal reputations. I remain unconvinced that the *Life of Saint Issa* preceded Notavitch, and even if it did, it is likely a late work, comparable to the fourteenth century Muslim *Gospel of Barnabas*. To be fair, Jacobs does not push the issue of authenticity, though he certainly seems more sympathetic to the succession of European travellers who allege to have seen the original Pali manuscript, but have never been able to produce anything close to proof. He is weak on actual critical assessment of these apocryphal texts, but has put a good deal of legwork into the research, examining very rare books in the British Library in order to check claims about their contents. At least one book is entirely lacking the material attributed to it.

On the last page he makes recourse to Albert Schweitzer's conclusions about the historical Jesus, that is the influence of Jesus' teachings, not the historical reliability of the gospels, that matters. I can't help feeling that Alan Jacobs desperately wanted to find some corroboration of the existence of the *Life of Saint Issa*, but was in the end was too honest a researcher.

Andrew Phillip Smith

Food for Thought

Militant atheism is the right answer to dishonest religions.

P. Nagaraja Rao

If we aim for the moon we might just get up the stairs.

Grant Showbiz

Modern artists are gnostics and practice things that the priests think are long forgotten; perhaps even commit sins that are no longer thought possible.

Hugo Ball

A person does not see with the soul or with the spirit. Rather, the mind, which exists between these two, sees the vision.

Gospel of Mary

The obscuring of the faith in creation is a fundamental part of what constitutes modernity. As I survey all the perplexing shifts in the spiritual landscape of today, only these two basic models seem to me to be up for discussion. The first I should like to call the Gnostic model, the other the Christian model. I see the common core of Gnosticism, in all its different forms and versions, as the repudiation of creation.

Joseph Ratzinger

Control and surrender have to be kept in balance. That's what surfers do – take control of the situation, then be carried, then take control. In the last few thousand years, we've become incredibly adept technically. We've treasured the controlling part of ourselves and neglected the surrendering part.

Brian Eno

For my part, when I enter most intimately into what I call myself, I always stumble on some particular perception or other, of heat or cold, light or shade, love or hatred, pain or pleasure. I never can catch myself at any time without a perception, and never can observe any thing but the perception. When my perceptions are remov'd for any time, as by sound sleep; so long am I insensible of myself, and may truly be said not to exist. And were all my perceptions remov'd by death, and cou'd I neither think, nor feel, nor see, nor love, nor hate after the dissolution of my body, I shou'd be entirely annihilated, nor do I conceive what is farther requisite to make me a perfect non-entity.

David Hume

Everything God has a wise person has.

Sentences of Sextus

Blessed are the cracked, for they shall let in the light... If you want to know where God is, ask a drunk.

Groucho Marx

Biographies

Anthony Blake was born 1939 in Bristol where he also studied Physics and met David Bohm, followed by studies in the history and philosophy of science at Cambridge. He became deeply involved in the Fourth Way activities of John Bennett, a leading exponent of Gurdjieff's ideas, and worked with him over many years, including educational research. He has published several books including *A Seminar on Time*, *The Intelligent Enneagram* and the recent *The Supreme Art of Dialogue*, dialogue being one of his passions. He lives in Scotland and has six children.

Miguel Conner is the author of the novel *Queen of Darkness* and host of the Internet radio show *Aeon Byte*, formerly *Coffee, Cigarettes and Gnosis*. A selection of his interviews with scholars of Gnosticism will soon be available from Bardic Press.

Bill Darlison has recently retired as the senior minister of Dublin Unitarian Church. He trained in Rome for the Catholic priesthood, but left before ordination and became a Unitarian in 1988. He has been a student of astrology for over forty years and is interested in the influence of astrology on early Christian thought and practice. He is the author of *The Gospel and the Zodiac: The Secret Truth about Jesus*, and *The Shortest Distance: 101 Stories from the World's Spiritual Traditions*.

John T Freeman was born in London in 1958 and studied painting at Bath Academy of Art and Chelsea School of Art 1976-80 and has since worked as a professional artist and tutor who can guarantee to teach absolutely anyone to draw in 48 hours. These images are taken from a series of 100 etchings from his recently completed book *Paris Workings*. *Paris Workings* is the third volume of a quartet of books, the first of which *I London* and *Descent to Byworth* are highly acclaimed but impossible to find. He is currently working on the final volume that explores his relationship with Alexandria. The work can be seen at www.johntfreeman.co.uk

Reginald Freeman, in Ecclesia Tau Phosphoros, is a Gnostic bishop of the Apostolic Church of the Pleroma. He is a long-time student and initiate of various branches of the Western Mystery Tradition, including Freemasonry, Martinism, and other traditional and esoteric Orders and Societies. He is self-taught in rudimentary Koine Greek and has some formal training in French. He currently lives a cloistered life in the U.S. Midwest where he develops liturgical and theurgic material for the ACP.

Michael Grenfell is Professor at Trinity College, Dublin. As an academic, his interests are in language, education and philosophy of education. He was a founder member of the Blake Society at St James in Piccadilly, London and served on their committee for a number of years. He is the author of some twelve books and numerous articles. He has a longstanding interest in Gnosis, Gnosticism, and related arts, literature and philosophies.

William Kennedy is a writer and speaker on paranormal & religious topics. Kennedy has produced articles for academic journals such as *Sophia: the Journal of Traditional Studies* and popular magazines like *New Dawn*. Kennedy authored *Lucifer's Lodge: Satanic Ritual Abuse in the Catholic Church* (Sophia Perennis: 2004), *Satanic Crime: A Threat in the New Millennium* (MVM: 2006) & *Occult History: Collected Writings 1994-2008* (MVM: 2008). In 2005 Kennedy began hosting Sphinx Radio which focuses on esoteric subjects and founded Mystic Valley Media, a book publishing and multimedia service.

Karl Le Marks is known as "A Dark Philosopher", esoteric scholar, quantum theorist, psychologist and general autodidact polymath. Study to degree level in Western Philosophy, Cognitive Psychology and Trade Union Labour History & Industrial Relations helped him, in at least two of the subjects, to follow his true passion, that of consciousness and its relation to philosophy, quantum mechanics, spirituality and esoteric studies. author of a paradigm shifting theory of consciousness "Collapsing the Consciousness wave" (CtCw), he now lives in Warwickshire, England, standing precariously on the bridge he's trying to build between Science and Spirituality.

Daniel C. Matt is a leading authority on Jewish mysticism. His books include *Zohar: Annotated & Explained*, *The Essential Kabbalah* and the ongoing *Zohar: Pritzker Edition*.

Jacob Needleman is professor of philosophy at San Francisco State University and a practising Gurdjieffan. His many books include *What Is God?*, *Time and the Soul, and Lost Christianity* .

Lance S. Owens is a physician in clinical practice and a frequent lecturer on Jung, Tolkien, and the imaginative tradition in Western history. He is a priest of the Ecclesia Gnostica and the creator and editor of The Gnosis Archive, www.gnosis.org, a prominent internet resource on Gnosticism. The essay presented here is from a forthcoming book on C.G. Jung and the tradition of vision.

Jeremy Puma has been a student of Gnosticism for over 15 years. He is one of the founding members of the Palm Tree Garden Gnostic community, an online collective of Gnostics from many different traditions, and the Gnostic Order of Allogenes, a collective of independent Gnostic practitioners. Jeremy is the author of a number of books on the theory and practice of Gnosticism in the twenty-first century, all of which can be found online at www.lulu.com/eleleth. He currently maintains two websites at waygnostic.wordpress.com and gnostichealing.wordpress.com. Jeremy lives in Seattle, WA with a lovely lady and two brown dogs.

Andrew Phillip Smith is the editor of *The Gnostic* and author of *A Dictionary of Gnosticism*, *The Gnostics: History, Tradition, Scriptures, Influence*, *The Gospel of Philip: Annotated & Explained*, *The Lost Sayings of Jesus: Annotated & Explained*, and *Gnostic Writings on the Soul: Annotated & Explained*. A renowned neo-hillbilly, his favourite attire is dungarees, his favourite car the 1933 Cadillac V-16 Convertible Victoria, his preferred breakfast Thunderbird Wine and Cheerios.

David Tibet is founder and the only constant member of the group Current 93. He runs the Durtro book imprint and record label, now Coptic Cat.

Elan' Rodger Trinidad has been nominated for an Eisner Award for best webcomic and was an animator on *The Simpsons*. You can see some of his work at theoryofeverythingcomics.com and elanrodgertrinidad.com

Breinigsville, PA USA
23 September 2010

245857BV00003BA/140/P